D1595052

EARLY AMERICAN PATTERN GLASS CAKE & Stands

& SERVING PIECES

Identification & Value Guide

Bettye S. James
&
Jane M. O'Brien

COORDINATED BY
Danny Cornelius
&
Don Jones

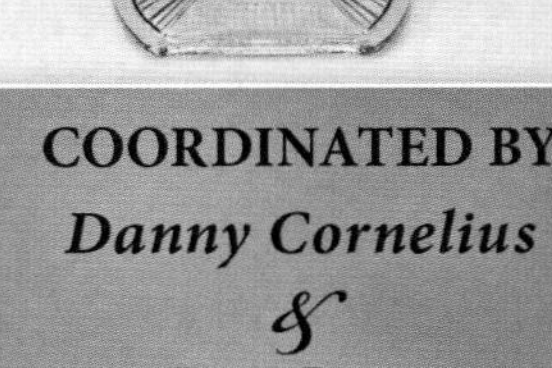

COLLECTOR BOOKS
A Division of Schroeder Publishing Co., Inc.

Front Cover, center: Adams' Thousand Eye, green, open lattice edge, $240.00. Left top: Nr 1883, cranberry stain, $250.00. Left center: Frosted Circle, $200.00. Left, bottom: Scroll with Cane Band, canary stain, $350.00. Top right: Dakota, with etching, $225.00. Dakota cover, $1,500.00. Dakota cake stand and cover, $3,250.00. Bottom right: Oval Medallion, etched, $285.00.

Back Cover: Fine Cut and Panel, vaseline, $190.00.

Cover design: Beth Summers★Book design: Lisa Henderson★Cover photography: Charles R. Lynch

COLLECTOR BOOKS
P.O. Box 3009
Paducah, Kentucky 42002-3009
www.collectorbooks.com

The current values in this book should be used only as a guide. They are not intended to set prices, which vary from one section of the country to another. Auction prices as well as dealer prices vary greatly and are affected by condition as well as demand. Neither the authors nor the publisher assumes responsibility for any losses that might be incurred as a result of consulting this guide.

Searching for a Publisher?

We are always looking for people knowledgeable within their fields. If you feel that there is a real need for a book on your collectible subject and have a large comprehensive collection, contact Collector Books.

Contents

Acknowledgments

Bettye S. James

I want to acknowledge my husband's enormous help over the years in traveling to flea markets, auctions, and yard sales, no matter the weather, to look for glass. He was always there with packing material and boxes! When the collecting days were almost over, he became the photographer, as well as taking over the chores of shopping and cooking.

My son, Bryan, insisted in 1997 that we buy a computer — that did it! Now I could search on line for all the beautiful patterns. Thanks for his help in learning the computer, and for getting me out of trouble when I got stuck. I knew nothing about CDs, thumb drives — none of the computer language.

Thanks to friends, relatives, and neighbors for sharing their glass to be photographed. This undertaking would not have been possible without all their help. Carolyn Crozier was a big help in identifying patterns with her extensive knowledge and reference books on EAPG, as well as her generosity in packing up 61 pieces of her glass and delivering them to Florida.

My friend, neighbor, and cruise mate, Val Redemsky, has been a tremendous help in proofreading the text, especially the index, while we were cruising the Caribbean, and later again proofreading after additional information was discovered on true manufacturers. She volunteered to help proof the manuscript, which was no quick, easy undertaking! She's getting to be an authority on EAPG glass.

And, of course, thanks to Jane M. O'Brien for encouraging me to write the book and her help in getting me started.

My friend, fellow collector, and neighbor, Danny Cornelius, has been invaluable in his help in identifying the elusive pattern on a cake stand. He too has an extensive collection of reference books, which is the envy of many collectors. He and Don Jones agreed to be coordinators on this book.

Jane M. O'Brien

The depth of information from this book comes from those before us with a love of fine, intricate pieces of early American pattern glass. Each piece tells it own story through its pattern. I dedicate this book to those who are willing to share information, which brought this book to fruition.

Our photographer and my good friend, Brad James, spent countless hours and persevered to photograph and produce the best quality photographs. Thank you, Brad, for making this one of the finest visual experiences with your eye for detail in capturing the delicate intricacies of the glassware.

Finally, I dedicate this book to my family: my parents, my children, and my grandchildren, who constantly teach and remind me what is truly important in life. But most of all, I dedicate this book to my wonderful husband, Tom, whose love motivates me in everything I do. His positive attitude, optimism, and humor keep me anchored. Without his support, I could not have attempted this project. Thank you, Tom, for always being there for me.

Danny Cornelius
Don Jones

A long-time fascination with antiques led Danny Cornelius and Don Jones down a varied path until, succumbing to the siren song of early American pattern glass, they found their true passion. While they find the glass patterns themselves fascinating, the history and research involved are equally fascinating — resulting in their becoming among the leading researchers in the country for this subject.

For the last five years they have traveled around the country helping to renew the interest in early American pattern glass by sharing their knowledge and glass through shows, seminars, and displays.

Their first book, *American Pattern Glass Table Sets* with Gene and Cathy Florence in 2007, allowed them to share this passion with collectors everywhere.

They are both honored and proud to coordinate this book with their friend and neighbor, Bettye James, along with co-author, Jane O'Brien.

Introduction

For more than 30 years we have enjoyed collecting glass and would like to share our knowledge and research. Our hope is that this book, *Early American Pattern Glass Cake Stands and Serving Pieces*, will help in identifying cake stands and other pieces.

Early American pattern glass (EAPG) refers to "early pressed glass" which was first pressed around 1830 and became very popular from 1850 until 1915. Use of the inexpensive pressed glass allowed the middle class to own fancy glassware.

The pattern names are listed alphabetically along with all available information: manufacturer's name, date of manufacture, size, shape, and color details. As with any reference book, pattern names may be listed differently from the one known by the reader. Patterns are listed by most popular name, with all other known names listed, including the original manufacturer's name (OMN) if different from the popular name. A cross-reference of all recognized pattern names for each pattern featured is listed in the index with the popular name in **bold** print. If you have additional knowledge with references to the pattern name, please let us hear from you.

The pattern may be a little different on each piece, i.e., inconsistency in the size of the pattern, making it difficult for positive pattern identification. At times, determining the exact pattern was difficult, and only through reviewing manufacturers' catalogs were we able to determine that a cake stand was, indeed, made in a particular pattern. Therefore, variants and a close-up of the pattern design are presented in the book for identification purposes. When unable to provide a photograph of a cake stand, we included other pieces as a means of verifying identity.

Originally, manufacturers referred to pedestal cake stands as salvers, wafer salvers, or cake plates. Most old salvers have a brandy well from shallow to 1⅜" deep in the center of the plate. The well was used, especially for fruitcakes, to hold brandy to moisten and flavor the cake.

EAPG cake stands are found in various colors, but mostly crystal (clear), and in numerous shapes — square, round, rectangular, octagonal, oval, and two very unique stands, Ashman and Nr 75 Square, which are round and square.

The last section is on cake stands that we have been unable to identify. If you have pertinent information, pattern name, date, manufacturer, reference, etc., on these unknown patterns, we would love for you to share that information with us.

Beautiful old patterns, never seen by the authors before, keep appearing at shows, antique malls, auctions, and on the internet. Cake stands continue to be one of the most sought after forms in pattern glass. After researching and discussing today's high demand for cake stands with collectors, dealers, and auctioneers, we believe the cake stand is here to stay.

How to Use This Book

This book will be helpful to all collectors of early American pattern glass to readily identify their pieces as the patterns on cake stands are much bigger and more easily identified. The terms "gallery" and "skirt" are used to describe a raised (gallery) edge and a lowered (skirt) edge. Most cake stands will have a "brandy well," an indention in the center of the plate used for brandy or other liqueur to flavor cakes, especially fruit cakes.

The pattern names are listed alphabetically with as much information as possible. Examples include different sizes and shapes, colors, stained, decorated with gold, dates made, and manufacturer's name. If known by more than one name, all names are included. The index reflects all known names with the most popular name listed in **bold** print.

Additionally, a separate Alphabetical List of Cake Patterns is included that contains the names of all known patterns in which a cake stand was produced. This list is provided for those who have inherited items or may collect a certain pattern. The ones covered in this writing appear in **bold** print.

Featured are 479 patterns from Actress to Zipper Cross, plus 26 unidentified, with 1,162 photographs. There are 64 manufacturers dating from 1872: Cambridge, Fostoria, Heisey, Riverside, and others. Many patterns that were previously credited to U. S. Glass Manufacturing Company now reflect the true manufacturers.

Prices are current at the time of publication from glass shows, flea markets, auctions and, of course, internet auctions. They reflect the value of mint, or near mint, pieces. There are many delicate patterns of cake stands, and the more delicate the pattern, the less likely it will be found in perfect condition after 100+ years. Items decorated in gold or colored stains are more valuable. Add an additional 25% for gold-trimmed items and an additional 25% if there is gold and stain on same item in excellent condition.

A black light is one tool to determine the age of glass. It should not be the only test, however. If a piece of glass will fluoresce it usually indicates it is old. Almost all early American pressed glass will fluoresce a greenish/yellow. Some pieces will fluoresce more than others. If a crystal piece of glass has no reaction to a black light, it presumably is not early American pattern glass. Uranium was the ingredient used during glass manufacture that caused the glass to glow. It was discontinued during World War I because of shortage, but is still available and used by some glass manufacturers today, especially to make vaseline glass. Since the black light test results are not always guaranteed, learn to identify your glass by sight, touch, and research.

Look for "use" scratches on the bottom of a piece, where it was moved around on a table either in use or while dusting furniture. There will most likely be scratch marks on a cake plate from the knife used in cutting the cake.

Pattern glass that has been exposed to sunlight for a long period of time will turn lavender, known as "sun purple." Please protect your valuable glass from sunlight coming through a window. The value is markedly decreased if it has turned sun purple.

Care should be taken to not expose pattern glass to extreme change in temperature when purchased at glass shows, antique malls, flea markets, or auctions. Taking the glass from the hot sun to an air-conditioned car can cause it to crack. The same is true when taking it from a warm building to a very cold car.

Alphabetical List of Cake Patterns

The patterns listed are known to have a cake stand; those listed in **bold** print are represented in this book.

A

Actress
Ada
Adam's Plume
Adams' Saxon
Adams' Thousand Eye
Adonis
Alabama
Albany (1898)
Alden Salver
Alfa
Alpha Swirl
All-Over Diamond
Amazon
America Nr 348
American
Anthemion
Apollo
Arched Fleur-de-Lis
Arched Ovals
Argent
Arrowhead-in-Oval
Art
Artichoke
Ashburton
Ashman
Atlanta
Atlas
Aurora
Austrian
Aztec

B

Baby Animals
Bakewell Ribbon
Ball and Swirl
Baltimore Pear
Banded Fleur-de-Lis
Banded Flute (Heisey) Nr 150
Barberry
Barley
Barred Forget-Me-Not
Barred Oval
Barred Star
Bartholdi
Basketweave
Basketweave w/Frosted Leaf
Beaded Band
Beaded Edge
Beaded Grape Medallion
Beaded Medallion
Beaded Oval and Fan
Beaded Oval and Scroll
Beaded Panel and Sunburst, Nr 1235
Beaded Swirl
Beaded Swirl and Disc
Beaded Swirl and Lens
Beaded Tulip
Bead Swag, Nr 1295
Beautiful Lady
Bellaire Bulls Eye
Belle
Bellflower Single Vine
Belmont Daisy and Button
Bethlehem Star
Bevelled Diagonal Block
Bevelled Diamond and Star
Bevelled Star
Big Diamond
Birch Leaf
Bird and Strawberry
Birds at Fountain
Bleeding Heart
Block and Fan
Block and Pleat
Block and Rosette
Block and Triple Bars
Blocked Arches
Blocked Thumbprint Band
Bontec
Bow Tie
Boxed Star
Box-in-Box
Brazen Shield
Brick Window
Brilliant
Bristol Diamond
Britannic
Broken Column
Broken Pillar and Reed
Buckle, Early
Buckle with Star
Bull's Eye and Fan
Bulls Eye and Spear Head
Burred Disc and Fan
Button Arches
Button Band
Button Panel

C

Cabachon, Nr 1951
Cabbage Rose
Cabbage Rose (Central)
Cable
Cable with Ring
Cactus
Cadmus
California
Cambridge 2351
Cambridge 2507
Cambridge 2653
Cambridge 2660
Canadian
Candlewick (aka Cole, Banded Raindrop)
Cane and Rosette, Nr 125
Cane Horseshoe
Cane Insert
Cannonball Pinwheel
Cardinal
Carmen
Carolina
Cathedral
Cavitt
Celtic Cross
Chain
Chain and Shield
Chain w/Star
Champion
Champion (Greentown Nr 75)
Chandelier
Checkerboard
Cherry and Fig
Chesterfield
Chestnut
Chippendale
Chrysanthemum (Riverside)
Church Windows
Circular Saw
Clear Diagonal Band
Clear Ribbon
Clover
Coarse Zig Zag (Highland)
Coin
Colonial (Bryce)
Colonial Nr 300 Heisey
Colonial Nr 400 Heisey
Colonial Scalloped Top, Nr 400, 400½
Colonis
Colorado
Columbia w/Pie Crust Edge
Columbian Coin
Connecticut
Contessa
Continental, Nr 339, 339½
Co-op Columbia
Cord and Tassel
Cord Drapery
Cordova
Cornell
Corner Medallion Variant, Nr 782
Cornucopia
Corona
Corrigan
Cottage
Cradled Diamonds
Croesus
Crown Nr 52
Crystolite
Crystal Rib
Crystal Wedding
Crystal Wedding (O'Hara Glass)
Cupid and Venus
Currant
Currier and Ives
Curtain
Curtain Tie Back
Cut Block, Nr 1200
Cut Log

D

Dagger
Dahlia
Daisy and Button Nr 782

Daisy and Button with Crossbars
Daisy and Button w/Thumbprint Panel
Daisy Band
Daisy Medallion
Dakota
Dalzell's Priscilla
Deer and Pine Tree
Delos
Dewdrop
Dewdrop in Points
Dewdrops and Flowers
Dewdrop w/Star
Diagonal Band
Diagonal Ribbon Band, Duncan
Diamond
Diamond and Sunburst
Diamond Band
Diamond Block w/Fan
Diamond Cut w/Leaf
Diamond Point
Diamond Point Discs
Diamond Ridge
Diamond Thumbprint
Diamond Waffle
Diana Nr 601
Dolphins and Herons
Doltec
Dotted Loop
Double Arch
Double Donut
Double Fan
Double Pinwheel
Doyle's Shell
Duncan's Clover
Duncan Nr 40
Duncan's Late Block
Dunmoyle

E

East Liverpool
Effulgent Star, Nr 875
Egg in Sand
1883 Pattern
Electric
Elephant Toes
Elite
Ellrose
Empress
Era
Era (Variant)
Esther
Etruscan
Eureka
Evangeline
Eyewinker

F

Fagot
Fan Band
Fancy Loop, Nr 1205, 1205½
Fandango, Nr 1201
Fan with Diamond
Fashion
Feather
Feather Band
Feather Duster
Feathered Medallion
Fentec
Ferris Wheel
Festoon
Field Thistle
File
Fine Cut
Fine Cut and Block
Finecut and Panel
Fine Cut Star and Fan
Fishscale
Flattened Diamond and Sunburst
Fleur-de-Lis and Drape
Floral Embossed
Floral Oval
Florence, Pattern 183, aka Stippled Bar/Bands or Panel/Bands
Florida (State Series)
Florida
Florida Palm
Flowered Scroll Nr 2000
Flower Pot
Flute
Flute Band, Nr 877
Fostoria's Atlanta
Frisco
Frontier
Frosted Circle
Frosted Fleur-de-Lis
Frosted Magnolia
Frosted Medallion
Fulton (Martha's Tears)

G

Gala
Galloway
Garden of Eden
Garden Pink
Garfield Drape
Gem
Georgia
Giant Bull's Eye
Globe and Star
Gonterman
Good Luck
Gooseberry
Gothic
Grape Band
Grand
Grated Diamond and Sunburst
Grenade (Grenada)
Groove and Slash Nr 1250
Group Thumbprint

H

Haley's Comet aka Halley's Comet
Hand
Hand (different from above)
Hanover
Hartley
Harvard Yard
Heart Stem
Heart w/Thumbprint
Heavy Finecut
Heavy Gothic
Heck
Heisey's Nr 300 Colonial
Helene
Henrietta
Hero
Herringbone, Indiana Tumbler & Goblet
Herringbone Buttress, Greentown
Hexagonal Bull's-Eye
Hickman
Hidalgo
High Hob
Hobbs Diamond and Sunburst (Hobbs, Bruckunier and Co)
Hobbs (Lee plate 83)
Hobbs Hobnail (Westmoreland Book)
Hobnail
Hobnail, Pointed
Hobnail Nr 118
Holly Clear (has panels)
Holly (Sandwich Glass)
Holly Golden Agate and Clear
Homestead Nr 63 (1900)
Honeycomb
Honeycomb with Star
Horn of Plenty
Horseshoe Stem

I

Illinois
Imperial
Indiana
Indiana Nr 156
Indiana Nr 168
Intaglio Daisy
Inverted Feather
Iowa
Iris
Ivanhoe
Ivy in Snow

J

Jacob's Ladder
Janus
Jasper
Jersey Swirl
Jewel
Jewelled Moon and Stars
Jewel with Dewdrop
Jubilee (aka Isis)

K

Kalonyal, Nr 1776
Kansas
Kayak
Kentucky
Keystone
King Arthur
King's Crown
King's Curtain
King's 500
Kismet (909)
Klondike
Kokomo

L

Lacy Daisy
Lacy Dewdrop
Lacy Spiral
Late Thistle
Late Washington
Lattice
Lattice Thumbprint

Laurel
Laverne (Leverne)
Leaf
Leaf Medallion
Lily of the Valley
Lincoln (Nr 1861)
Lindburgh
Lined Ribs (Nr 855)
Lion (Frosted Lion)
Locket on a Chain, Nr 160
Loop
Loop and Dart
Loop with Dewdrop(s)
Loop with Stippled Panels
Louise
Louisiana

M

Madolin
Madora
Magedalent or Mondalene
Magna
Magnolia
Maine
Majestic
Majestic (Pilgrim)
Maltese Cross
Manhattan
Manhattan
(different from above)
Manhattan
(Millersburg Glass)
Maple
Mardi Gras
Marlboro
Marsh Fern
Marsh Pink
Martec — cake plate
Maryland
Mascotte
Masonic
Maypole
McKee's Sunburst
Medallion
Medallion Sunburst
Melrose
Michigan
Millard
Minerva
Minnesota
Missouri
Moon and Star
Mount Vernon plate
Murano

N

Nail
Nelly
Nestor
Nevada
New Crescent
New England Pineapple
New Era (Ward's)
New Hampshire
New Jersey
New Martinsville
Nonpareil
Nugget-Late
Nr 33 Salver
Nr 40 Salver
Nr 44 Salver
Nr 75 (Riverside)
Nr 75 Square
(Adams Co)
Nr 98 Westmoreland
Nr 120
Nr 150
Nr 200 Westmoreland
Nr 307
Nr 331 Block
Nr 444
Nr 500 (Westmoreland)
Nr 544
Nr 601 Diana
Nr 677
Nr 782
Nr 800, Heavy Fine Cut
Nr 857
Nr 901 (Plain Salver)
Nr 956 Fostoria
Nr 1641
Nr 1883
Nr 2001

O

Odd Fellow
Oesterling Salver
O'Hara Diamond
O'Hara's Crystal Wedding
O'Hara's Crystal
Wedding Variant
Okay
Old Columbia
aka Prism Buttress
Old Williamsburg, Nr 341
Omnibus
Oneata
One-O-One
Opal Salver
Open Rose
Opposing Pyramids
Oregon
Ornate Star (cake plate)
Oval Medallion

P

Paddlewheel Shield
Palmette
Palm Leaf Fan
Panama
Panel and Diamond Point
Panel and Star (Nr 500)
aka Column and Block
Paneled Cane, Nr 315
Paneled Daisy
Paneled Thistle
Panelled Diamond Block(s)
Panelled Diamond Cut and Fan
Panelled Diamond Point
Panelled Dogwood
Panelled Forget-Me-Not
Panelled Heather
Panelled Ivy
Panelled Palm
Panelled Primula
Panelled Sawtooth
Panelled Sunflower
Panel with Diamond Point
Pathfinder
Pattee Cross
Pavonia
Peerless, Nr 300
Peerless Heisey
Peerless Model
Peerless, Model Flint Co,
Albany
Perkins
Pert
Petticoat
Picket
Pillow and Sunburst
Pillow Encircled
Pillows, Nr 325
Pineapple and Fan, Nr 1255
Pineapple and Fan
Pimlico (Lotus Leaf)
Pittsburgh (cake basket)
Pittsburgh Nr 2001 (1891)
Pittsburgh Fan
Plain Band, Nr 1225
Pleat and Panel
Pleat Band
Pleated Medallion
Plume
Plutec
Plytec
Pogo Stick
Pointed Jewel
Popcorn
Portieux
Portland
Potpourri
Powder and Shot
Pressed Diamond,
Nr 775
Pressed Leaf
Pride
Primrose
Prince of Wales Plumes,
Nr 335
Princess Feather
Princess Plaza (square) Nr 5527,
(round) Nr 5533
Priscilla (Fostoria)
Prism and Flute
Prism Arc
Prism Buttress,
aka Old Columbia
Prism Column
Prison Stripe
(The) Prize
Punty & Diamond Point
Punty Band, Nr 1220
Pyramids

Q

Quaker Lady
Quartered Block
Queen
Queen Anne, Nr 365
Queen Anne
Queen's Necklace
Question Mark
Quintec

R

Radiant
Raindrop
Rambler
Ray
Rayed Flower
Rebecca at the Well
Recessed Panel
Red Block
Reticulated Cord

Revere, Nr 1183
Reverse Torpedo
Reward (Nr 511)
Ribbed Ellipse
Ribbon Candy
Ridgeleigh, Nr 1469
Ring and Petal
Ripley's Nr 10
Rising Sun
Riverside's Aurora
Roanoke
Roanoke Star
Robin Hood, Nr 603
Rock Crystal
Rocket
Rock Rib (rework of America by removing slashes from the swirl pattern)
Roman Rosette
Romola
Rope, Nr 794
Rope, Nr 795
Rope, Nr 796
Rose in Snow
Rose Point Band
Rose Sprig
Rosette
Rosette and Palms
Rosette with Pinwheels
Ruby Thumbprint

S

Saint Bernard
Salvers, 350 Ware
Salver, 350 – Heavy
Salvers Nrs 2500, 2508, 2537, 2577
Salver, F-8313-1
Sawtooth
Sawtoothed Honeycomb
Scalloped Diamond Point Pattern 439
Scalloped Six Point
Scalloped Swirl
Scalloped Tape
Scroll with Cane Band
Scroll with Flowers
Seashell
Sequoia
77 (Seventy Seven), Royal Ware
Sheaf and Block
Sheaf and Diamond
Shell
Shell and Jewel
Shell and Tassel
Sheraton
Shimmering Star
Shoshone
Shrine
Shuttle
Silver Queen (Elmino)
Simoon
Six Panel Finecut
Skilton
Slewed Horseshoe
Snail
Snow Band
Snowflake
Snowflower
Solar
Spiral and Maltese Cross
Spirea Band
Sprig
Squat Pineapple
"S" Rib
Star
Star Galaxy, Kamm II
Starglow
Star in a Square (Star-in-Square)
Star in Bull's Eye
Star in Diamond
Star Nr 875
Star Nr 876
Starred Block
Starred Loop
Stars and Bars
Stars and Stripes
Startec
(The) States
Sterling
Stippled Bar
Stippled Chain
Stippled Daisy
Stippled Double Loop
Stippled Forget-Me-Not
Stippled Medallion
Stippled Palm
Stippled Sandbur
Strawberry and Fan Variant
Sunbeam
Sunk Daisy
Sunken Arches
Surprise
Swag Block
Swirl and Dot
Swirled Column
Swirled Star
Swirl with Beaded Band
Sylvan

T

Tarentum's Atlanta
Tarentum's Manhattan
Tarentum's Virginia
Taunton
Teardrop
Teardrop and Thumbprint
Teasel
Teepee
Tennessee
Ten Pointed Star
Teutonic
Texas
Texas Bull's-Eye
Texas Star
Thistle
Three Face
Three-in-One
Thumbprint
Tile (aka Optical Cube)
Tokyo
Torpedo
Touraine, Nr 335, 337½
Tree of Life with Hand
Triple Thumbprint
Trump
Truncated Cube
20th Century (Twentieth Century)
Twin Snowshoes
Twin Teardrops
Twist (Model Swirl)
Two Panel
Two-Ply Swirl

U

Unique
U. S. Coin
U. S. Rib Nr 15061
U. S. Thumbprint (1891 – 1892)
Urn, 379
Utah

V

Valencia Waffle
Valentine (plate)
Valtec
Vertical Leaf and Rib
Victoria (Bakewell Pears and Co.)
Victoria (Pioneer)
Victoria (Riverside)
Victoria (U. S. Glass)
V-in-Heart
Virginia
Virginia Nr 1467

W

Waffle with Points
Washington (U. S. Glass)
Water Lily and Cattails
Waverly (Westmoreland)
Wellsburg
Westmoreland 98
Weston
Wheat and Barley
Wheeling (115 Ware)
Whirlpool, Nr 1506
Wildflower
Willow Oak
Winged Scroll, Nr 1280
Wisconsin
Wyoming

X

X-Bull's Eye (Summit)
X-Logs
X-Ray

Y

Yale
Yeoman, Nr 1184
Yesteryear
Yoke and Circle
York Colonial
Yutec

Z

Zenith Block
Zipper Block
Zipper Cross

ACTRESS

OMN: Opera; AKA: Annie, Jenny Lind, Pinafore, Theatrical.

Manufactured by: LaBelle Glass Company, ca 1872; Crystal Glass Company, 1879; Adams and Company, Pittsburgh, Pennsylvania, ca 1880. This pattern was featured in the August 1937 edition of *American Collector*, which stated the manufacturer was an "Unknown Western factory." Twenty-five pieces were made featuring eight actresses, three actors, and scenes from three plays. Some of the items and names/plays are:

Cake salver: Maud Granger and Annie Pixley. Names are printed in glass.

Water pitcher: Balcony scene and name "Juliet" in the glass. On reverse: "Pearl of Savoy"

Goblet: Lotta Crabtree and Kate Claxton

Covered sugar: Lotta Crabtree and Kate Claxton

Butter: Fanny Davenport and Miss Neilson

Creamer: Fanny Davenport and Miss Neilson

Spoon holder: Mary Anderson and Maud Granger

Celery vase: Scenes from Pinafore; "Pinafore" written in glass

Bread plate: Miss Neilson

Covered jam jar: Maud Granger and Annie Pixley

Covered cheese: Robson and Crane as The Two Drominos; title in glass.

Cover: The Lone Fisherman

Compotes: open, 9¾" and 4½", and covered, 7"; Fanny Davenport and Maggie Mitchell

Sauce dishes: 4" and 5", Maggie Mitchell; 4½", Fanny Davenport and Maggie Mitchell

Pickle dish: Kate Claxton and "Love's Request in Pickles"

Oblong relish dishes: 8" x 5", Miss Neilson; 7" x 4½", Maggie Mitchell

Low round bowl: 6", Lotta Crabtree. Name not written

Butter dish

The information above was furnished courtesy of Ken Freeston of Freeston Antiques and Collectibles, Newtown, Connecticut. The cake stand has either a crystal or frosted pedestal. The names Maud Granger and Annie Pixley are printed in the cake stand; Fanny Davenport and Miss Neilson are printed in the butter dish. Very hard to see, but it is there!

Top view of cake stand

Item	Size	Crystal
Cake stand	9½"	$260.00
	10" x 6¾"	300.00
Butter	6" x 7½"	175.00

Pedestal

Close up of pattern

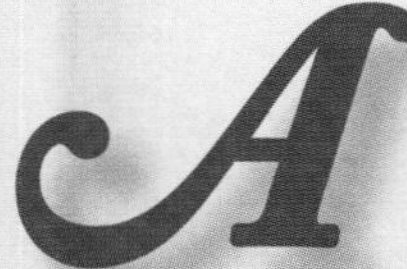

ADA

OMN: Ohio Flint Nr 808.

Manufactured by: Ohio Flint Glass, 1897, and Cambridge Glass Company, 1903. This is a beautiful, very ornate pattern. The cake stand has a slight gallery, comprised of small and large scallops, which are carried through on the base of the pedestal. The pattern is repeated on the pedestal and base. The compote pictured is a "marriage,"as the top, even though the same pattern, does not fit properly. The compote has a scalloped sawtoothed rim, while the cover obviously fits inside a rim, rather than resting on it.

Item	Size	Crystal
Cake stand	8½" x 4¾"	$70.00
	10" x 5½"	95.00
Compote, covered	7¼" x 12"	55.00

Stacked cake stands

Compote

Top view of cake stand

ADAMS' SAXON

Manufactured by: Adams and Company, 1888. This is a plain cake stand with a ½" gallery and a shallow brandy well. The bottom edge of the plate has small scallops extending out. There is a 3¾" inner circle, slightly indented, under the plate with the same scallops as on the edge. The pedestal is comprised of six panels. This pattern is often seen etched, as it is very plain.

Item	Size	Crystal
Cake stand	10" x 7¼"	$90.00

Cake stand

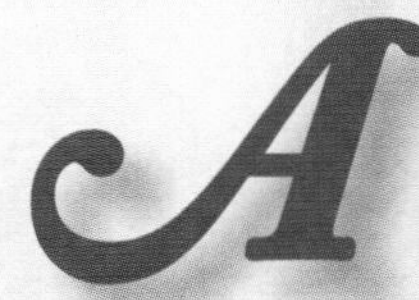

ADAMS' THOUSAND EYE

OMN: Adams Nr 130; AKA: Banded Thousand Eye, Three Knob.

Manufactured by: Adams and Company, ca. 1874. If you look closely at the picture of the three cake stands, you will note that the blue and amber cake stands have closed scallops; those on the green one are open, which are susceptible to breaking. The pedestal has three knobs where it joins the plate. Buyers beware of the many reproductions.

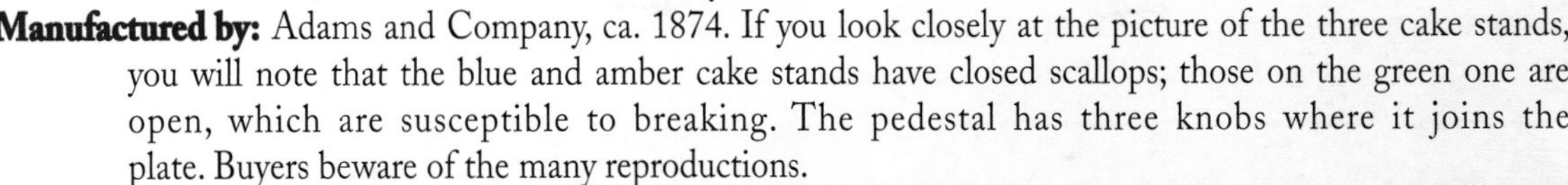

Item	Description	Size	Crystal	Amber	Blue	Green	Vaseline
Cake stand	Closed lattice edge	10"	$100.00	$115.00	$140.00	$180.00	$165.00
		11"	115.00	125.00	165.00	175.00	175.00
	Open lattice edge	10"	165.00	165.00	190.00	215.00	215.00
		11"	140.00	140.00	215.00	240.00	240.00

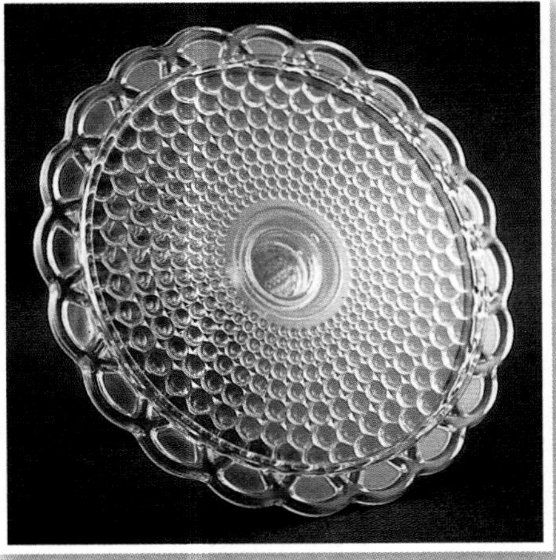

Top view of cake stand, blue

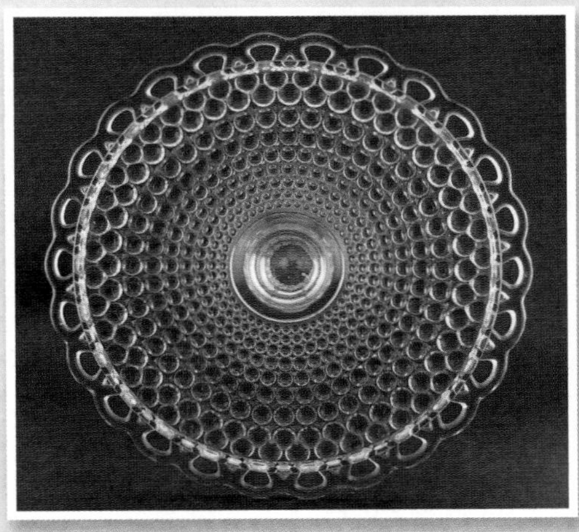

Top view of cake stand, green

Pedestal

Cake stands, amber, blue, and green

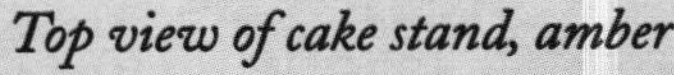

Top view of cake stand, amber

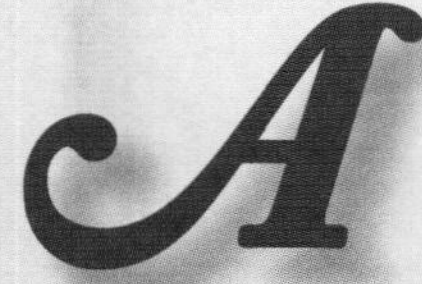

ADONIS

AKA: Pleat and Tuck, Washboard.

Manufactured by: McKee & Brothers, Pittsburgh, Pennsylvania, 1897. This pattern reminds one of pyramids. The pedestal is very attractive and is hollow. Most pedestals are solid glass.

ITEM	DESCRIPTION	SIZE	CRYSTAL	BLUE	CANARY
Cake stand		10½"	$100.00	$375.00	$325.00
Compote	Covered (no lid shown)	8⅜" x 7⅞"	70.00	150.00	175.00
Milk pitcher		6¾" x 7½"	45.00	80.00	65.00

Milk pitcher

Compote

Compote interior

ALABAMA

OMN: United States Glass Nr 15062 – Alabama; AKA: Beaded Bull's Eye and Drape.

Manufactured by: United States Glass Company, Pittsburgh, Pennsylvania, ca. 1899. The design on the plate and pedestal is reminiscent of patriotic bunting. Alabama was the sixteenth of the "state series" patterns made. Cake stand courtesy of Bryan K. James.

ITEM	SIZE	CRYSTAL
Cake stand	9" x 6½"	$265.00
Toothpick		75.00

Cake stand

Toothpick

Pedestal

ALFA

AKA: Boylan, Euclid, Rexford.
Manufactured by: J. B. Higbee Glass Company, ca 1908; New Martinsville Manufacturing Glass Company, 1915.

Item	Description	Size	Crystal
Cake stand or wafer salver		10"	$55.00
Cake stand	Child's	6¼" x 3¼"	65.00
Compote	Open	8¼" x 6½"	40.00
Pitcher		½ gal.	90.00

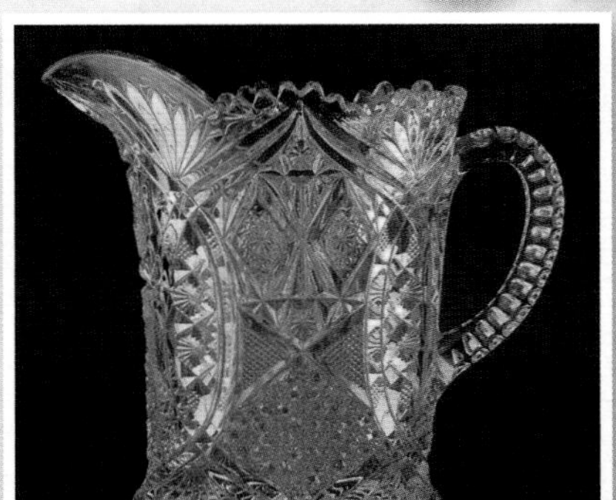

Pitcher

Cake stands

Top view of cake stand

AMAZON

AKA: Sawtooth, Sawtooth Band.
Manufactured by: Bryce Brothers, 1890, Pittsburgh, Pennsylvania.

Cake stand and compote

Top view of cake stand

Item	Description	Size	Crystal	Crystal/Etched
Cake stand		8"	$95.00	$110.00
		9"	115.00	125.00
		10"	130.00	145.00
Compote	Open	7" h	30.00	35.00

AMERICA

OMN: Riverside Nr 348; AKA: Slashed Swirl, Swirl and Diamond-Kamm Nr 1, Swirl and Sawtooth.

Manufactured by: Riverside Glass Company, 1890.

Item	Description	Size	Crystal
Cake stand			$95.00
Compote	Covered (no cover shown)	8"	150.00

Pedestal

Compote interior

AMERICAN

OMN: Fostoria Nr 2056; AKA: Zig Zag Block.

Manufactured by: Fostoria Glass Company, 1915. A limited line of 95 pieces was produced in 1915, which included the round cake stand. The older pieces, which react to a black light, command a much higher price. Originally, the cake plate was attached to the pedestal with glass. In later years the plate and pedestal were glued, which may separate or the glue will yellow with age. Round cake stand courtesy of Robert Wilt.

Item	Description	Size	Crystal
Cake stand	Round	10"	$150.00
	Square	10"	225.00
Creamer			30.00
Sugar			35.00

Top view of square cake stand

Square cake stands

Square cake stand and cream and sugar

Top view of round cake stand

Square and round cake stands

ANTHEMION

AKA: Albany.
Manufactured by: Model Flint Glass Company, Findlay, Ohio, ca 1895.

Item	Size	Crystal
Cake plate	9"	$65.00
Bowl	9½"	35.00

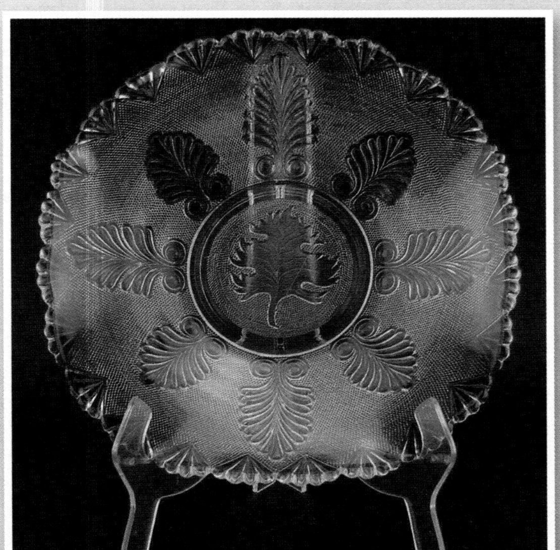

Bowl

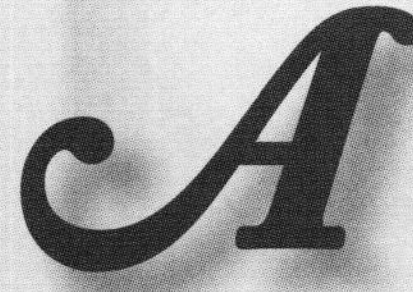

APOLLO

AKA: Canadian Horseshoe, Frosted Festal Ball, Shield Band, Thumbprint and Prisms.

Manufactured by: Adams and Company, Pittsburgh, Pennsylvania, ca. 1875. Beautiful, clear glass, plain, except for a scalloped gallery and skirt with the same design repeated on the base. The plate is often engraved with the design shown on the spooner.

Item	Size	Crystal	Crystal w/Engraved	Crystal w/Frosting
Cake stand	8"	$75.00	$85.00	$95.00
	9"	85.00	95.00	110.00
	10"	100.00	120.00	150.00
	11"	185.00	200.00	235.00
	12"	150.00	185.00	200.00
Spooner		40.00	45.00	50.00

Cake stand

Spooner

APPLIED BANDS

OMN: King Nr 216; AKA: Batesville.

Manufactured by: King, Son and Company, 1883. How this compote has survived these many years in perfect condition is extraordinary! The cover for the compote sits inside the scallops on the bowl portion. If you look closely at the picture, on the left and right sides, you can see that the scallops are on the outside of the cover. The unique design is continued with the base resting on scallops.

Item	Size	Crystal	Crystal/Etched
Cake stand		$75.00	$85.00
Compote	7¼" x 10½"	60.00	70.00

Compote

A

ARCHED FLEUR-DE-LIS

AKA: Fleur-de-Lis, Intaglio, Late Fleur-de-Lis.

Manufactured by: Bryce, Higbee and Company, ca. 1898; J. B. Higbee Glass Company, 1907. This is one of the many cake stands beautifully made during this time period. One cake stand has a plain border; one has a single scallop and one has a double scallop. All have the arched fleur-de-lis design. The grouping of cake stands is courtesy of Louise Wilt, Marie Gibbons, and Robin Whipp-Cook; Louise and George Wilt provided the bowl. Banana stand courtesy of Carolyn Crozier.

Item	Description	Size	Crystal
Cake stand		9"	$75.00
		10½"	95.00
Banana stand		9¾" x 7½"	75.00
Berry bowl	Master, gilded	8"	80.00
Berry bowl	Master	8"	60.00

Pedestal

Top view of cake stand

Cake stand and banana stand

Cake stands

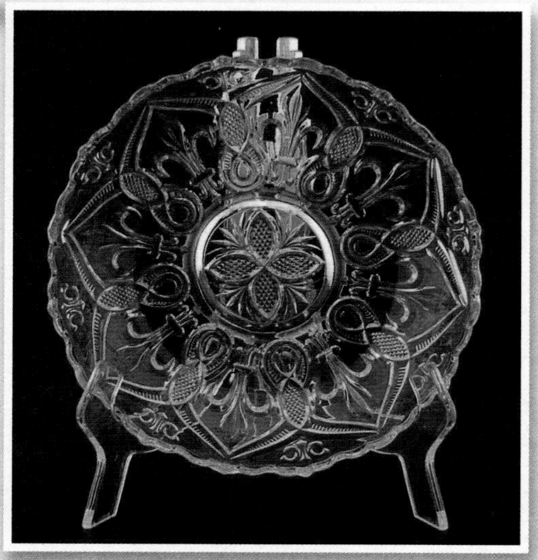

Bowl

Master berry bowl, gilded

ARCHED OVALS

OMN: United States Glass Nr 15091; AKA: Concaved Almond, Optic.

Manufactured by: United States Glass Company, Factory "F" (Ripley and Company), Pittsburgh, Pennsylvania, 1905.

Item	Size	Crystal	Crystal w/Gold
Cake stand		$80.00	$90.00
Creamer	5½" x 4½"	50.00	60.00

Creamer

ARGENT

AKA: Crystal Panels with Cord Band, Rope Bands.

Manufactured by: Bryce Brothers, 1884. The pedestal on this pattern was very popular with the employees, as it has been seen on many other patterns.

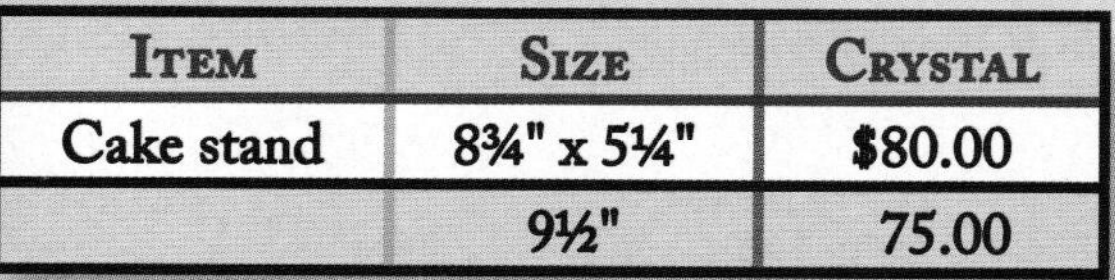

Item	Size	Crystal
Cake stand	8¾" x 5¼"	$80.00
	9½"	75.00

Top view of cake stand

Pedestal

ARROW SHEAF

Manufactured by: Cooperative Flint Glass Company, 1905.

Item	Crystal
Pitcher	$40.00

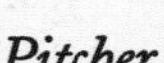

Pitcher

ART

OMN: Art; AKA: Jacob's Tears, Job's Tears, Teardrop and Diamond Block.

Manufactured by: Adams & Company, Pittsburgh, Pennsylvania, ca 1889. The pointed scallops (tear drops) on this cake stand make it difficult to find this pattern in perfect condition.

Top view of cake stand

Item	Size	Crystal
Cake stand	7¾"	$85.00
	9"	115.00
	10"	125.00
	10½"	145.00
Celery vase		50.00

Cake stand and celery

Pedestal

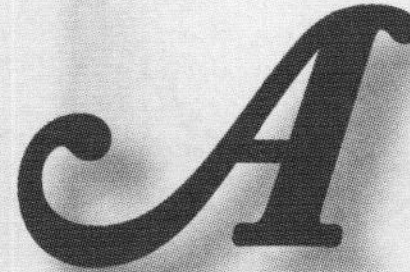

ARTICHOKE

OMN: Fostoria Nr 205; AKA: Frosted Artichoke, Valencia.

Manufactured by: Fostoria Glass Company, ca. 1891. There was limited production in crystal. This pattern is seldom seen.

Item	Size	Crystal	Crystal/w Frosting
Cake stand	10½" x 6"	$300.00	$350.00

Top view of cake stand

Pedestal

ASHBURTON

OMN: Ashburton; AKA: Barrel Ashburton, Choked Ashburton, Dillaway, Double Flute, Double Knob Stem Ashburton, Flaring Top Ashburton, Giant Straight Stemmed Ashburton, Large Thumbprint, Near Slim Thumbprint, Proxy Ashburton, Semi-Squared Ashburton, Short Ashburton, Slim Ashburton, and Talisman Ashburton.

Manufactured by: Boston and Sandwich Glass Company; McKee and Brothers; and New England Glass Company, ca 1850. Courtesy of Carolyn Crozier.

Wine and goblet

Item	Size	Crystal
Cake stand		$140.00
Goblet	3⅛" x 5⅞"	45.00
Wine	2⅝" x 3¾"	45.00

ASHMAN

AKA: Cross Roads.

Manufactured by: Unknown, 1880s. This cake stand is both round and square; the surface for the cake is round; the square portion is on the bottom of the plate. The pedestal and base are square, with the cross repeated on the base. The crosses on the covered compote and pedestal are set so that they are in alignment and squared. The etched compote has the crosses on the ends of the bowl with the pedestal crosses aligned.

Item	Description	Size	Crystal	Crystal w/Etching
Cake stand		8¾"	$225.00	
Compote	Square			
	Covered	5" x 9"	75.00	$85.00
	Open	7"	45.00	50.00

Compotes

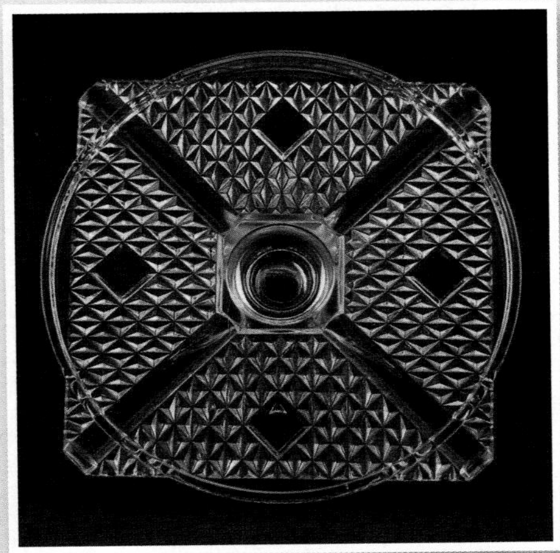

Top view of cake stand

ATLAS

AKA: Bullet, Cannon Ball, Crystal Ball, Knobby Bottom.

Manufactured by: Bryce Brothers, Pittsburgh, Pennsylvania, ca 1889. The design in the center resembles a sailing ship's multiple-spoke wheel, with crystal balls surrounding the rim of the plate.

Item	Size	Crystal	Crystal w/Ruby
Cake stand	8"	$85.00	$190.00
	8½"	90.00	200.00
	9"	115.00	240.00
	10"	140.00	325.00

Pedestal

Top view of cake stand

AURORA

AKA: Diamond Horseshoe.

Manufactured by: Brilliant Glass Company, 1888; Greensburg Glass Company, 1890; and McKee Brothers, Pittsburgh, Pennsylvania, 1902, chocolate only. The plain gallery has two scallops opposite, and there are two opposite scallops on the skirt. An unusual plain pattern.

Item	Size	Crystal
Cake stand	10½" x 6½"	$165.00

Cake stand

Pedestal

AUSTRIAN

OMN: Federal Nr 110, Indiana Nr 200; AKA: Fine Cut Medallion, Panelled Oval Fine Cut, Western.

Manufactured by: Indiana Tumbler and Goblet Company, 1897; Indiana Glass Company, 1907; and Federal Glass Company, 1914. May be found in crystal, amber, canary, green, chocolate, Nile green, opaque, and cobalt. The cake stand is skirted; the pedestal is notched. This pattern is very similar to Cane Medallion and Fancy Loop by Heisey. A Cane Medallion covered creamer, valued at $65 on the left and an Austrian creamer on the right are furnished for comparison of the patterns. Note on the Cane Medallion pattern there is a diamond where the two ovals join.

Item	Size	Crystal	Vaseline
Cake stand	10¼" x 6¼"	$125.00	$350.00
Creamer (no lid shown)	4¼" h	45.00	170.00

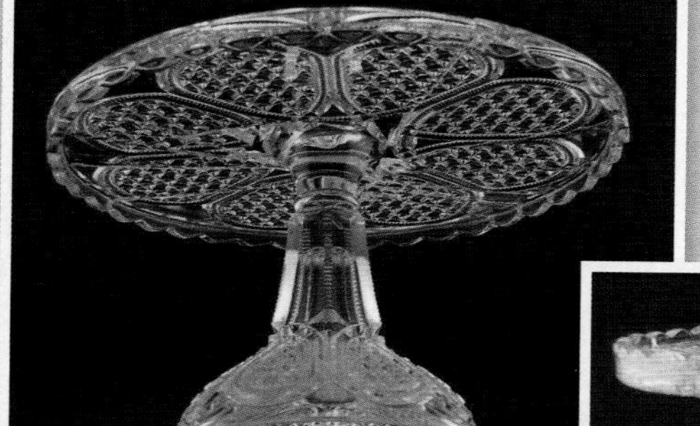

Top view of cake stand

Pedestal

Left: Cane Medallion creamer, right: Austrian creamer

BAKEWELL RIBBON

AKA: Frosted Ribbon, Rebecca at the Well, Simple Frosted Ribbon.
Manufactured by: Bakewell, Pears and Company, 1870; and George Duncan, 1878.

Item	Size	Crystal	Crystal w/Frosting
Cake stand		$65.00	$90.00
Spooner	3¼" x 5¾"	50.00	85.00

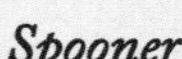

Spooner

BALL AND SWIRL

OMN: Ray; AKA: Swirl and Ball.
Manufactured by: McKee Brothers, 1894. This pattern is found in crystal, crystal with acid finish, and crystal with ruby stain and is easily identified by the balls on the edge of the base or plate that roll inward into swirls. The pedestal and base are swirled.

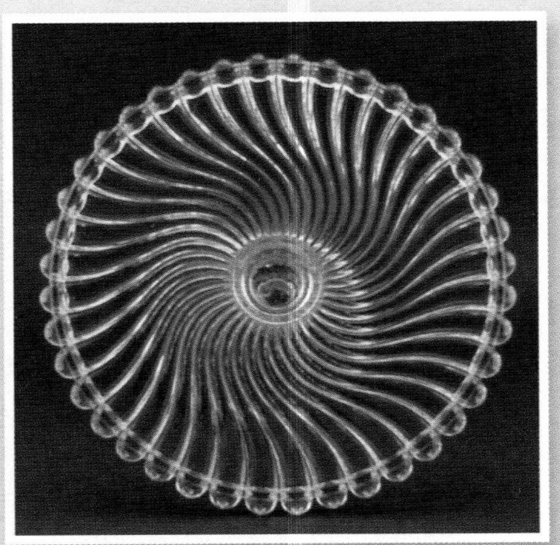

Top view of cake stand

Item	Size	Crystal
Cake stand	10"	$85.00

Pedestal

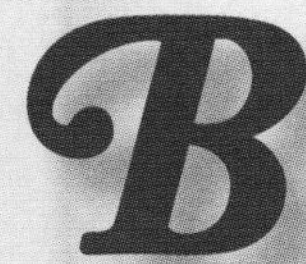

BALTIMORE PEAR

OMN: Gypsy; AKA: Double Pear, Fig, Maryland Pear, Twin Pear.

Manufactured by: Adams and Company, Pittsburgh, Pennsylvania, 1874. Jeannette Glass Company reproduced this pattern. The bread plate pictured is a "modern day rendition" of the original pattern.

Item	Description	Size	Crystal
Cake stand		9¼"	$325.00
		10"	375.00
Bread plate	Round, handled	12½"	45.00

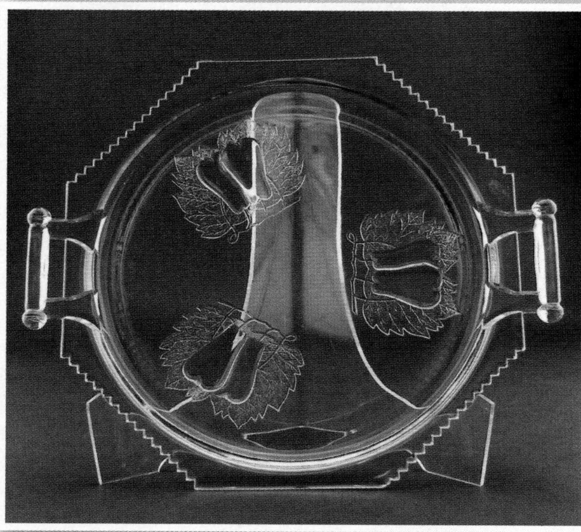

Bread plate

BANDED FLEUR-DE-LIS

OMN: Imperial Nr 3; AKA: Stippled Fleur-de-lis-Diamond Band.

Manufactured by: Imperial Glass Company, ca 1904. This is an impressive cake stand. The stippling in the background is actually daisies with eight petals. Can you imagine how long it took to make the mold? The daisies are much more prominent on the base than on the plate. The bands around the outer edge of the plate and the pedestal are comprised of alternating large and small ovals; the large oval is flat on the bottom and the small oval is pointed. There is one single daisy separating the ovals. The band across the fleur-de-lis is rows of five squares each.

Item	Size	Crystal
Cake stand	9⅞" x 5⅜"	$85.00

Top view of cake stand

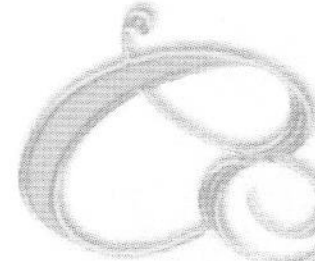

BANDED STAR

Manufactured by: King, Son and Company, 1880. This sauce dish rests on four feet. There is a band of stars around the top edge of the bowl.

Item	Crystal
Sauce bowl	$25.00

Sauce bowl

BARBERRY

OMN: Berry "Seashell."

Manufactured by: McKee and Brothers, Pittsburgh, Pennsylvania, ca 1880; and The Boston Sandwich Company, Sandwich, Massachusetts, ca 1850s – 1860s. This is an excellent high standard, non-flint cake stand to use during the holidays. The cake stand is decorated with four groupings of three leaves and two clusters of barberries each. The finial on the covered compote is in the shape of a seashell. Cake stand courtesy of Jane M. O'Brien.

Item	Description	Size	Crystal
Cake stand		11" x 5"	$235.00
Compote	Covered	8¼" x 8½"	160.00

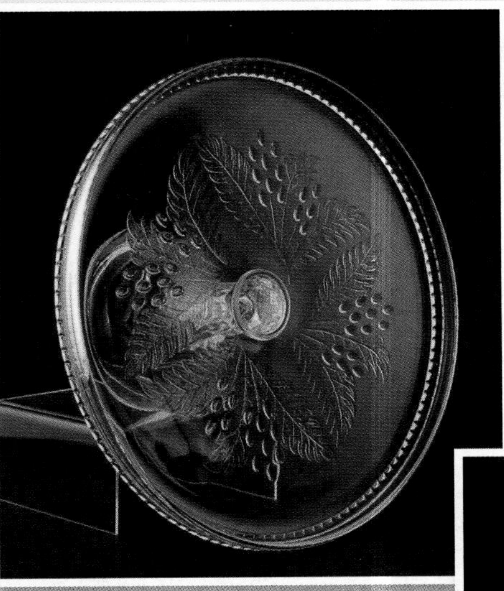

Top view of cake stand

Compote, covered

Cake stand and compote

BARLEY

Manufactured by: Unknown. Any color is considered rare. This is a very dainty cake stand. Note the design on the gallery.

Top view of cake stand

Item	Size	Crystal
Cake stand	8"	$60.00
	9"	70.00
	9½"	90.00
	10"	120.00
	11"	140.00
Water pitcher		55.00

Pitcher

BARRED FORGET-ME-NOT

Manufactured by: Attributed to Canton Glass Company, Canton, Ohio, 1883 to 1890, by J. Stanley Brothers, Jr. (*News Journal,* American Pattern Glass Society, Volume 12, Number 2, Summer 2005). This is a busy pattern with stippled background and flowers and "bars" (fences).

Item	Size	Crystal
Cake stand	8¼" x 6½"	$90.00

Top view of cake stand

Pedestal

B

BARRED OVAL

OMN: United States Glass Nr 15004; AKA: Banded Portland, Banded Portland-Frosted, Buckle, Frosted Banded Portland, Oval and Crossbar, Purple Block.

Manufactured by: United States Glass Company, Pittsburgh, Pennsylvania, Factory D. This is a very glamorous cake stand with ruby stain, courtesy of Eileen and Richard Flaks. Syrup courtesy of Carolyn Crozier.

Item	Size	Crystal	Crystal w/Ruby
Cake stand	10" x 6"	$135.00	$650.00
Syrup	4¾" x 5⅞"	55.00	135.00

Syrup

Cake stand

BARTHOLDI

OMN: O'Hara Nr 650; AKA: Daisy and Button Band.

Manufactured by: O'Hara Glass, 1885. This pattern was also done with ruby stain.

Item	Crystal	Crystal w/Etching
Cake stand	$75.00	$85.00
Compote	55.00	65.00

Compote

BEADED BAND

Manufactured by: Unknown, mid 1880s.

Item	Size	Crystal
Cake stand	7½"	$60.00
	8½"	65.00
	9"	75.00
	10"	90.00

Top view of cake stand

Pedestal

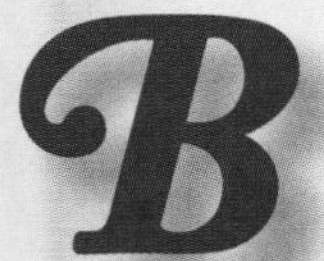

BEADED GRAPE MEDALLION

Manufactured by: The Boston Silver Glass Company, East Cambridge, Massachusetts, 1869. Goblet courtesy of Carolyn Crozier.

Goblet

Item	Size	Crystal
Cake stand	11"	$95.00
Goblet	3⅛" x 6"	60.00

BEADED OVAL AND SCROLL

AKA: Dot.

Manufactured by: Bryce, McKee and Company, Bryce, ca. 1880.

Item	Size	Crystal
Cake stand		$60.00
Creamer	4¾" x 4½"	50.00
Spooner	3½" x 4¼"	50.00

Creamer and spooner

Cheese dish plate

BEADED PANEL AND SUNBURST

OMN: Heisey Nr 1235.

Manufactured by: A. H. Heisey Glass Company, Newark, Ohio; ca 1897, discontinued before 1913. Occasionally pieces are found marked with the "Diamond H." There are more than 80 pieces in this pattern.

Item	Description	Size	Crystal
Cake stand or salver	High standard	9"	$140.00
	Low-foot	7" – 8"	90.00
	Low-foot	10" – 11"	110.00
Cheese dish plate			25.00

BEADED SWIRL

OMN: Duncan Nr 335; AKA: Swirled Column.

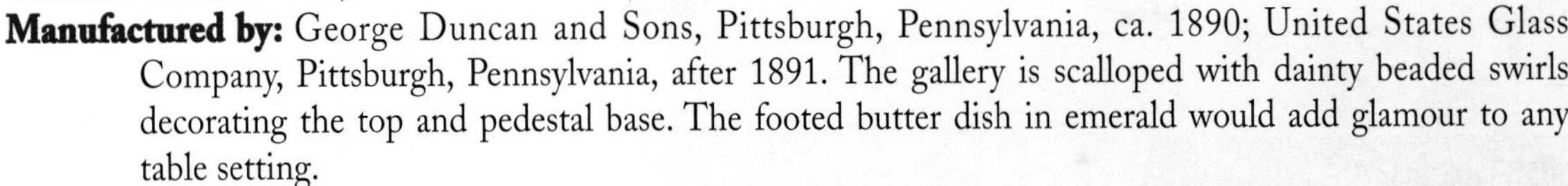

Manufactured by: George Duncan and Sons, Pittsburgh, Pennsylvania, ca. 1890; United States Glass Company, Pittsburgh, Pennsylvania, after 1891. The gallery is scalloped with dainty beaded swirls decorating the top and pedestal base. The footed butter dish in emerald would add glamour to any table setting.

Item	Size	Crystal	Emerald Green
Cake stand	9¾"	$95.00	$135.00
Butter dish	8¼" x 7"	65.00	90.00

Top view of cake stand

Pedestal

Butter dish

BEADED SWIRL AND DISC

OMN: United States Glass Nr 15085.

Manufactured by: United States Glass Company, ca. 1904. This pattern is distinguished by large beaded swirls similar to a long and narrow "s" with disc shapes at the top.

Item	Size	Crystal
Cake stand		$60.00
Creamer	4" x 4½"	50.00

Creamer

BEADED SWIRL AND LENS

AKA: Beaded Swirl.

Manufactured by: Unknown. This pattern is similar to Duncan Nr 335, Beaded Swirl. Cruets courtesy of Carolyn Crozier.

Cruets

Item	Description	Size	Crystal
Cake stand			$75.00
Cruet	w/original stopper	7¼" x 3½"	75.00

BEAD SWAG

OMN: Heisey Nr 1295.

Manufactured by: A. H. Heisey Glass Company, 1899. The flowers and painted beads on dish bottom really add to this otherwise plain pattern.

Item	Size	Crystal	Opal
Cake salver	9"	$75.00	$150.00
	10"	85.00	165.00
Butter dish	6" x 7½"	55.00	110.00

Butter dish

BEAUTIFUL LADY

Manufactured by: Bryce, Higbee and Company, ca. 1905. The pattern is repeated on the base.

Item	Description	Size	Crystal
Cake stand		9½"	$70.00
	Child's	6¼"	55.00

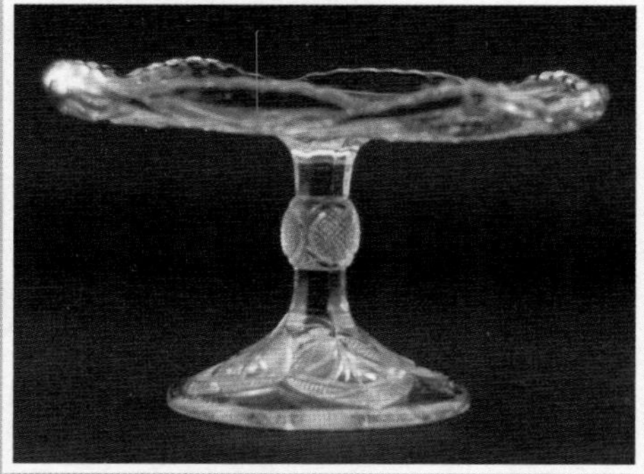

Pedestal

Top view of cake stand

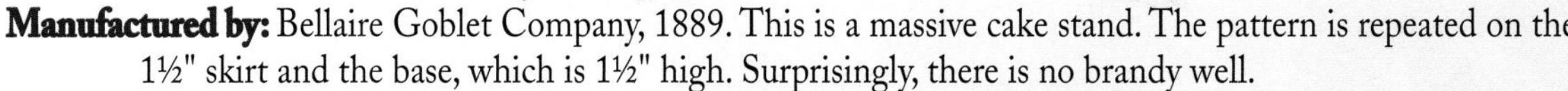

B

BELLAIRE BULLS EYE

OMN: Bellaire Nr 91; AKA: Findlay's Bellaire.

Manufactured by: Bellaire Goblet Company, 1889. This is a massive cake stand. The pattern is repeated on the 1½" skirt and the base, which is 1½" high. Surprisingly, there is no brandy well.

Item	Size	Crystal
Cake stand	10" x 7⅜"	$175.00

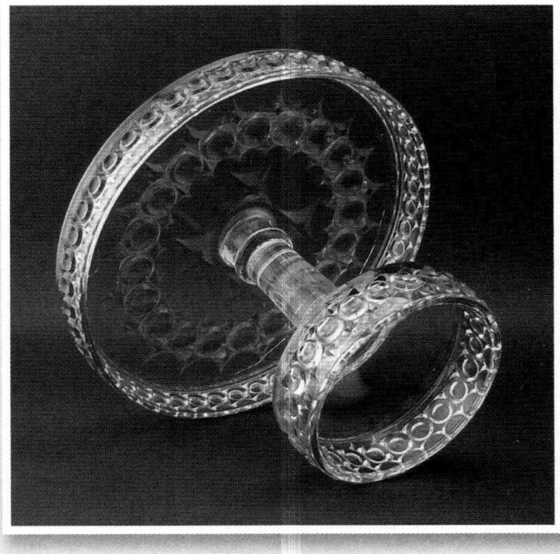

Pedestal

Top view of cake stand

BETHLEHEM STAR

AKA: Bright Star, Six Point Star, Star Burst.

Manufactured by: Indiana Glass Company, Dunkirk, Indiana, ca. 1912; Jefferson Glass Company, Toronto, Montreal, Canada. Cake stand courtesy of Carolyn Crozier.

Top view of cake stand

Item	Size	Crystal
Cake stand	9" x 3¼"	$45.00

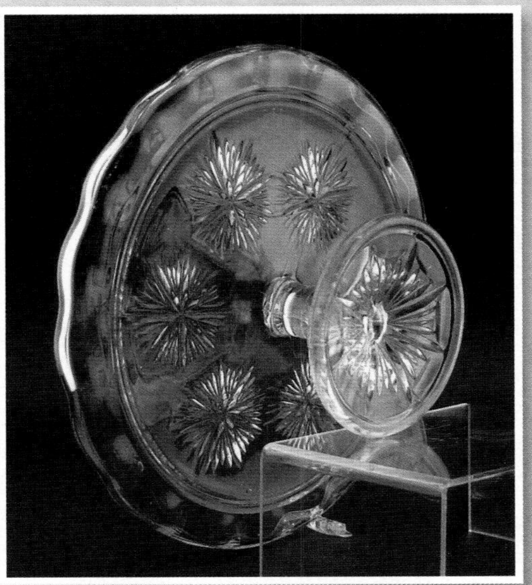

Pedestal

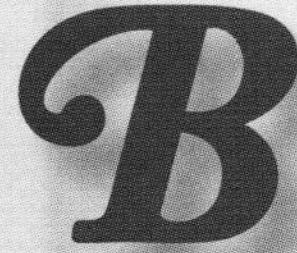

BEVELLED DIAMOND AND STAR

AKA: Albany, Diamond Prism(s), Princeton.

Manufactured by: Tarentum Glass Company, Tarentum, Pennsylvania, ca. 1894 – 1918; burned in 1918.

Top view of cake stand

Item	Size	Crystal	Crystal w/Ruby
Cake stand	9"	$70.00	$230.00
	10"	90.00	300.00
Water tray	10"	40.00	

Pedestal

Water tray

BIG DIAMOND

OMN: Dalzell Nr 39D; AKA: Arkansas.

Manufactured by: Dalzell, Gilmore and Leighton, 1889. This pattern was difficult to identify because the star was placed in a curved blank rather than the diamond shape as shown in most books. The pedestal is the same as most cake stands made by Dalzell, Gilmore and Leighton, i.e., Magnolia.

Item	Size	Crystal
Cake stand	8"	$75.00
	9½"	85.00

Top view of cake stand

Stacked cake stands

B

BIRD AND STRAWBERRY

OMN: Indiana Nr 157; AKA: Blue Bird, Flying Bird and Strawberry, Strawberry and Bird.
Manufactured by: Indiana Glass Company, Dunkirk, Indiana, 1914.

Item	Size	Crystal
Cake stand	9½"	$85.00

Top view of cake stand

Pedestal

BLEEDING HEART

OMN: King's Floral Ware, United States Glass Nr 85 – New Floral.
Manufactured by: King, Son and Company, Pittsburgh, Pennsylvania, ca. 1875; Specialty Glass Company, 1888. This is a rather large plain cake stand, except for the bleeding heart vines on the plate surface. Colors are rare in this pattern. Cake stand courtesy of Sue Edelmon.

Item	Size	Crystal
Cake stand	9"	$120.00
	10"	170.00
	11"	250.00

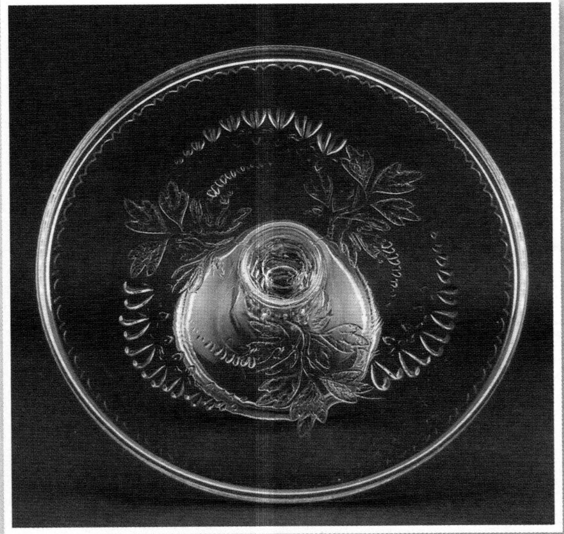

Top view of cake stand

Pedestal

BLOCK AND FAN

OMN: Richards and Hartley Nr 544; AKA: Block w/Fan, Block w/Fan Band.

Manufactured by: Richards and Hartley, Tarentum, Pennsylvania, ca 1885. This is one of the prettiest cake stands; at first glance, it appears to be cut lead crystal. The pattern is repeated on the pedestal and base; the pedestal is hollow.

Item	Description	Size	Crystal	Crystal w/Ruby Stain
Cake stand		9"	$100.00	$340.00
		10"	120.00	400.00
Compote	Open	7"	50.00	110.00
		8"	60.00	120.00
Bowl		8"	45.00	85.00

Pedestal

Compote and bowl

Top view of cake stand

BLOCK AND SUNBURST

Manufactured by: George Duncan and Sons, 1880s.

Item	Size	Crystal
Cake stand		$45.00
Creamer	3¾" x 5"	25.00

Creamer

BLOCK AND TRIPLE BARS

AKA: Block and Fan, and Romeo.

Manufactured by: Unknown. The pattern is repeated on the pedestal.

Item	Size	Crystal
Cake stand	9" x 4"	$70.00

Pedestal

Top view of cake stand

BLOCKED ARCHES (BERKELEY)

OMN: United States Glass Nr 15020.

Manufactured by: United States Glass Company, 1891.

Item	Size	Crystal
Cake stand		$75.00
Compote	5¾" x 11"	70.00

Compote

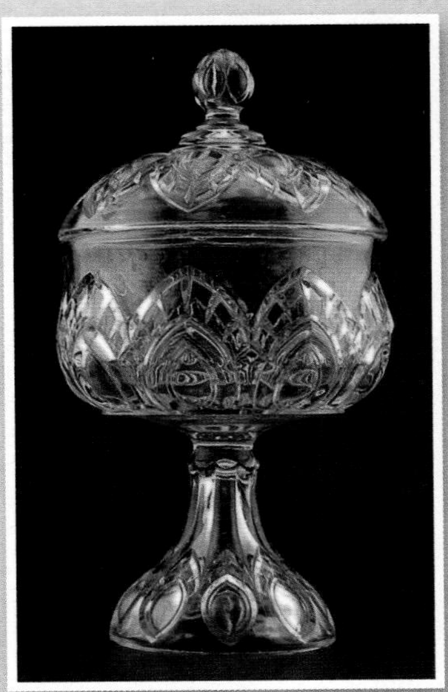

BOWTIE

OMN: Thompson Nr 18; AKA: American Bow Tie.
Manufactured by: Thompson Glass Company, Uniontown, Pennsylvania, 1889.

Item	Size	Crystal
Cake stand	9¼" x 6¼"	$300.00
Compote	10½" x 10¼"	375.00

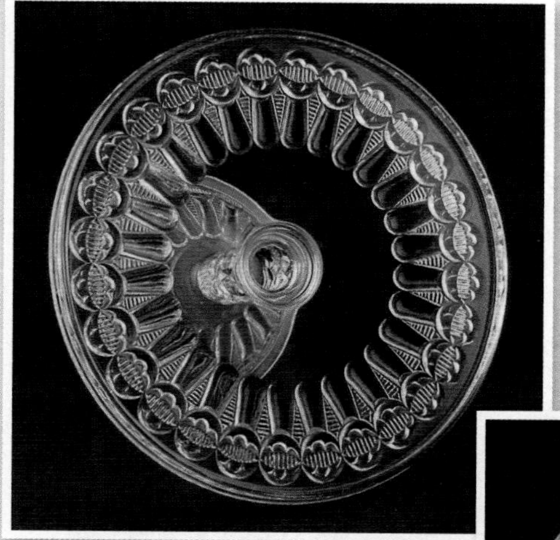

Top view of cake stand

Pedestal

Compote

BRICK WINDOW

OMN: Central 870; AKA: Picture Window.
Manufactured by: Central Glass Company, 1887.

Item	Description	Size	Crystal
Cake stand			$175.00
Compote	Open	8½" x 6¼"	100.00

Compote interior

Pedestal

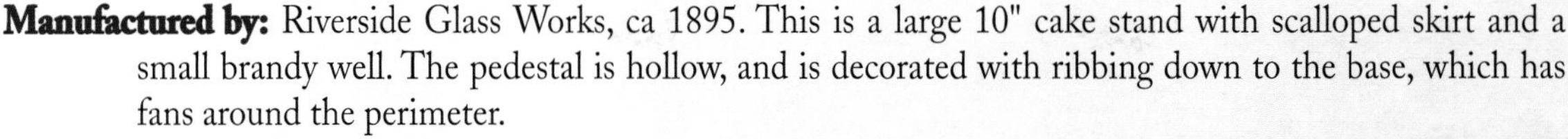

BRILLIANT

OMN: Riverside Nr 436; AKA: Miami, Petalled Medallion.

Manufactured by: Riverside Glass Works, ca 1895. This is a large 10" cake stand with scalloped skirt and a small brandy well. The pedestal is hollow, and is decorated with ribbing down to the base, which has fans around the perimeter.

Item	Description	Size	Crystal	Etched
Cake stand		10" x 6¾"	$110.00	$365.00
Creamer	Individual		35.00	

Top view of cake stand

Creamer, individual

Pedestal

BRITANNIC

Manufactured by: McKee and Brothers Glass Works (under National Glass Company), Pittsburgh, Pennsylvania, ca. 1894 until sometime after 1903. Beautiful amber and ruby stained colors are found, along with crystal.

Item	Description	Size	Crystal	Crystal w/Ruby	Crystal w/Amber
Cake stand		9"	$100.00	$350.00	$300.00
		10"	140.00	400.00	325.00
Compote	Open, plain rim	8"	55.00	125.00	100.00
Cruet with original stopper			60.00	240.00	225.00

Cruet

Pedestal

Compote

BROKEN COLUMN

OMN: United States Company Nr 15021; AKA: Broken Column with Red Dots, Broken Irish Column, Irish Column, Notched Rib, Rattan, Ribbed Fingerprint.

Manufactured by: United States Glass Company at Factories "E" and "J," ca. 1893. In the 1970s, Imperial Glass Company reproduced this pattern for the Smithsonian Institute and Metropolitan Museum of Art; there is no Imperial (IG) mark, but it is marked "SI" and "MMA." Cake stand courtesy of Florence "Flo" Kaluzny.

Item	Description	Size	Crystal	Crystal w/Ruby
Cake stand	High standard	9"	$160.00	$850.00
		10"	240.00	975.00
Compote	Footed			
	Open, round	6"	65.00	250.00
	Open, round	8½"	110.00	325.00
	Covered	7"	175.00	825.00
Pitcher	Water	½ gal	160.00	650.00

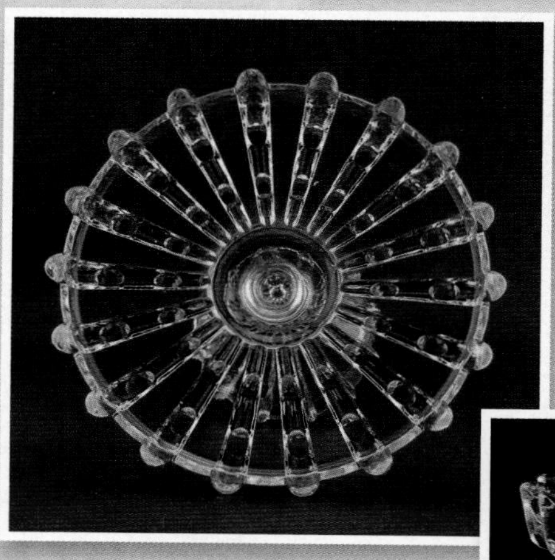

Cake stand

Pedestal

Compote

Pitcher, crystal w/ruby

BUCKINGHAM

OMN: United States Glass Nr 15106; AKA: Crosby.
Manufactured by: United States Glass Company, Glassport Factory, 1907.

Item	Size	Crystal
Bowl	8¼" x 2¾"	$30.00

Bowl

BUCKLE, EARLY

OMN: Gillander Nr 15.
Manufactured by: Unknown but often attributed to Gillander and Sons, Pittsburgh, Pennsylvania, ca late 1870s; and Boston and Sandwich Glass Company, Sandwich, Massachusetts; and Union Glass Company, Somervillle, Massachusetts, 1870s.

Item	Description	Size	Flint	Non-Flint
Cake stand		9¾"	$375.00	$180.00
Compote	Open, low standard	8½"	60.00	35.00

Pedestal

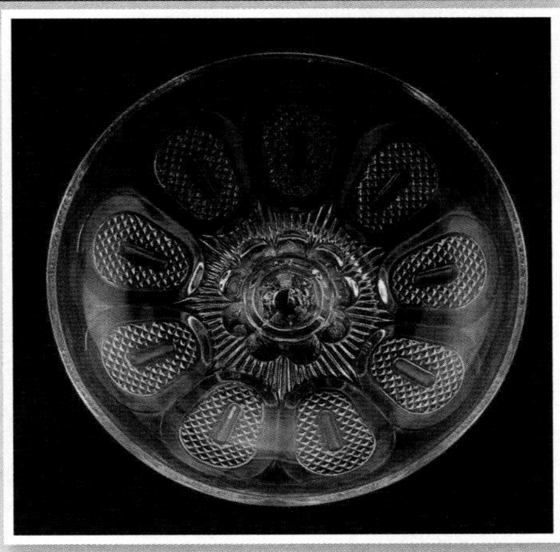

Open compote

BUCKLE WITH STAR

OMN: Orient; AKA: Buckle and Star, Late Buckle and Star.
Manufactured by: Bryce Brothers, 1880.

Item	Size	Crystal
Cake stand	10¾" x 5½"	$75.00

Top view of cake stand

Pedestal

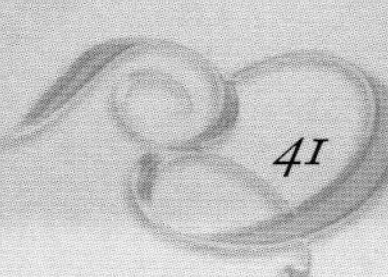

BULL'S EYE AND FAN

OMN: United States Glass Nr 15090; AKA: Daisies in Oval Panels.

Manufactured by: United States Glass Company, Pittsburgh, Pennsylvania, ca. 1904. There are two variations of this pattern; "soft" fan and "hard" fan. Pictured is the "hard" fan, with six lines in the fan. The "soft" fan has two lines.

Item	Description	Size	Crystal	Pink/Amethyst Stain	Green	Blue
Cake stand	High stand	8"	$70.00	$85.00	$110.00	$130.00
		9¼"	90.00	100.00	125.00	160.00
		10"	100.00	120.00	150.00	220.00
Creamer			70.00	90.00	100.00	110.00

Top view of cake stand

Stacked cake stands

BUTTON ARCHES

OMN: Duncan Nr 39; AKA: Scalloped Daisy-Red Top, Scalloped Diamond, Scalloped Diamond – Red Top.

Manufactured by: George Duncan Sons and Company, Washington, Pennsylvania, 1897; and Duncan and Miller Glass Company, 1900. The design on the top is repeated on the base. This pattern was sold as souvenirs with names, dates, etc., imprinted thereon.

Item	Description	Size	Crystal	Crystal w/Ruby Stain
Cake stand	Skirted	9"	$100.00	$290.00
Goblet			30.00	60.00

Top view of cake stand

Pedestal

Cake stand and goblet

BUTTON BAND

OMN: Wyandotte; AKA: Umbilicated Hobnail.

Manufactured by: Ripley and Company, 1886. This cake stand has a plain gallery and a scalloped skirt that extends beyond the edge of the plate. The pattern is very fragile and very few with perfect scallops are found. The bases of the cake basket and spooner are the same scallops as on the plate.

Item	Size	Crystal	Crystal w/Engraving
Cake stand	9½" x 6¾"	$285.00	$300.00
	10"	265.00	290.00
Cake basket with pewter bail handle	9½" x 7" to top of handle	135.00	150.00
Sugar		80.00	90.00

Pedestal

Top view of cake stand

Cake basket

Sugar

BUTTON PANEL

OMN: Duncan Nr 44; AKA: Diamond Crystal, Rainbow Variant.

Manufactured by: George Duncan and Sons, Pittsburgh, Pennsylvania, ca 1900. See *Encyclopedia of Victorian Colored Pattern Glass, Book 1, Toothpick Holders from A to Z*, William Heacock. This is an outstanding cake stand, very good glass, and is generously gilded on the 1" scalloped skirt.

Item	Crystal	Crystal w/Gold
Cake stand	$95.00	$125.00

Top view of cake stand

Pedestal

CABBAGE ROSE

OMN: Central Nr 140; AKA: Rose.

Manufactured by: Central Glass Company, 1870.

Item	Size	Crystal
Cake stand	9"	80.00
	9½"	90.00
	10"	100.00
	11"	125.00
	12"	160.00
	12½"	175.00

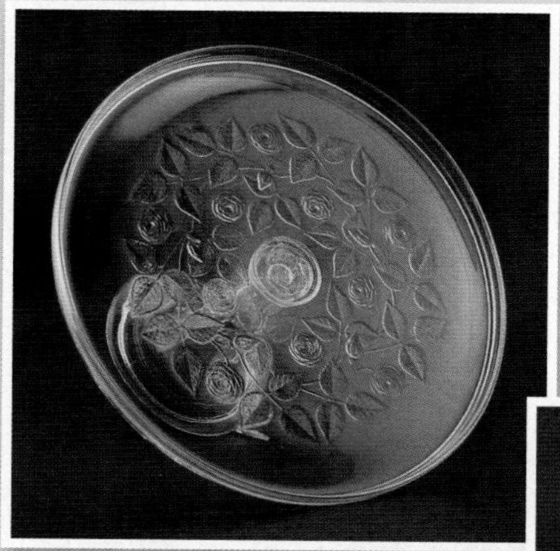

Top view of cake stand

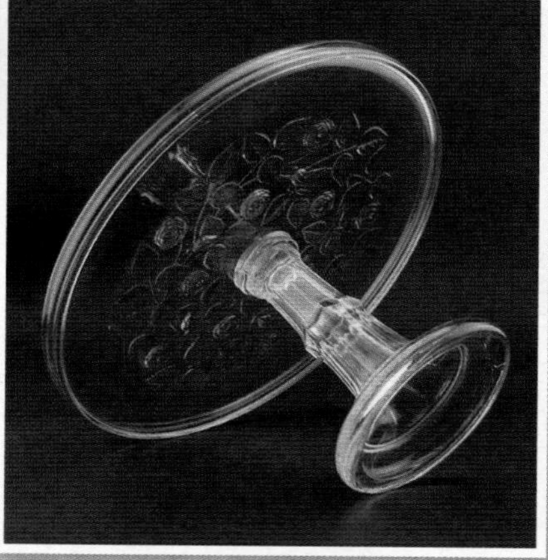

Pedestal

C

CABLE

AKA: Atlantic Cable, Cable Cord.

Manufactured by: The Boston and Sandwich Glass Company, Sandwich, Massachusetts, ca 1850. The cake stand was produced from a footed compote; and is considered extremely rare. Courtesy of Carolyn Crozier.

Item	Description	Size	Crystal
Cake stand			$4,500.00
Compote	Low standard	8⅜" x 4½"	125.00

Compote, side view

Compote, interior

CABLE WITH RING

Manufactured by: Boston and Sandwich Glass Company, 1860s. Sugar courtesy of Carolyn Crozier.

Item	Size	Crystal
Cake stand		$165.00
Sugar (lid not shown)	4⅝" x 4⅜"	165.00

Sugar

CADMUS

OMN: Dugan-Lonaconing Nr 700.

Manufactured by: Beaumont Glass Company, 1902; however, this pattern is pictured in a Butler Brothers catalog dated February 1916, but without a pattern name. It is from an assortment of glass from the Dugan Glass Company, Lonaconing, Maryland, plant, 1915. The pattern is repeated on the pedestal and base.

Top view of cake stand

Pedestal

Item	Size	Crystal
Cake stand	9¼"	$95.00

CALIFORNIA

OMN: United States Glass Nr 15059, Beaded Grape; AKA: Beaded Grape and Vine, Grape and Vine.

Manufactured by: United States Glass Company, Pittsburgh, Pennsylvania, 1899. The pattern is repeated on the pedestal, which is comprised of four panels. Normally there are a pedestal and base; however, in this pattern, there is no separate base. This is the thirteenth in the "state series" patterns. Pickle dish courtesy of Ronda Rose Garcia.

Item	Description	Size	Crystal	Emerald
Cake stand	Square	8¾" x 6¼"	$225.00	$290.00
Pickle dish		7¼"	25.00	35.00

Pickle dish

Pedestal

Top view of cake stand

CAMBRIDGE NR 2351

Manufactured by: Cambridge Glass Company, Cambridge, Ohio; production dates from 1906.

Item	Description	Crystal
Cake stand		$55.00
Pitcher	Milk	95.00

Pitcher

CAMBRIDGE NR 2507

Manufactured by: Cambridge Glass Company, 1903. This cake stand with rosettes has a matching base. There is a Star of David in the center of the plate portion.

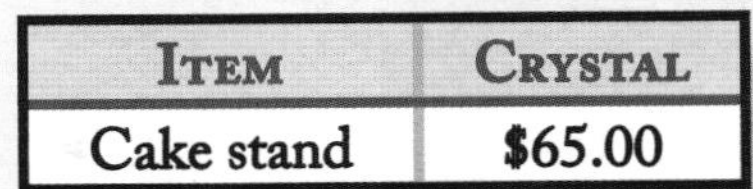

Item	Crystal
Cake stand	$65.00

Pedestal

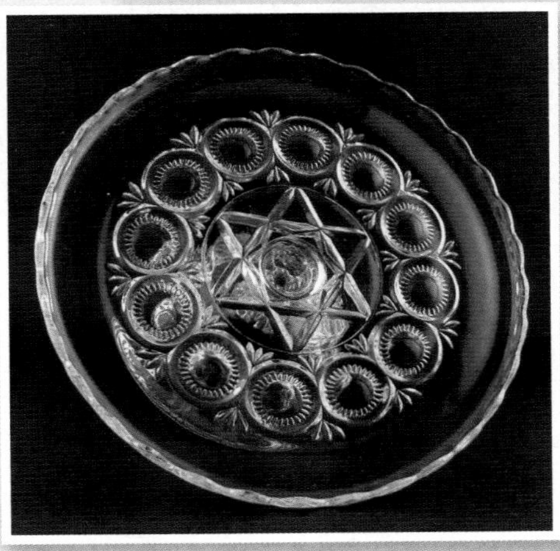

Top view of cake stand

CAMBRIDGE NR 2653

AKA: Ribbon.

Manufactured by: Cambridge Glass Company, 1908.

Item	Size	Crystal
Cake stand	10½" x 5½"	$85.00

Top view of cake stand

Pedestal

CANADIAN

Manufactured by: Unknown, ca 1870s. This is a unique pattern; there are three different scenes on each piece.

Spooner and creamer

Item	Size	Crystal
Cake stand		$225.00
Creamer	5 5/16" x 5 3/4"	80.00
Spooner	3 9/16" x 5 5/8"	75.00

CANE AND ROSETTE

OMN: Duncan Nr 125; AKA: Flower Panelled Cane, Jewel.
Manufactured by: Duncan and Sons, ca 1877. This pattern has nine cane panels with a rosette separating them.

Item	Size	Crystal
Cake stand	11 1/4" x 6 1/2"	$65.00

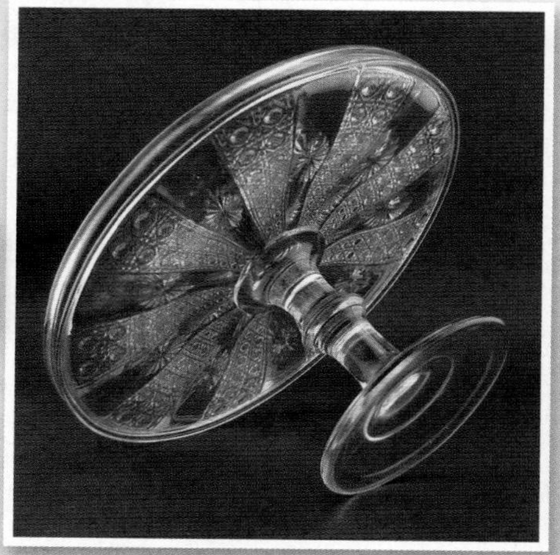

Pedestal

Top view of cake stand

CANE HORSESHOE

OMN: United States Glass Nr 15118; AKA: Paragon.
Manufactured by: United States Glass Company, Pittsburgh, Pennsylvania, ca. 1909.

Berry bowl

Item	Description	Crystal
Cake stand		$80.00
Berry bowl	Individual	20.00

CANE INSERT

AKA: Arched Cane and Fan.
Manufactured by: Tarentum Glass Company, 1898.

Item	Crystal
Cake stand	$55.00
Pitcher	70.00

Pitcher

CARDINAL

AKA: Blue Jay, Cardinal Bird.
Manufactured by: Ohio Flint Glass Company, Lancaster, Ohio, ca 1875.

Spooner and creamer

Item	Size	Crystal
Cake stand		$1,500.00
Creamer	5½" x 5¾"	85.00
Spooner	3¼" x 5"	90.00

CARMEN

OMN: Fostoria Nr 575; AKA: Paneled Diamonds and Finecut.
Manufactured by: Fostoria Glass Company, Moundsville, West Virginia, 1896. Described in editorials of the time as "...different from the average imitation cut-glass pattern coming in fine quality material." Numerous patterns were made to imitate the "brilliant cut glass" — that capability came after the ability to make the pressed glass for the working class. A cake stand was also made with gold on the four "propellers."

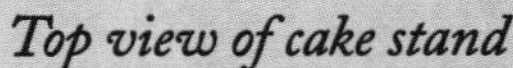

Top view of cake stand

Item	Size	Crystal	Amber Stain	Gold Stain
Cake stand	9"	$85.00	$195.00	$100.00
Bowl	8¼" x 5¼"	60.00	100.00	70.00

Pedestal

Bowl

Bowl

CAROLINA

OMN: United States Glass Nr 15083; AKA: Inverness, Mayflower.

Manufactured by: United States Glass Company, Pittsburgh, Pennsylvania, ca 1903. This is the thirty-fourth pattern of the "state series" by U. S. Glass.

Item	Size	Crystal
Cake stand	8"	$50.00
	9½"	55.00
	10¼"	65.00
	11"	85.00
Compote	9" x 5½"	45.00

Top view of cake stand

Compote

C

CATHEDRAL

OMN: Orion; AKA: Waffle and Fine Cut.

Manufactured by: Bryce Brothers, Pittsburgh, Pennsylvania, ca 1885. Easy to see how this pattern derived its name from the cathedral window thereon.

Item	Size	Crystal	Amber	Blue	Vaseline	Amethyst
Cake stand	10"	$80.00	$90.00	$120.00	$150.00	$180.00
Spooner	3¾" x 5⅝"	55.00	45.00	50.00	60.00	70.00

Spooner

CAVITT

OMN: Bryce Nr 128 and Jones Nr 128; AKA: Mikado Fan, Star.

Manufactured by: Jones, Cavitt and Company, ca. 1887; Bryce Brothers, 1889. This is a large impressive cake stand. The pedestal matches the top. The small oval bowl belonged to Ethan Turner James's paternal great, great grandmother who served cranberry sauce in it at Thanksgiving. This pattern is easily confused with Boling. Thanks to Ashton Marie James for the cake stand photograph.

Top view of cake stand

Item	Size	Crystal
Cake stand		$75.00
Bowl	10"	45.00
	7"	30.00
Berry bowl	4¼"	18.00
Goblet		40.00

Bowl

Pedestal

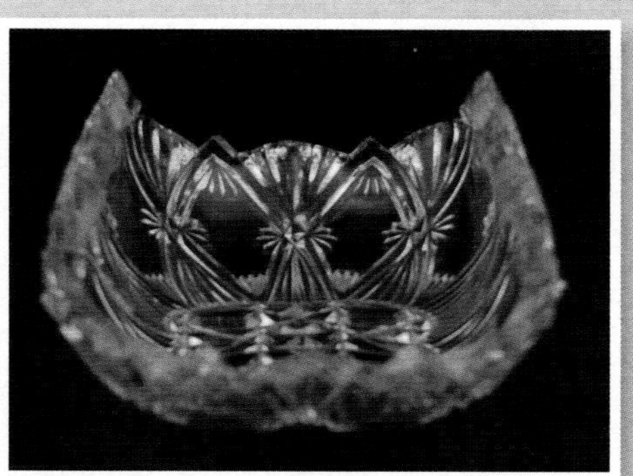

Cranberry bowl

Goblet

CENTENNIAL

AKA: Centennial Drape, Philadelphia Centennial.

Manufactured by: Gillander and Sons, 1876. This goblet has been gifted down five generations to Ashton Marie James. Her paternal great grandfather remembered that his mother (Ashton's great, great grandmother) divided her set of goblets among her children at a 4th of July picnic. He, in turn, gave it to his son, Bradley P. James (Ashton's grandfather) on the 4th of July, 1976.

Goblet

Goblet

Item	Crystal
Goblet	$90.00

CHAIN

Manufactured by: Unknown, probably 1870s.

Item	Size	Crystal
Cake stand	9"	$75.00

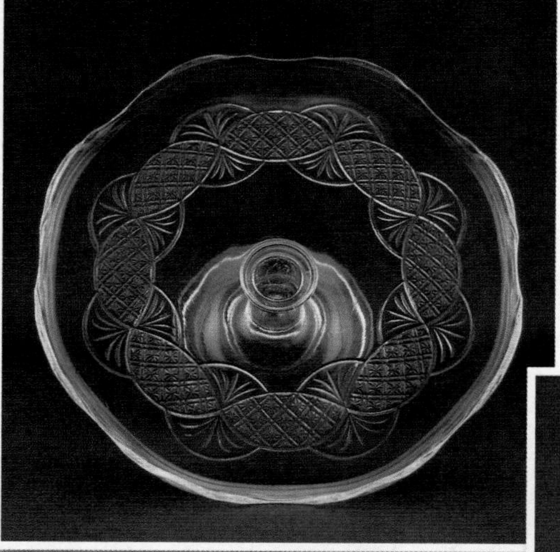

Top view of cake stand

Pedestal

CHAIN AND SHIELD

AKA: Shield and Chain.
Attributed to Portland Glass Company, ca 1870s.

Item	Crystal
Cake stand	$60.00
Creamer	45.00
Spooner	40.00

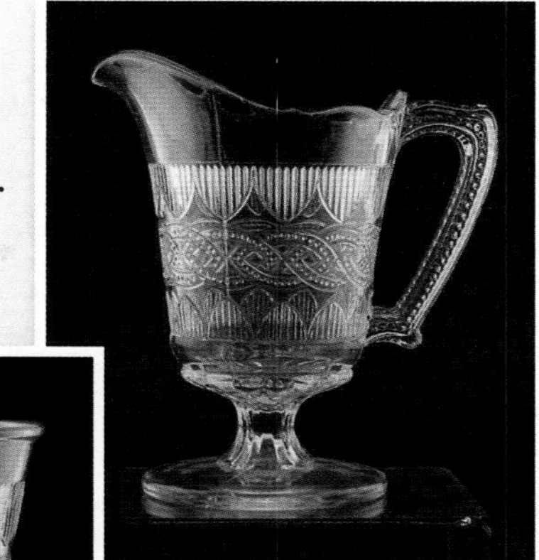

Creamer

Spooner

CHAIN WITH STAR

OMN: Bryce Nr 79; AKA: Chain, Frosted Chain.
Manufactured by: Bryce Brothers, 1882.

Item	Size	Crystal
Cake stand	8¼"	$60.00
	9½"	75.00
	10½"	85.00
Plate		15.00
Sugar bowl (no lid shown)		85.00

Top view of cake stand

Pedestal

Sugar bowl and plate

CHAMPION

AKA: Diamond and Long Sunburst, Fan with Crossbars, Greentown Nr 11, Seagirt.

Manufactured by: Indiana Tumbler and Goblet Company, ca 1894; McKee Brothers, ca 1896; and Indiana Glass Company, ca 1904. One cake stand has a scalloped gallery; the other has a scalloped skirt.

Item	Size	Crystal	Crystal w/Ruby Stain
Cake stand	9½"	$75.00	$125.00
	10½"	85.00	145.00
Compote		50.00	75.00

Top view of cake stand

Pedestal

Stacked cake stands

Top view of cake stand

Pedestal

Compote

C

CHANDELIER

OMN: O'Hara Nr 82 – Crown Jewels.

Manufactured by: O'Hara Glass Company, Pittsburgh, Pennsylvania, ca. 1888. It is easy to see how this pattern got its name. The design on the pedestal of the cake stand is like prisms on a chandelier and is very similar to Heck pedestal. The tips of the prisms on the creamer comprise the base on which it rests. There is a block with crosshatching at the top of each prism. On the creamer, the bottom portion of the twisted handle is a part of the mold, and the top of the handle is applied. The bowl was a gift to Bradley A. James from his paternal grandmother.

Item	Size	Crystal	Crystal w/Etching
Cake stand	11"	$510.00	$700.00
Bowl	10¼" x 5½"	85.00	120.00
Creamer	5¼" x 4"	75.00	85.00

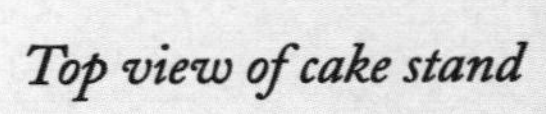

Top view of cake stand

Bowl

Pedestal

Creamer

CHECKERBOARD

OMN: Westmoreland Nr 500; AKA: Block and Fan Variant, Bridle Rosettes, Old Quilt, Square Block.

Manufactured by: Westmoreland Glass Company, ca. 1910. Checkerboard is the longest continuous running line in American tableware.

Spooner

Item	Size	Crystal
Cake plate	10"	$55.00
Spooner		35.00

CHESTERFIELD

OMN: Cambridge Nr 2500; AKA: Diamond Lattice.
Manufactured by: Cambridge Glass Company, Cambridge, Ohio, 1903.

Item	Size	Crystal
Cake stand	8¾" x 4½"	$65.00
Butter dish	7½" x 5½"	40.00

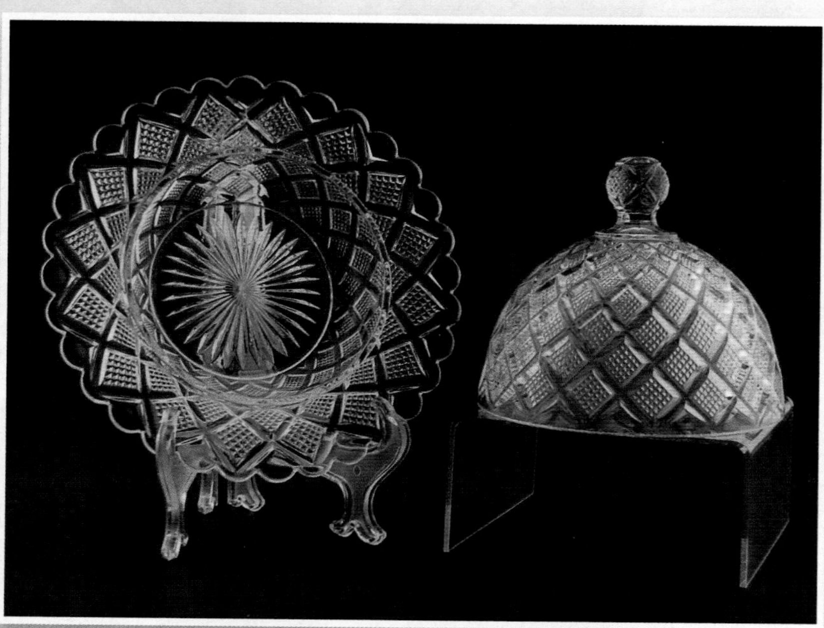

Butter dish

CHIPPENDALE

Manufactured by: Ohio Flint Glass Company, 1907; Jefferson Glass in 1908; and Central Glass Company in 1919. Items are marked Krys-Tol in the bottom. Pattern is easily identified by the handles, which are flat on the top.

Item	Crystal
Cake salver	$75.00
Creamer	25.00
Sugar	25.00

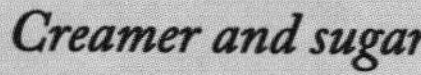

Creamer and sugar

CHRYSANTHEMUM

OMN: Riverside Nr 408; AKA: Double Daisy, Rosette Band.

Manufactured by: Riverside Glass Works, ca 1893. Made in crystal and ruby stain. The chrysanthemum flower is on the base, inside the bowl, on the lid, and comprises the finial on the compote.

Item	Description	Size	Crystal	Crystal/Ruby Stain
Cake salver			$90.00	$390.00
Compote	Covered	8"	110.00	250.00
	Open	8¾" x 7¾"	95.00	200.00
	Covered	7¼" x 11½"	95.00	225.00

Compote, covered

Compote

CHURCH WINDOWS

OMN: United States Glass Nr 15082; AKA: Columbia, Tulip Petals.

Manufactured by: United States Glass Company, 1903.

Item	Description	Size	Crystal	Crystal w/Gilding
Cake stand			$75.00	$85.00
Master berry bowl	Plain	8¾"	35.00	45.00
Bowl	Deep	5½"	25.00	30.00
Berry bowl	Individual	3½"	15.00	20.00

Master and individual berry bowls

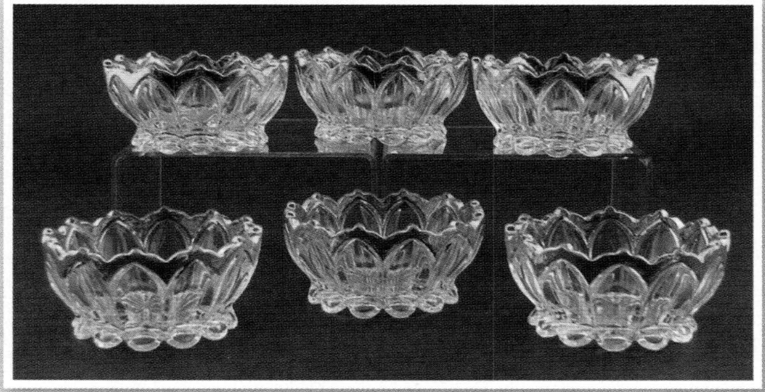

Berry bowls, crystal with gilding

CIRCULAR SAW

AKA: Rosetta.
Manufactured by: Beaumont Glass Company, 1904.

ITEM	SIZE	CRYSTAL
Bowl	8"	$35.00

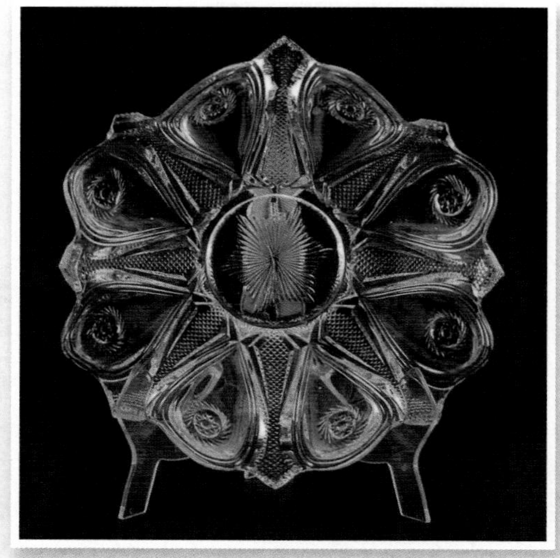
Bowl

CLASSIC

Manufactured by: Gillander and Sons, Philadelphia, Pennsylvania, 1875. Minnie Watson Kamm in her *A Fourth Pitcher Book* (1950) wrote that this is one of the top ranking American patterns, with several different pieces being made, possibly a cake stand. The log feet easily identify the pattern.

ITEM	SIZE	CRYSTAL
Pitcher	9¼"	$575.00

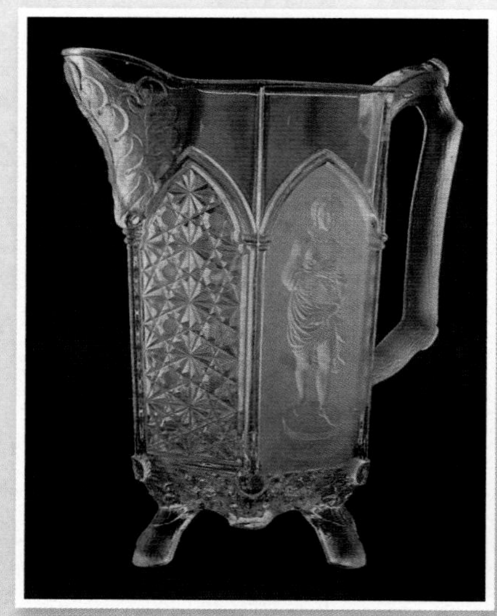
Pitcher

CLASSIC MEDALLION

AKA: Cameo.
Manufactured by: Richards and Hartley Glass Company, Tarentum, Pennsylvania, 1870s.

ITEM	SIZE	CRYSTAL
Creamer	5½"	$65.00

Creamer

CLEAR DIAGONAL BAND

AKA: California State.
Manufactured by: Unknown, ca. 1880s.

Item	Size	Crystal
Cake stand		$95.00
Celery	8½" x 4"	50.00

Celery

CLEAR RIBBON

Manufactured by: Unknown. This pattern is not to be confused with the Ribbon pattern that is found in crystal or frosted. The Ribbon pieces with pedestals have a flat base whereas the Clear Ribbon has a scalloped, footed base.

Item	Size	Crystal	Crystal w/Ruby Stain
Cake stand	8"	$130.00	$175.00
Compote	8½" x 13½"	85.00	110.00

Compote

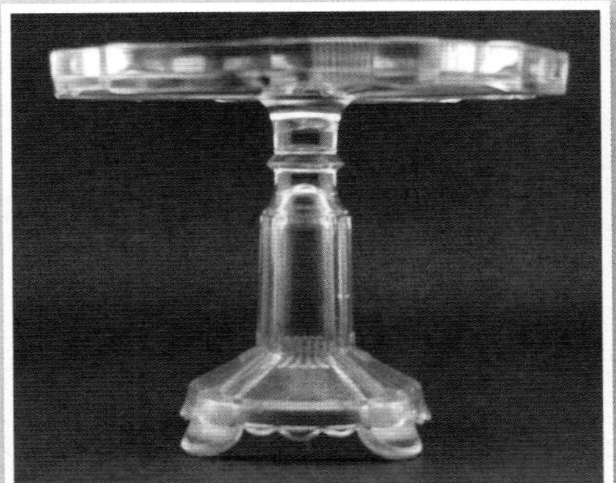

Pedestal

Top view of cake stand

CLOVER

AKA: Leaf Ware.
Manufactured by: Richards and Hartley, 1888.

Item	Description	Size	Crystal
Cake stand			$65.00
Bowl	Triangular	10½"	35.00

Bowl

COARSE ZIG ZAG

AKA: Highland.
Manufactured by: J.B. Higbee Glass Company, ca. 1908; and New Martinsville Glass Manufacturing Company, after 1917.

Item	Size	Crystal
Cake stand	9" x 4½"	$75.00
Banana stand	9⅞" x 7¾"	75.00
Spooner	4⅞" x 3½"	30.00

Top view of cake stand

Pedestal

C

Banana stand

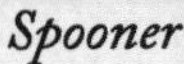

Spooner

COLONIAL

AKA: Estelle, Paden City Nr 205.

Manufactured by: J. B. Higbee Glass Company, 1910; and Paden City Glass Manufacturing Company, 1919. Most often found in crystal and tinted amethyst, with the Higbee trademark bee, characterized by a 28-pointed star in the base of most pieces. The cake stand is courtesy of Carolyn Crozier.

Item	Size	Crystal
Cake stand	6"	$55.00
	9"	60.00
	11"	75.00
Cake tray	10"	65.00
Butter dish	5½" x 8"	50.00

Top view of cake stand

Pedestal

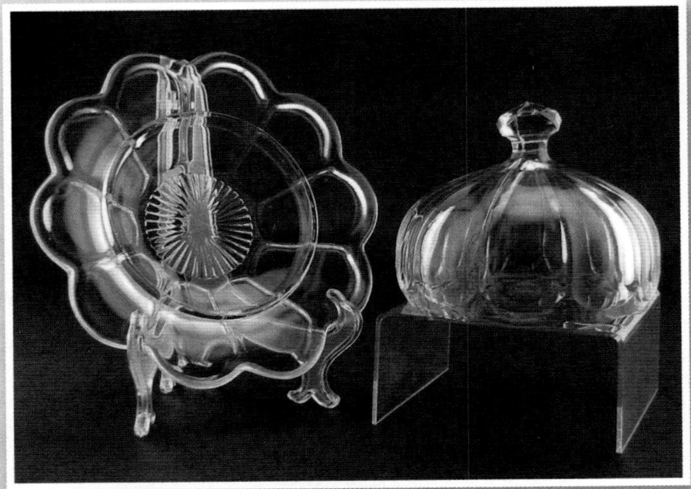

Butter dish

COLONIAL SCALLOPED TOP

OMN: Heisey Nrs 400 and 400½.

Manufactured by: A. H. Heisey and Company, Newark, Ohio, 1909. Cake stand courtesy of Carolyn Crozier.

Item	Size	Crystal
Cake stand	9"	$100.00
	10" x 6"	150.00

Cake stand

COLONIS

AKA: United States Glass Nr 15145.

Manufactured by: United States Glass Company, Glassport, Pennsylvania, Factory "O"-GP, 1913. Pieces may be found decorated in gold, blue, or rose.

Item	Size	Crystal
Cake stand		$55.00
Creamer	5¼" x 3¾"	35.00
Sugar	6½" x 6½"	35.00

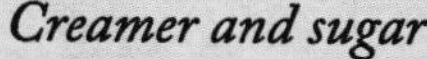

Creamer and sugar

COLORADO

OMN: United States Glass Nr 15057 – Colorado; AKA: Jewel, Lacy Jewel.

Manufactured by: United States Glass Company, Pittsburgh, Pennsylvania, ca 1899 to about 1920. This is the eleventh pattern in the "state series" pattern. Creamer is courtesy of CarolynCrozier.

Item	Size	Crystal	Green w/Gold	Blue
Cake stand	9"	$100.00	$135.00	$225.00
	10½"	120.00	215.00	325.00
Butter	8¼" x 7"	70.00	145.00	325.00
Creamer	5⅜" x 5¾"	50.00	95.00	115.00

Butter, crystal, with cover and emerald bottom

Creamer

COLUMBIA WITH PIE CRUST EDGE

Manufactured by: Dalzell, Gilmore and Leighton, ca. 1893. This cake salver is easily identified by the fluted, piecrust edge, and bulbous pedestal resting on a scalloped base. Columbia was referred to as "Princely" in the manufacturer's advertisement for 25 cents in Assortment of Salvers. As this cake stand has a plain plate, it is often found etched.

Item	Size	Crystal
Cake salver	10" x 4½"	$85.00

Cake salver

CONNECTICUT

OMN: United States Glass Nr 15068.

Manufactured by: United States Glass Company, Pittsburgh, Pennsylvania, at Factory "K," ca 1900. This is a quite plain pattern of beautiful clear glass with the only decoration being a row of blocks with Xs around the top, in the center, and base, and often has enamel decorations. The pedestal is hollow with nine panels descending to a 5" base. This pattern is sometimes found etched. This is the twenty-first pattern in the "state series." My husband, Brad, originally from Connecticut, claims these two pieces.

Top view of cake stand

Item	Size	Crystal
Cake stand	10⅜" x 6⅛"	$145.00
Compote	7½" x 11½"	115.00

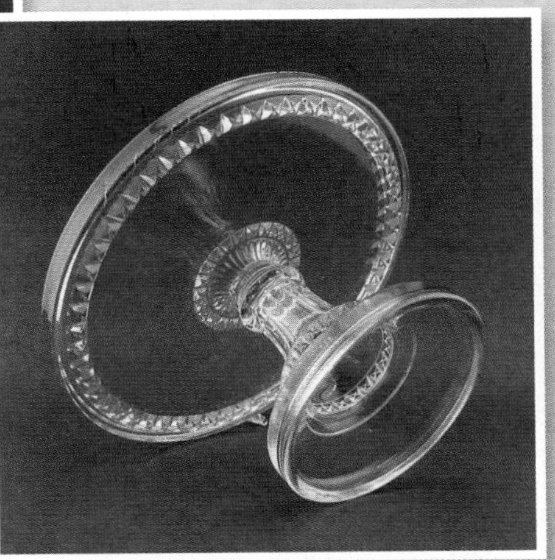

Pedestal

Compote, covered

CORD AND TASSEL

Manufactured by: La Belle Glass Company, Bridgeport, Ohio, 1872; and Central Glass Company, Wheeling, West Virginia, 1879.

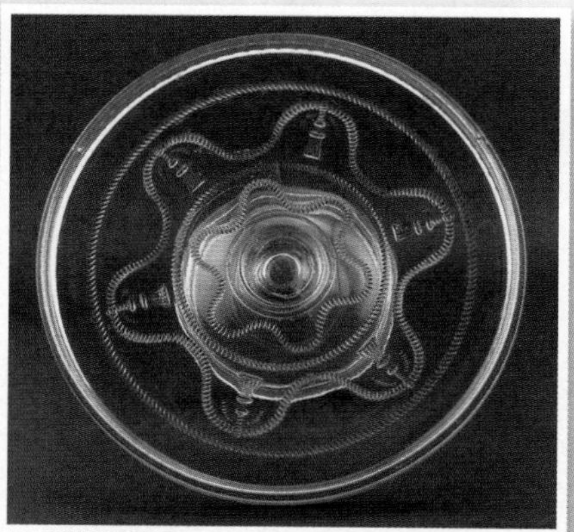

Top view of cake stand

Item	Description	Size	Crystal
Cake stand	Non-flint	8½"	$250.00
		9½"	275.00
		10½"	325.00

Cake stands side by side

CORD DRAPERY

AKA: Indiana Nr 350.

Manufactured by: Indiana Tumbler and Goblet Company, ca. 1900; National Glass Company, 1901; and Indiana Glass Company, 1907. Cake stand, whimsy, and cake plate are courtesy of Carolyn Crozier. The whimsy is made from a footed cake plate.

Item	Description	Size	Crystal	Amber	Emerald	Cobalt
Cake stand		8¼"	$95.00	$350.00		$500.00
Cake plate		10"	165.00	375.00		475.00
	Six-footed	8¼"	50.00			
		9½"	55.00	180.00	190.00	225.00
		10"	60.00			
Tri-cornered whimsy		9½" x 4"	50.00	75.00		

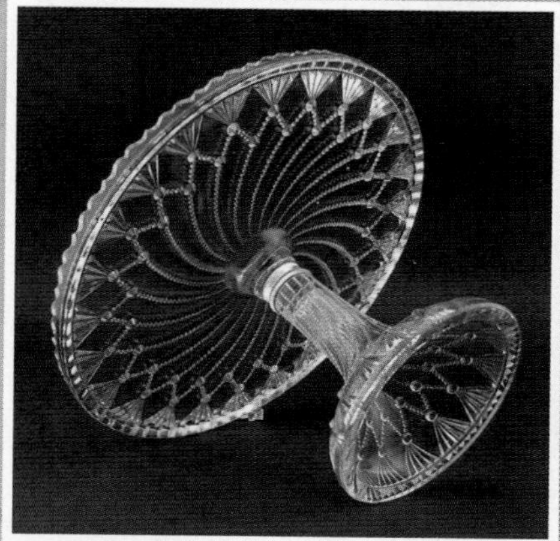

Cake stand

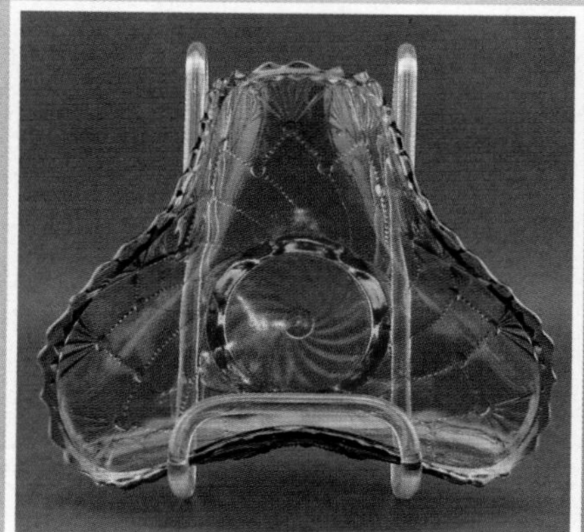

Tri-cornered whimsy

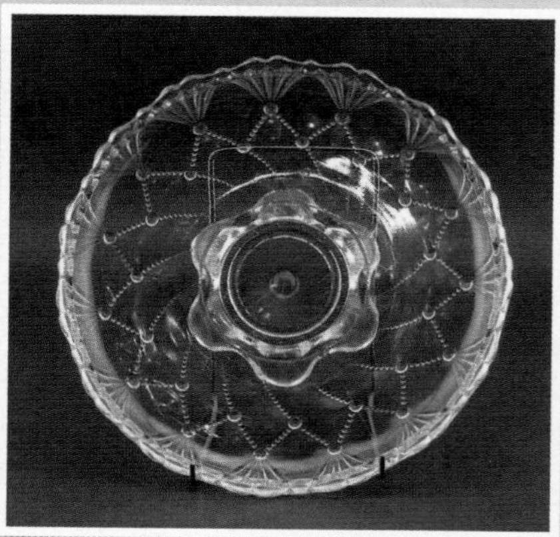

Footed cake plate

C

CORDOVA

Manufactured by: O'Hara Glass Company, ca. 1890. A non-flint pedestal cake stand may be found in crystal. Perfume courtesy of Carolyn Crozier.

Item	Size	Crystal
Cake stand	10"	$125.00
Compote	8" x 6"	100.00
Perfume	3" x 7"	50.00

Compote

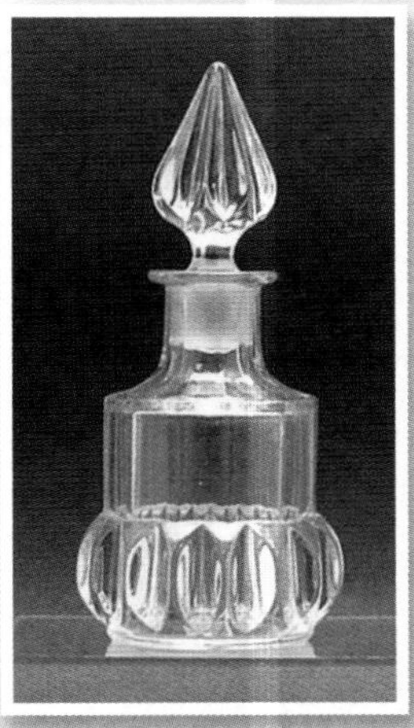

Perfume

Pedestal

CORNELL

Manufactured by: Tarentum Glass Company, 1898.

Item	Size	Crystal
Cake stand		$85.00
Creamer	5" x 3"	55.00

Creamer

CORNUCOPIA

OMN: Dalzell Nr 9D; AKA: Strawberries and Currants.

Manufactured by: Dalzell, Gilmore and Leighton, ca. 1890s. The pitcher shows a fruit-filled cornucopia on one side and the reverse may have a fruit group with cherries and figs; blackberries and grapes; or strawberries and currants. Note that the base is different on the cake stand and compote.

Item	Size	Crystal
Cake stand	9¼" x 6¾"	$90.00
	11"	110.00
Compote	7" x 11" h	75.00
Pitcher		95.00

Cake stand

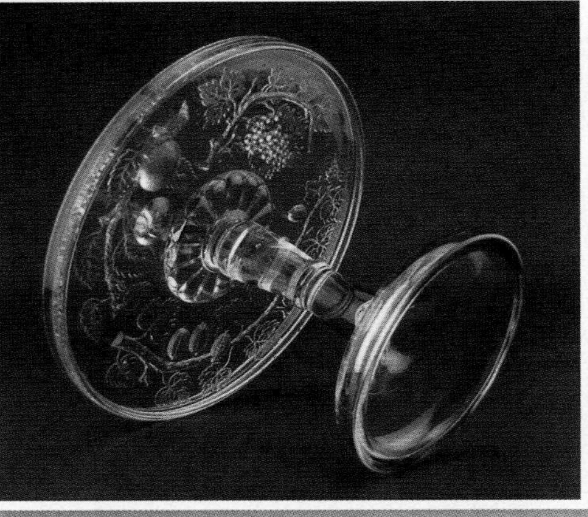

Pedestal

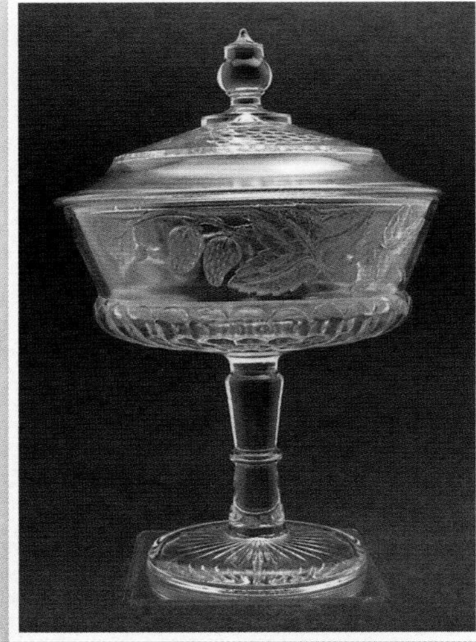

Compote

Pitcher

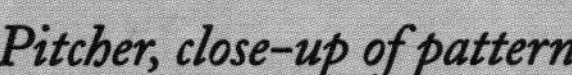

Pitcher, close-up of pattern

Compote and cake stand

C

CORRIGAN

Manufactured by: Dalzell, Gilmore and Leighton Glass Company, Findlay, Ohio, ca 1890. *Findlay Glass, The Tableware Manufacturers, 1886 – 1902,* by James Measell and Don E. Smith lists this as being made by Findlay Glass.

Item	Size	Crystal
Cake stand	10¼" x 6¾"	$135.00

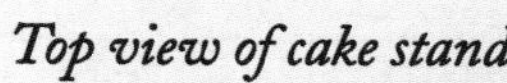

Top view of cake stand

Pedestal

COTTAGE

AKA: Dinner Bell, Fine Cut Band.

Manufactured by: Adams and Company, Pittsburgh, Pennsylvania, 1874; and Bellaire Goblet Company, ca 1891 (goblet only). Although very rare, pieces may be found in amber, blue, crystal with ruby stain, and emerald green. Colors demand at least a 70% increase in value.

Item	Size	Crystal
Cake stand	9"	$70.00
	10"	95.00
Creamer		35.00

Top view of cake stand

Stacked cake stands

Cake stand and creamer

CROESUS

OMN: Riverside Nr 484.

Manufactured by: Riverside Glass Works, ca 1897; McKee and Brothers, ca 1901. This photograph of the incredibly beautiful cake stand in green is furnished courtesy of Eileen and Richard Flaks; the spooner and sugar courtesy of Carolyn Crozier.

Item	Size	Crystal	Green	Amethyst
Cake stand	9½" x 6"	$350.00	$385.00	$650.00
Spooner	3½" x 4⅝"	85.00	100.00	145.00
Sugar	7½" x 4¼"	135.00	165.00	245.00

Cake stand, green

Cake stand

Creamer and spooner

CROWN

OMN: Duncan Nr 52; AKA: Ladder with Diamond.

Manufactured by: Duncan and Miller Glass Company, ca 1904. This gold trimmed, skirted cake stand is truly elegant.

Item	Size	Crystal
Cake stand	9½" x 4¾"	$110.00

Top view of cake stand

Pedestal

CRYSTAL RIB

Manufactured by: Findlay Glass, ca 1886. This has been a difficult cake salver to identify. It was originally misidentified as Cordova, but is pictured in *Findlay Glass, The Glass Tableware Manufacturers, 1886 – 1902*, by James Measell and Don E. Smith.

Item	Size	Crystal
Cake salver	10"	$80.00

Pedestal

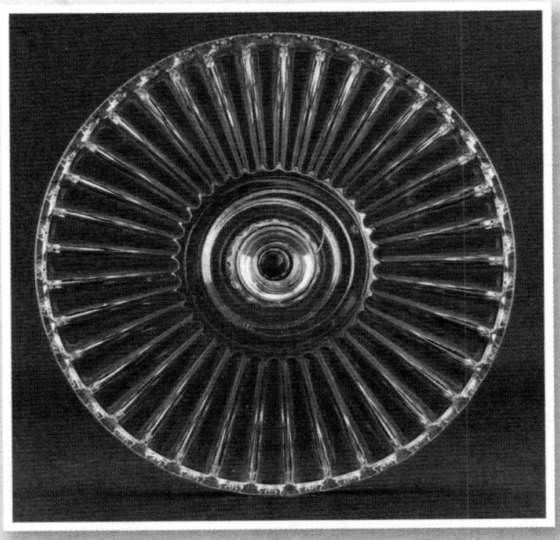

Top view of cake salver

CRYSTAL WEDDING

AKA: Collins, Crystal Anniversary.

Manufactured by: Adams and Company, ca. 1890. On original pieces the pedestal is joined to the plate with a glass wafer (ring). The first step from the top of the pedestal is scalloped. Reproductions are made in one piece and the first step on the base is squared. Items found in crystal with amber stain, vaseline, or cobalt are scarce. Thanks to Sue Edelmon for the red stained compote.

Item	Description	Size	Crystal	Crystal w/Frosting	Crystal w/Ruby
Cake stand	Square	10"	$235.00	$350.00	$525.00
Banana stand			175.00	275.00	650.00
Compote	Covered		55.00	65.00	75.00

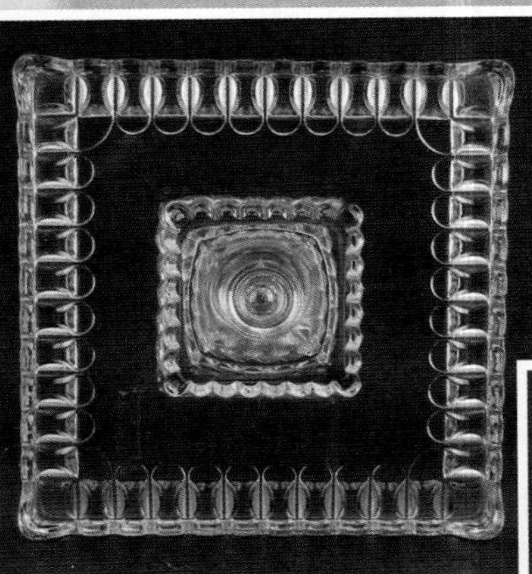

Top view of cake stand

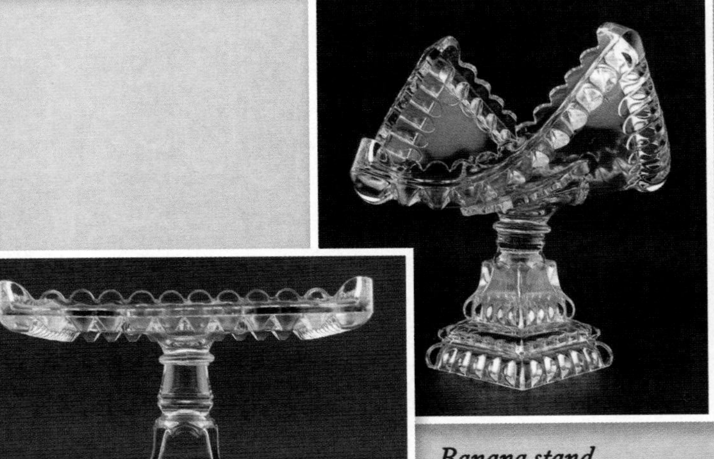

Pedestal

Banana stand

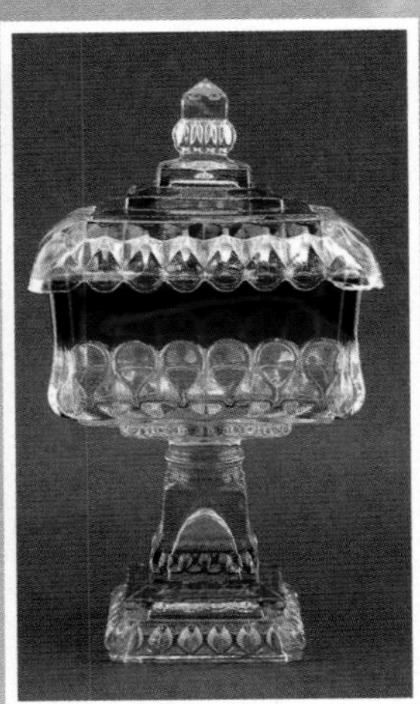

Compote

CUPID AND VENUS

OMN: Richards and Hartley Nr 500; AKA: Guardian Angel, Minerva.

Manufactured by: Richards and Hartley Glass Company, Pittsburgh, Pennsylvania, 1875. Vaseline and amber pieces command 40% higher prices. Pickle castor, celery, and sugar courtesy of Carolyn Crozier.

Item	Description	Size	Crystal
Cake stand			$195.00
Compote	Low standard w/cover	8¾"	160.00
Butter		6¾" x 6¾"	225.00
Creamer			155.00
Sugar (no lid shown)		5¼" x 4¼"	160.00
Celery		8¼" x 4¼"	75.00
Pickle castor in silver plate frame			250.00

Sugar, butter, and creamer

Pickle castor, celery, and sugar

Compote, no lid shown

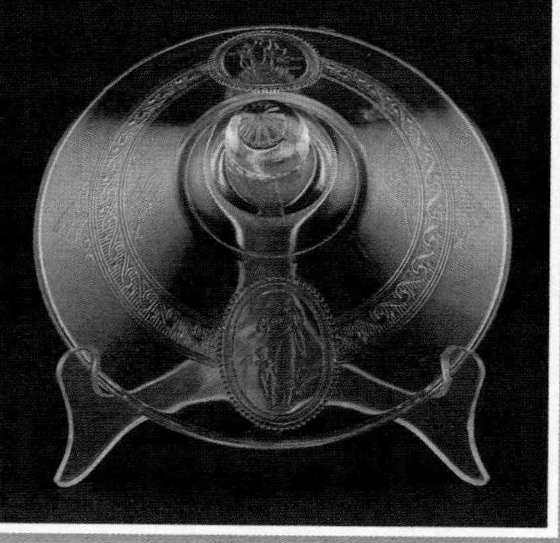

Close up of pattern

CURRIER AND IVES (BALKY MULE)

Manufactured by: Bellaire Glass Company, 1890. This is a cake stand that is rarely seen. The design is repeated on the pedestal, which is hollow. Any color in this pattern is considered rare. Tray and syrup courtesy of Carolyn Crozier.

Item	Size	Crystal	Blue
Cake stand	9½" x 5⅛"	$145.00	
Syrup	7" x 5"	95.00	
Tray	12" x 1¼"	55.00	$100.00

Top view of cake stand

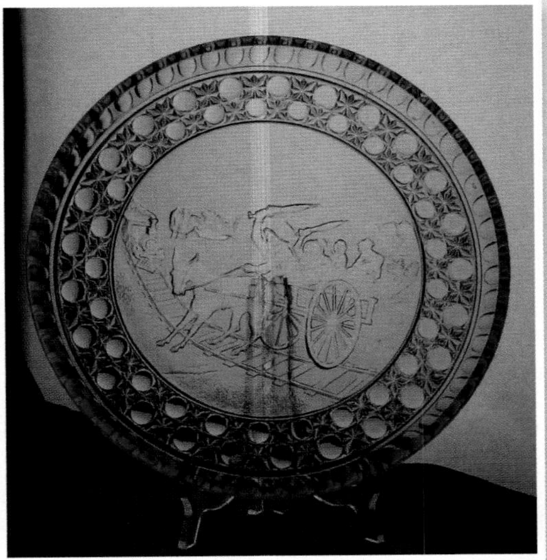

Balky Mule tray

Pedestal

Syrup

CURTAIN

OMN: Sultan.
Manufactured by: Bryce Brothers, late 1870s.

Item	Size	Crystal
Cake stand	8"	$70.00
	9"	90.00
	9½"	100.00
	10"	125.00

Top view of cake stand

Pedestal

CURTAIN TIE BACK

Manufactured by: Unknown, 1860s.

Item	Size	Crystal
Cake stand		$95.00
Celery tray	8½" x 5¼"	25.00

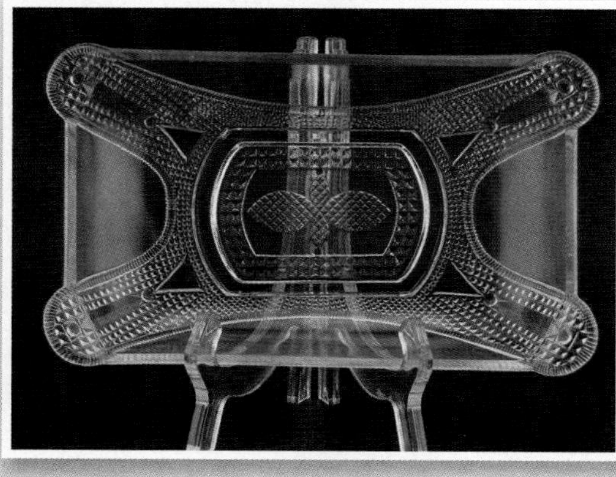

Celery tray

CUT LOG

OMN: Ethol; AKA: Cat's Eye and Block.

Manufactured by: Bryce, Higbee and Company, Pittsburgh, Pennsylvania, 1889. The pattern is repeated on the pedestal and base. There is a ¼" gallery on the plate.

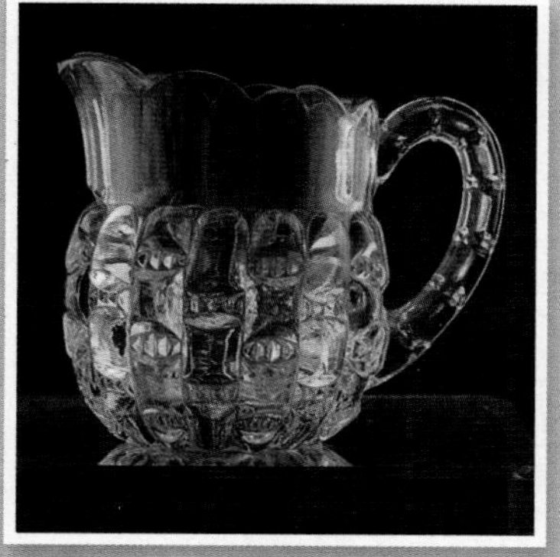

Creamer

Cake stands side by side

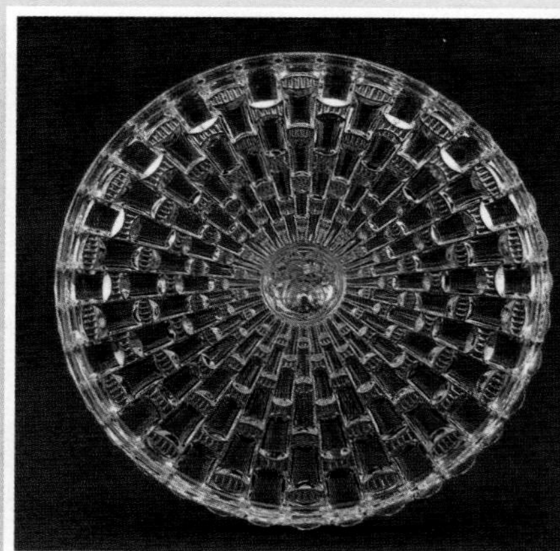

Top view of cake stand

Item	Description	Size	Crystal
Cake stand		9¼"	$190.00
		10½"	240.00
Creamer	Individual		20.00

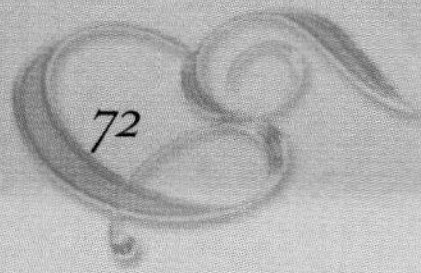

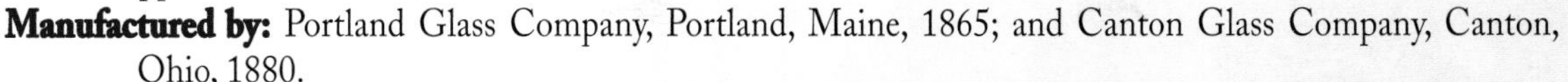

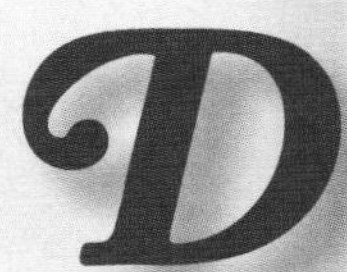

DAHLIA

AKA: Stippled Dahlia.

Manufactured by: Portland Glass Company, Portland, Maine, 1865; and Canton Glass Company, Canton, Ohio, 1880.

Item	Size	Crystal	Amber	Blue	Green	Vaseline
Cake stand	9½"	$80.00	$90.00	$120.00	$135.00	$150.00
	10"	100.00	120.00	145.00	175.00	200.00

Pedestal

Top view of cake stand

DAISY AND BUTTON

Manufactured by: Unknown. The manufacturer is not known. The cake stand pictured is eight sided, and is unusual in that the pedestal is not Daisy and Button, but is the same pedestal as Argent (Rope Bands), which was manufactured by Bryce Brothers, 1885.

Item	Description	Size	Crystal
Cake stand		9" x 6¾"	$75.00

Pedestal

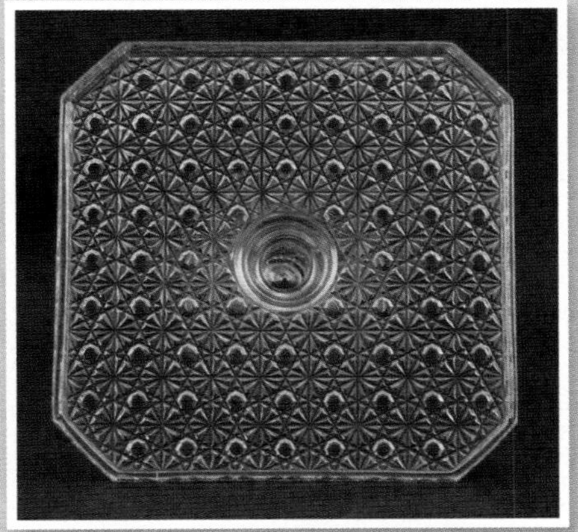

Top view of cake stand

DAISY AND BUTTON WITH CROSS BARS

OMN: Richards and Hartley Nr 99; AKA: Daisy and Thumbprint Crossbar, Daisy and Button with Crossbar and Thumbprint, Daisy and Button with Crossbar and Thumbprint Band, Daisy with Crossbar, Mikado.

Manufactured by: Richards and Hartley Glass Company, 1885. Although no record has been found of a cake stand in this pattern, it is very likely that one was made, as there is no written record found for a covered compote in the size pictured.

Item	Description	Size	Crystal	Amber	Blue	Canary (Yellow)
Cake stand			$150.00	$160.00	$180.00	$200.00
Compote	Covered	8" x 12"	125.00	135.00	145.00	165.00

Compote

DAISY AND BUTTON WITH THUMBPRINT PANEL

OMN: Adams Nr 86; AKA: Daisy and Button Thumbprint, Daisy and Button with Amber Stripe, Daisy and Button with Thumbprint Panels.

Manufactured by: Adams and Company, ca. 1886. Photographs of vaseline and amber stain courtesy of Cindy Johnson.

Item	Size	Crystal	Amber	Blue	Vaseline	Crystal w/Stain
Cake stand	9¼"	$150.00	$150.00	$180.00	$200.00	$160.00

Top view of cake stand, vaseline

Pedestal

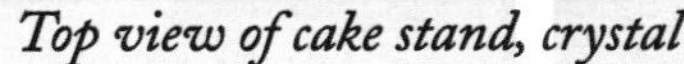

Top view of cake stand, crystal

Top view of cake stand, amber

Top view of cake stand, amber stain

DAISY AND SCROLL

OMN: United States Glass Nr 15104; AKA: Buzz Saw in Parentheses, U. S. Victoria.
Manufactured by: United States Glass Company, 1907.

Item	Description	Crystal
Pitcher	Water	$45.00
Tumbler		25.00

Pitcher and tumblers

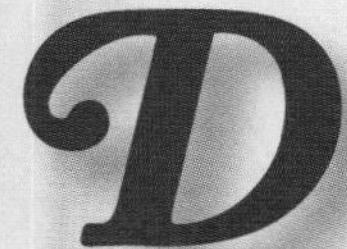

DAKOTA

AKA: Baby Thumbprint, Thumbprint Band, Thumbprint Band – Crystal, Thumbprint Band – Red Top.

Manufactured by: Ripley and Company, Pittsburgh, Pennsylvania, ca. 1885. In April 2005, an etched, 9" cake stand and cover sold for $2,950 on an internet auction! The etched pieces are decorated with Fern and Berry Engraving Nr 76. My pride and joy is this beautiful etched cake stand with cover! I was fortunate that my husband bought the cover a few years ago and I finally found the etched cake stand on which it rests. Thanks, Brad!

Item	Description	Size	Crystal	Crystal w/Etching	Crystal w/Ruby
Cake stand		8"	$95.00	$120.00	$300.00
		9"	110.00	135.00	
		9½"	125.00	175.00	
		10"	140.00	190.00	400.00
		10½"	175.00	225.00	
	With cover	9½"	1,000.00	3,000.00	
	With cover	10½" x 15¼"	1,200.00	3,250.00	
Cake cover		8"	600.00	900.00	
		9"	800.00	1,100.00	
		10" x 4" h	1,000.00	1,500.00	
Compote		7"	75.00	105.00	
	Covered	10" x 16" h	115.00	250.00	
Butter dish		6⅛" x 7½"	75.00	95.00	
Sugar	Covered	6⅜" x 5½"	75.00	85.00	
Creamer		6⅜" x 5½"	65.00	75.00	
Spooner		6" x 3¼"	60.00	70.00	

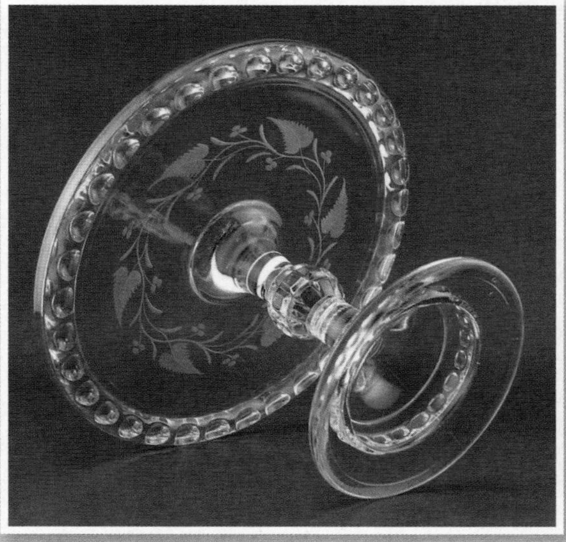

Cake stand, etched

Cake stand, etched, with cover

Cake stand and cover

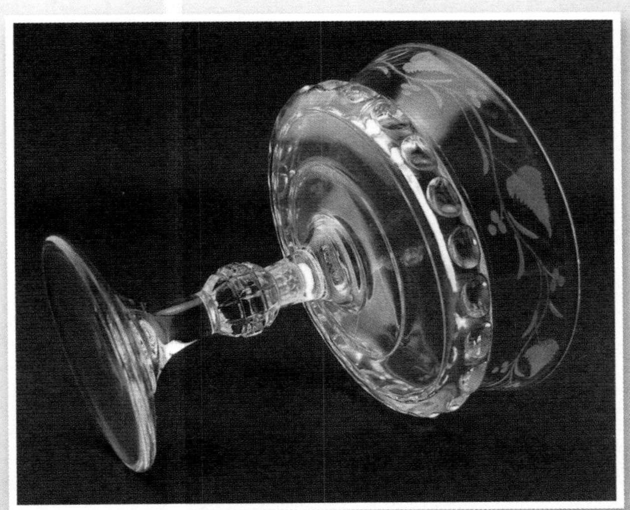

Compote, etched

Compote, covered

Sugar, butter dish, spooner, and creamer, etched

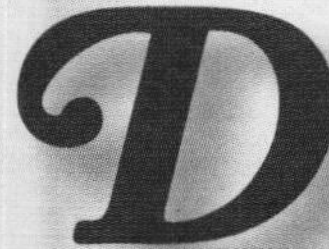

DALZELL'S PRISCILLA

OMN: Alexis; AKA: Late Moon and Star, Stelle, Sun and Star.

Manufactured by: Dalzell, Gilmore and Leighton, Findlay, Ohio, ca. 1888; and later National Glass Company, Pittsburgh, Pennsylvania, ca. 1899. Pieces were originally made in crystal and crystal with ruby stain. Ruby stain was applied at the Oriental Glass Company of Pittsburgh, Pennsylvania. The pictures of the crystal, blue, and green petit four plates are reproductions and are provided to show the difference in the cake stand.

Item	Description	Size	Crystal
Cake stand	High standard	6½"	$85.00
		9½"	150.00
		10"	165.00
Compote	Crystal, open	5"	45.00
	Covered	9"	235.00

Top view of cake stand, skirted

Pedestal

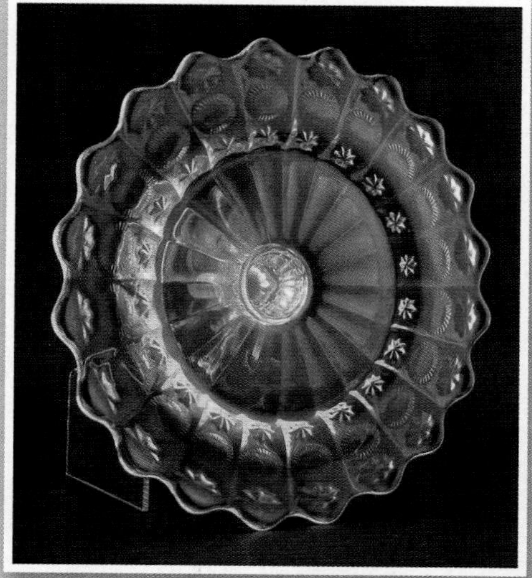

Crystal petit four

Crystal pedestal

Blue petit four

Blue pedestal

Green petit four

Green pedestal

Compote, open

Compote, covered

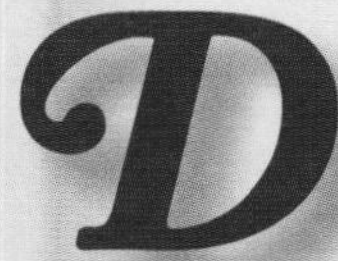

DART

Manufactured by: Unknown, late 1880s.

Item	Size	Crystal
Cake stand		$45.00
Compote	7¼" x 7"	55.00

Compote

DEER AND PINE TREE

OMN: McKee Band Diamond; AKA: Deer and Doe.

Manufactured by: McKee and Brothers, Pittsburgh, Pennsylvania, 1886. This pattern is easily recognized as the name suggests by the antlered deer and pine tree. A crystal goblet has been reproduced.

Item	Description	Size	Crystal	Green
Cake stand		10¾"	$250.00	
Celery vase			175.00	
Compote	Covered	9" long	350.00	
Jar	Marmalade with cover (no cover shown)		350.00	
Pitcher	Water	½ gal.	190.00	
Plate	Bread		60.00	$175.00
Sugar	Covered	7½"	200.00	

Top view of cake stand

Pedestal

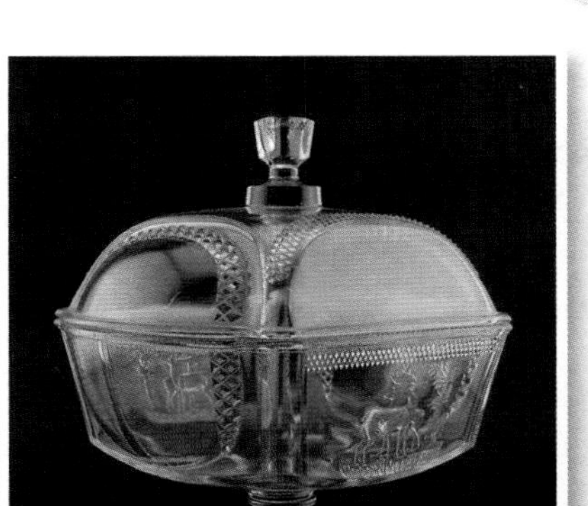

Compote

Sugar, pitcher, and celery vase

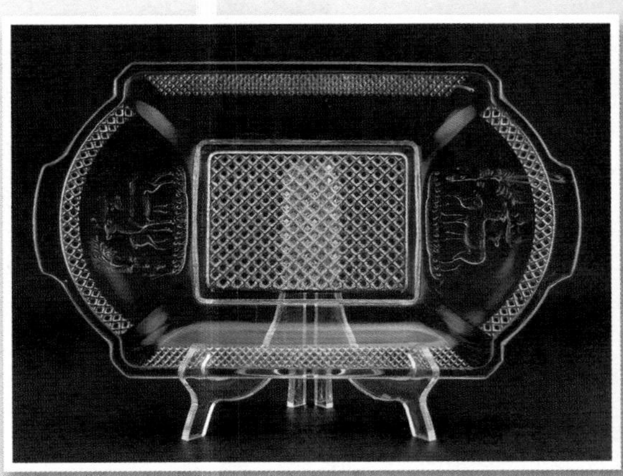

Bread plate, crystal

Celery, marmalade jar

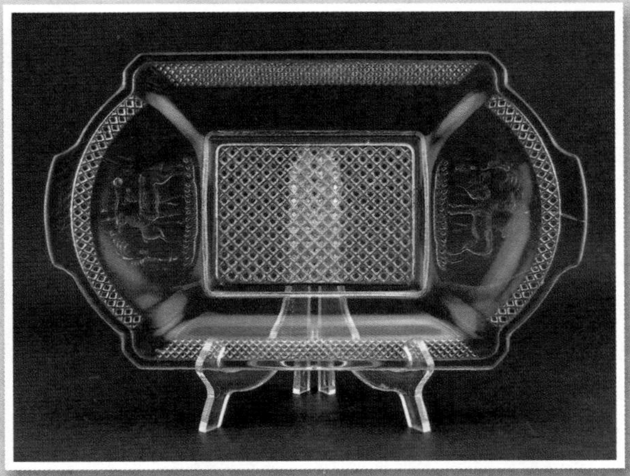

Bread plate, green

DELAWARE

OMN: United States Glass Nr 15065 Delaware, Diamond Nr 206 – New Century; AKA: American Beauty, Four Petal Flower.

Manufactured by: United States Glass Company, Pittsburgh, Pennsylvania, ca. 1899. This is the eighteenth in the "state series" patterns.

Item	Description	Crystal	Green w/Gold	Rose w/Gold
Water pitcher	Tankard	$60.00	$160.00	$240.00

Water pitcher, rose with gold

DELOS

OMN: Dalzel Nr 85D.

Manufactured by: Dalzel, Gilmore and Leighton, ca 1902. This is the last pattern made by Dalzell, Gilmore & Leighton Glass Works. This cake stand is very similar to Columbia, which was also made by Dalzel, Gilmore and Leighton.

Item	Size	Crystal
Cake stand	10" x 5"	$85.00

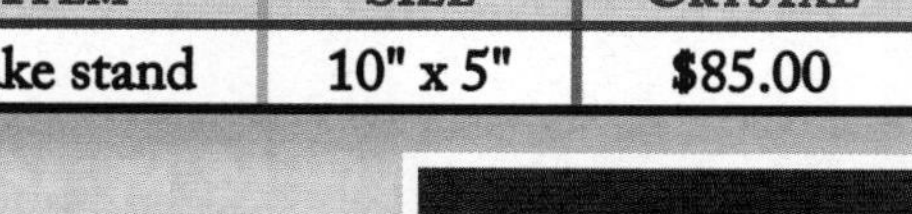

Pedestal

Top view of cake stand

DEWDROP IN POINTS

OMN: Greensburg Glass Nr 67.

Manufactured by: Brilliant Glass Works, 1888; and Greensburg Glass Company, 1889. Number 67 was likely a Brilliant Glass Works Company pattern used before the plant was moved and became United States Glass Company.

Item	Size	Crystal
Cake stand	10½"	$90.00

Pedestal

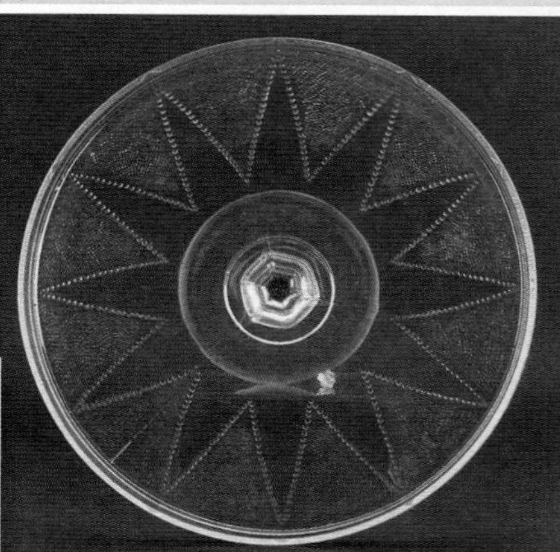

Top view of cake stand

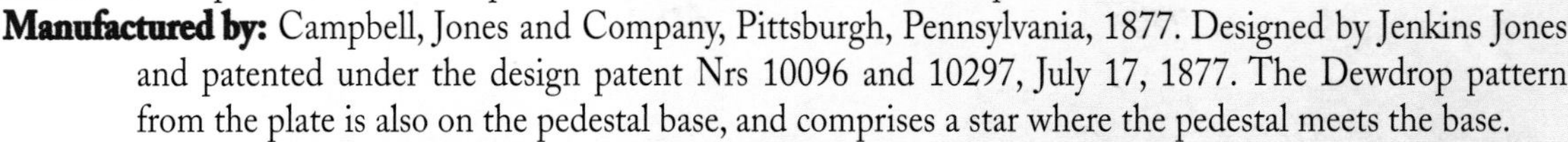

DEWDROP WITH STAR

AKA: Dewdrop and Star, Dewdrop with Small Star, Star and Dewdrop.

Manufactured by: Campbell, Jones and Company, Pittsburgh, Pennsylvania, 1877. Designed by Jenkins Jones and patented under the design patent Nrs 10096 and 10297, July 17, 1877. The Dewdrop pattern from the plate is also on the pedestal base, and comprises a star where the pedestal meets the base.

Item	Size	Crystal
Cake stand	9½"	$90.00
	11"	130.00

Top view of cake stand

Pedestal

DIAGONAL BAND

AKA: Diagonal Block and Fan.

Attributed to Burlington Glass Works, Hamilton, Ontario, Canada. The pedestal has six panels.

Item	Size	Crystal	Amber	Apple Green
Cake stand	9"	$100.00	$115.00	$175.00

Top view of cake stand

Pedestal

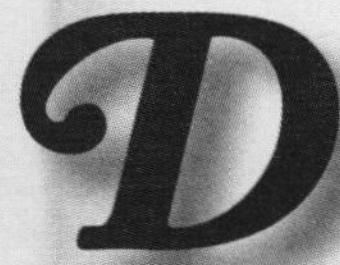

DIAMOND

OMN: Ohio Nr 488.

Manufactured by: Ohio Flint Glass Company, ca 1896. The pattern is repeated on the base.

Item	Size	Crystal
Cake stand	10"	$55.00

Top view of cake stand

Pedestal

DIAMOND AND SUNBURST

Manufactured by: Bryce Walker and Co, ca. 1874. The pattern is repeated on the base.

Item	Description	Size	Crystal
Cake stand			$90.00
Compote	Low standard		50.00
	High standard	7" x 7"	80.00

Pedestal

Compote, high standard

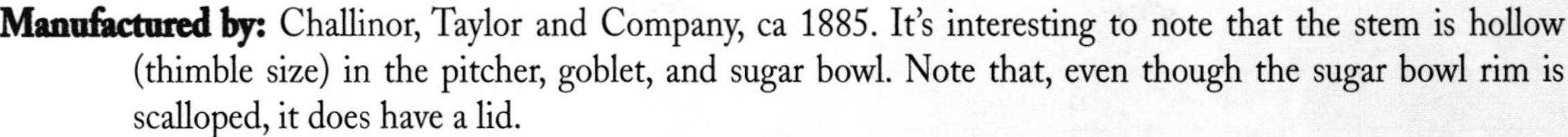

DIAMOND BLOCK WITH FAN

OMN: Challinor Nr 309; AKA: Blockade.

Manufactured by: Challinor, Taylor and Company, ca 1885. It's interesting to note that the stem is hollow (thimble size) in the pitcher, goblet, and sugar bowl. Note that, even though the sugar bowl rim is scalloped, it does have a lid.

Item	Size	Crystal
Cake stand	10" x 5¼"	$65.00
Pitcher		85.00
Goblet		35.00
Sugar bowl		45.00
Sauce		15.00

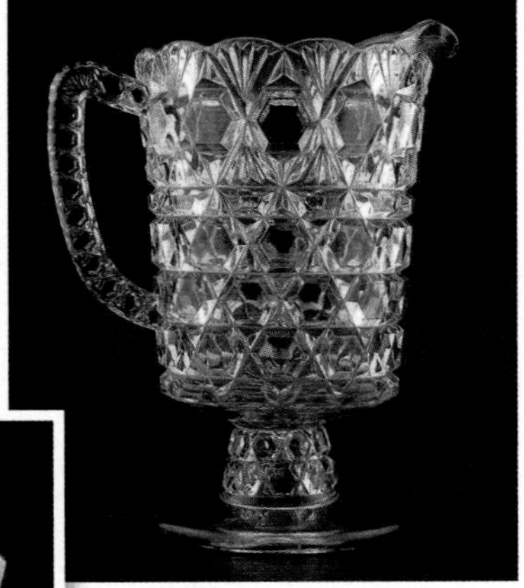

Pitcher

Goblet, pitcher, sugar bowl, and sauce

DIAMOND POINT DISCS

AKA: Crescent Nr 601, Diamond Point Disk.

Manufactured by: J. B. Higbee Glass Company, ca 1905; and later New Martinsville Glass Manufacturing Company, 1916. Courtesy of Regan Tommi Hoch.

Item	Size	Crystal
Cake stand	9¼"	$70.00

Top view of cake stand

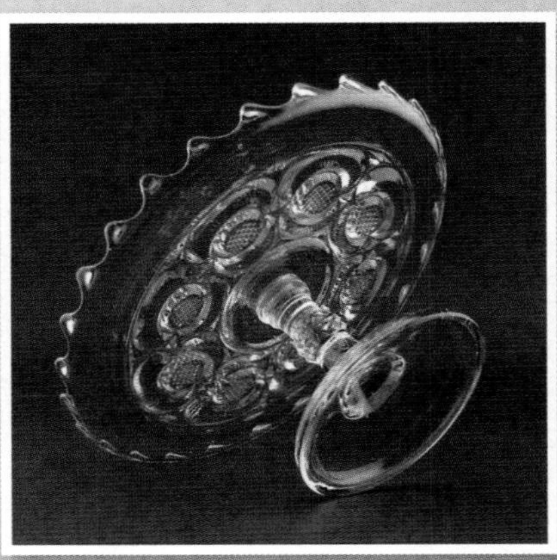

Pedestal

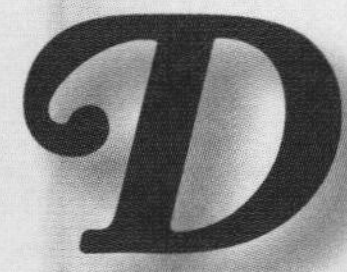

DIAMOND POINT LOOP

Manufactured by: Unknown, ca 1890s.

Item	Size	Crystal
Sauce bowl	4"	$20.00

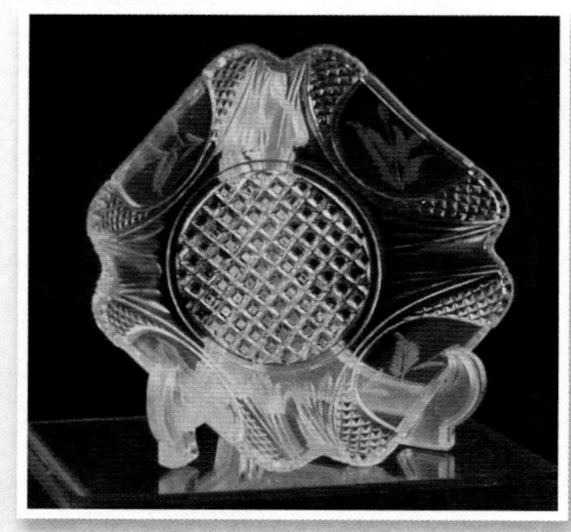

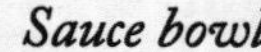

Sauce bowl

DIAMOND THUMBPRINT

AKA: Diamond and Concave.

Manufactured by: Boston and Sandwich Glass Company; Union Glass Company, Somerville, Ohio, ca 1850. Courtesy of Carolyn Crozier.

Item	Description	Size	Crystal
Cake stand			$165.00
Compote	Low standard	7⅞" x 3⅜"	95.00

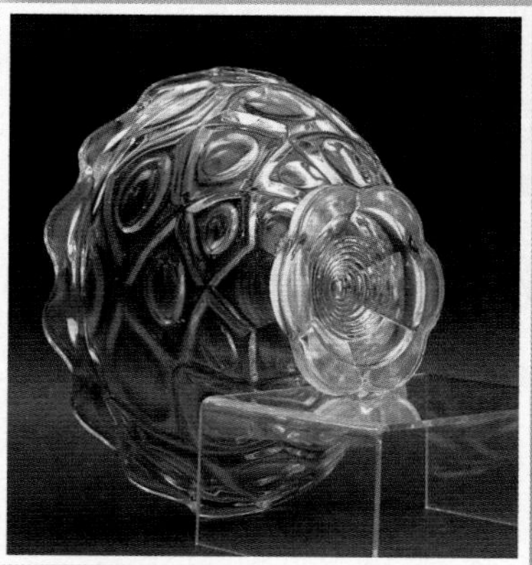

Compote, side view

Compote, interior

DIAMOND WAFFLE

OMN: United States Glass Nr 15025; AKA: Patricia, U. S. Diamond Block.

Manufactured by: United States Glass Company, ca. 1892. Courtesy of Mary Sloper.

Item	Size	Crystal
Cake stand	10"	$125.00

Top view of cake stand

Pedestal

DOTTED LOOP

Manufactured by: Unknown. The pattern is repeated on the base of the pedestal. There is a small scalloped gallery.

Item	Size	Crystal
Cake stand	10" x 5¼"	$60.00

Top view of cake stand

Stacked cake stands

Pedestal

DOUBLE ARCH

OMN: United States Glass Nr 15024; AKA: Interlocking Crescents.

Manufactured by: King Glass Company (tumbler only); O'Hara Glass Company, Ltd., 1892 (goblet only); United States Glass Company, 1892.

Item	Size	Crystal
Cake stand	10" x 6½"	$75.00

Top view of cake stand

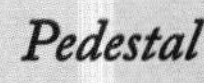

Pedestal

DOUBLE FAN

Manufactured by: Dalzell, Gilmore and Leighton, 1890.

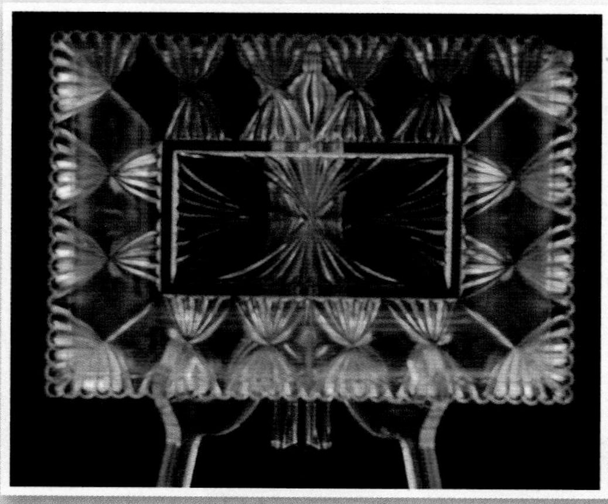

Bowl

Item	Size	Crystal
Cake stand		$45.00
Bowl	5½" x 7½"	20.00

DOUBLE PINWHEEL

AKA: Juno.

Manufactured by: Beatty-Brady Glass Company, ca 1898; Indiana Glass Company, ca 1908. The pattern is repeated on the base.

Item	Size	Crystal
Cake stand	10" x 4¾"	$85.00

Pedestal

Top view of cake stand

DOYLE'S SHELL

AKA: Cube with Fan Nr 1, Knight, and Shell Nr 2.

Manufactured by: Doyle and Company, 1880s.

Item	Size	Crystal
Cake stand		$60.00
Creamer	5" x 4½"	35.00

Creamer

EFFULGENT STAR

OMN: Central Nr 876; AKA: Star, Star Galaxy.

Manufactured by: Central Glass Company, Wheeling, West Virginia, 1880s. The six-pointed stars that cover the underneath surface of the plate and the pedestal base easily identify this pattern. There is no brandy well, but there is a ½" gallery.

Item	Size	Crystal
Cake stand	8"	$200.00
	9"	250.00
	10"	275.00

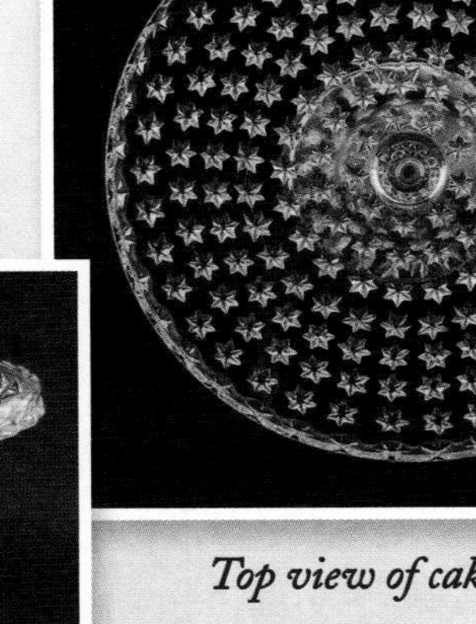

Pedestal

Top view of cake stand

EGG IN SAND

AKA: Bean, Stippled Oval.

Manufactured by: Beaver Falls Glass Company, Beaver Falls, Pennsylvania, 1869 – 1879.

Item	Size	Crystal
Cake stand		$135.00
Creamer	4¾" x 3¼"	50.00

Creamer

ELECTRIC

OMN: United States Glass Nr 15038.

Manufactured by: United States Glass Company, ca 1896.

Item	Size	Crystal
Cake stand		$110.00
Jelly compote	5¾" x 4¾"	45.00

Jelly compote, interior

Side view of compote

ELEPHANT TOES

OMN: U. S. Glass Nr 15134.
Manufactured by: United States Glass Company, 1912.

Creamer

Item	Size	Crystal
Creamer	4⅜" h x 5½"	$50.00

ELLROSE

AKA: Amberette, Daisy and Button – Paneled – Single Scallop, Daisy and Button – Single Panel, Paneled Daisy, Paneled Daisy and Button.
Manufactured by: George Duncan Sons and Company, 1885. Found in crystal, and crystal with amber, red, and blue stains. The red and blue stains are considered very rare. All items courtesy of Marie N. James.

Item	Size	Crystal	Crystal w/Amber
Cake stand with raised scalloped lip	10"	$375.00	$500.00
Creamer	5½" x 5"	50.00	95.00
Berry bowl	5"	40.00	60.00
Butter pat	2¾"	50.00	85.00
Celery vase		65.00	125.00

Top view of cake stand

Pedestal

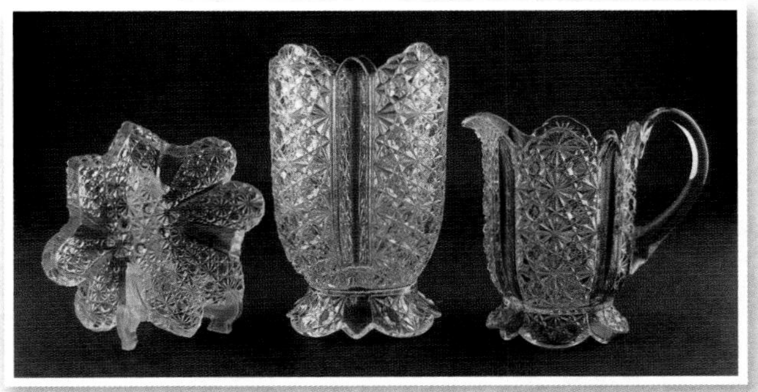

Berry bowl, celery, creamer

Bowl and butter pat

Creamer

EMPRESS

OMN: Riverside Nr 492; AKA: Double Arch.
Manufactured by: Riverside Glass Works, Wellsburg, West Virginia, ca. 1898.

Item	Size	Crystal	Emerald Green
Cake stand		$225.00	$360.00
Butter dish	7½" x 6"	115.00	160.00

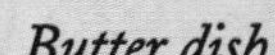

Butter dish

ERA

Manufactured by: Bryce, Higbee and Company, 1880s. This square cake stand is of very good, crystal glass. The panels in the four corners are clear, while the other panels have a design, which is carried through down the pedestal and onto the base.

Top view of cake stand

Item	Size	Crystal
Cake stand	9"	$100.00
	10"	125.00

Pedestal

ERA (VARIANT)

Manufactured by: Unknown. The panelled design is repeated on the pedestal base.

Item	Size	Crystal
Cake stand	9¼"	$85.00

Top view of cake stand

Pedestal

ESTHER

OMN: Esther Ware; AKA: Tooth and Claw.

Manufactured by: Riverside Glass Company, Wellsburg, West Virginia, ca. 1896. The unique pattern on the plate has three separate chains of four flowers each, surrounded by rays. A similar single type flower is on the base.

ITEM	SIZE	CRYSTAL	GREEN	CRYSTAL W/RUBY	CRYSTAL W/AMBER
Cake stand	10½"	$140.00	$200.00	$290.00	$325.00

Pedestal

Top view of cake stand

EUREKA

Manufactured by: National Glass Company at McKee & Brothers, Jeannette, Pennsylvania, ca. 1901 – 1904.

ITEM	SIZE	CRYSTAL	CRYSTAL W/RUBY
Cake stand	11"	$150.00	$700.00
Compote	8" x 8½"	40.00	90.00

Pedestal

Compote

EYEWINKER

OMN: Genoese; AKA: Cannon Ball, Crystal Ball, Winking Eye.

Attributed to Dalzell, Gilmore and Leighton Glass Company, Findley, Ohio, ca. 1889. Some cake stands do not have the Eyewinker pattern on the surface of the plate. They are plain on the top, with balls around the rim. This diminutive cake stand glows under a black light.

Item	Size	Crystal
Cake stand	8¼" x 3½"	$190.00
	9½"	245.00
	10"	300.00
Bowl	8"	125.00
Compote	7"	250.00
Pitcher	1 qt.	350.00

Top view of cake stand

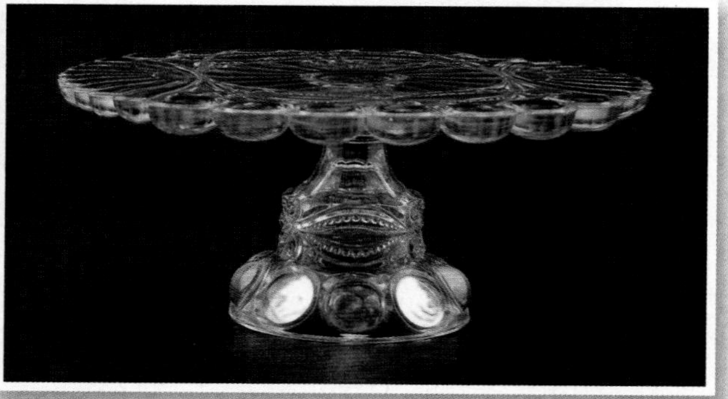

Pedestal

Bowl

Pitcher, side view

FAGOT

OMN: Robinson Nr 1; AKA: Vera.

Manufactured by: Robinson Glass Works, Zanesville, Ohio, 1893. This 10¾" cake stand is impressive with the deep, frosted scallops, which are repeated on the pedestal. Note that the scallops are clear on the compote. Bowl courtesy of Karen and Sam Ruble.

Item	Size	Crystal	Crystal w/Frosting
Cake stand	10¾" x 5½"	$130.00	$145.00
Bowl	7½" x 2¾"	35.00	45.00
	8" x 3¾"	35.00	45.00
	11¼"	50.00	65.00
Compote	11" x 8¾"	110.00	125.00

Pedestal

Top view of cake stand

Compote

Cake stand and bowl

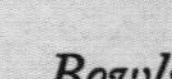

Bowls

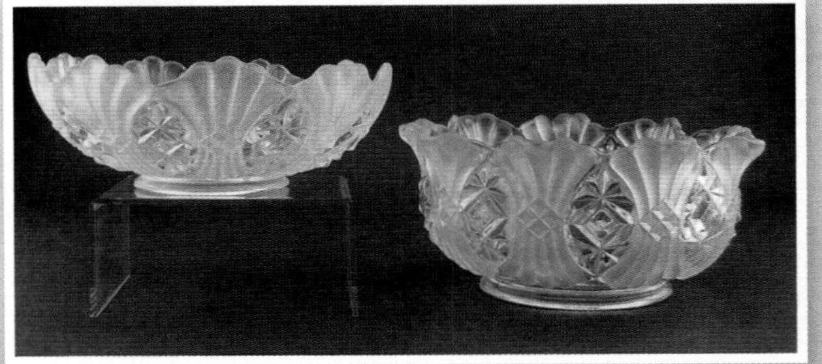

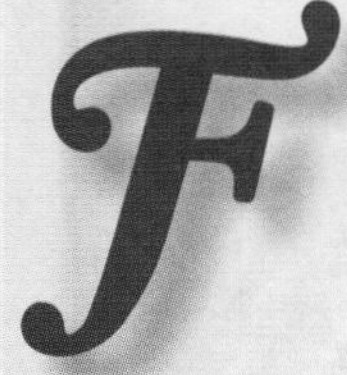

FAN BAND

OMN: Yale; AKA: Scalloped Flower Band.

Manufactured by: Bryce, Higbee and Company, 1887; J. B. Higbee Glass Company, 1907; New Martinsville Glass Manufacturing Company, 1916. The gallery on this cake stand has alternating scallops; one has a fan, the next is marked with short, dainty lines; the pedestal is plain.

Top view of cake stand

Item	Size	Crystal
Cake stand	9⅝" x 4¾"	$65.00

FANCY LOOP

OMN: Heisey Nr 1205, 1205½.

Manufactured by: A. H. Heisey and Company, ca. 1896. Note the gold trim on the creamer, sugar, and spooner. This pattern is easily confused with Crystal Queen by Northwood. It is not marked with Heisey diamond. Compote courtesy of Carolyn Crozier.

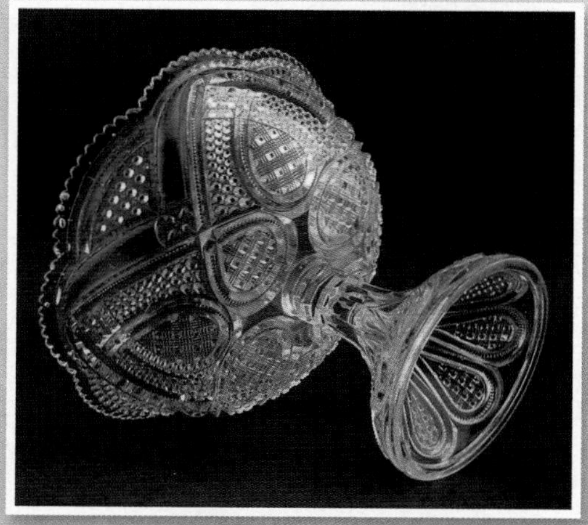

Compote

Item	Size	Crystal	Crystal w/Gold
Cake salver	9"	$110.00	$125.00
Creamer		60.00	70.00
Molasses can	7 oz.	85.00	95.00
Spooner		60.00	70.00
Sugar (lid not shown)		90.00	100.00
Compote	9¼" x 7¾"	55.00	75.00

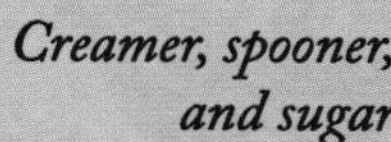

Creamer, spooner, and sugar

Molasses can

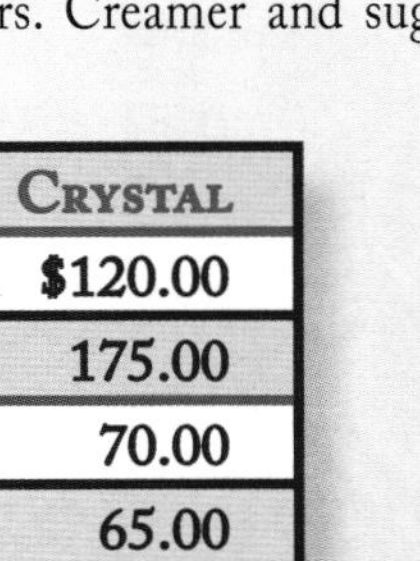

FANDANGO

OMN: Heisey Nr 1201.

Manufactured by: A. H. Heisey and Company, ca. 1896. Fandango was named by Minnie Kamm and is one of the first two patterns by Heisey. Heisey refers to cake stands as salvers. Creamer and sugar courtesy of Carolyn Crozier.

Item	Description	Size	Crystal
Cake salver		9"	$120.00
Cake basket	Unmarked	9¾" x 6"	175.00
Bowl	Ruffled	8"	70.00
	Plain	8"	65.00
Creamer	Individual	4¼" x 3¼"	50.00
Sugar	Individual	5¼" x 2⅝"	50.00

Sugar and creamer

Bowl

Bowl, ruffled

FAN WITH DIAMOND

OMN: McKee Nr 3 – Shell.

Manufactured by: McKee and Brothers, Pittsburgh, Pennsylvania, 1880.

Item	Crystal
Cake stand	$80.00
Creamer	45.00

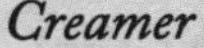

Creamer

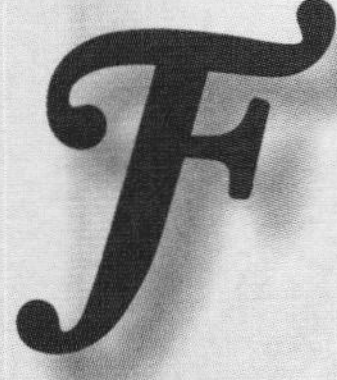

FASHION

OMN: Imperial Nr 402½.

Manufactured by: Imperial Glass Company, 1914. This pattern has been reproduced.

Item	Description	Size	Crystal
Cake stand		10"	$65.00
Compote	Open		55.00

Compote interior

Pedestal

FEATHER

OMN: Cambridge Nr 669, McKee Doric; AKA: Cambridge Feather, Feather and Quill, Fine Cut and Feather, Indiana Swirl, Prince's Feather, Swirl(s) and Feather(s).

Manufactured by: McKee Glass Company, Jeannette, Pennsylvania, ca 1896 – 1901; Cambridge Glass Company, Cambridge, Ohio, ca. 1902 – 1903.

Item	Description	Size	Crystal	Green	Amber Stain
Cake stand		8"	$85.00	$225.00	$475.00
		8½"	95.00	235.00	500.00
		9½"	120.00	275.00	575.00
		10"	140.00	325.00	600.00
	Rare	11"	200.00	550.00	900.00

Top view of cake stand

Cake stands, side by side

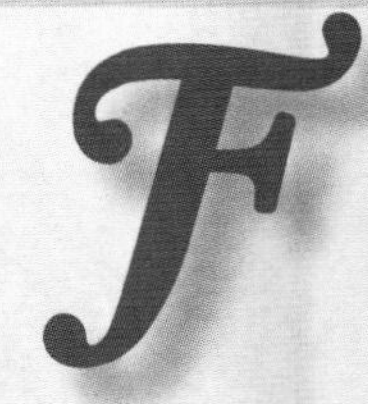

FEATHERED MEDALLION

OMN: Bryce Nr 15.

Manufactured by: Bryce Higbee Company, ca 1905. These cake stands are each 9¼" in diameter by 4¼" high. The pattern is reminiscent of fireworks on the 4th of July! This pattern remained unidentified for several months — in fact, I bought two in the hopes of making identification easier! There is a scalloped ½" gallery.

Item	Size	Crystal
Cake stand	9¼" x 4¼"	$60.00

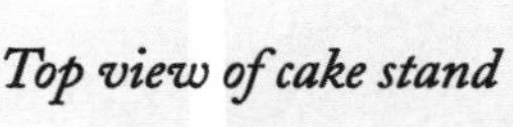

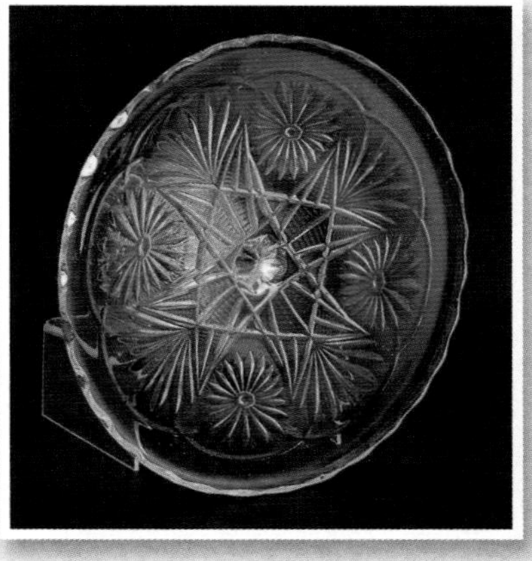

Top view of cake stand

Stacked cake stands

FERRIS WHEEL

AKA: Lucille, Prosperity.

Manufactured by: Indiana Glass Company, Dunkirk, Indiana, ca. 1910. This pattern can easily be confused with Paddlewheel by Westmoreland.

Item	Size	Crystal
Cake stand	9"	$70.00

Top view of cake stand

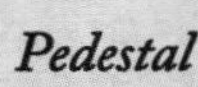

Pedestal

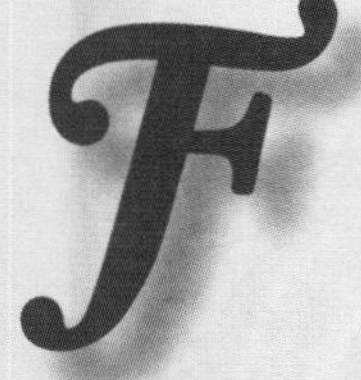

FESTOON

Manufactured by: Beatty-Brady Glass Company, Dunkirk, Indiana, 1898. This cake stand sparkles like cut crystal. An elegant pattern! The pedestal is comprised of three rings which extend to the base. Compote courtesy of Carolyn Crozier.

Item	Size	Crystal
Cake stand	9"	$95.00
	10"	125.00
Compote	8⅜" x 7¾"	325.00

Top view of cake stand

Compote interior

Compote, side view

FILE

AKA: Ribbed Sawtooth.
Manufactured by: Columbia Glass Company, 1888; and Imperial Glass Company, 1904.

Item	Size	Crystal
Cake plate	8¼"	$45.00
	10"	60.00
Bowl		25.00

Bowl

FINE CUT

OMN: Bryce Nr 720; AKA: Flower in Square.
Manufactured by: Bryce Brothers, 1870s. A very elegant, footed pitcher in vaseline.

Item	Size	Crystal	Amber	Blue	Vaseline
Cake stand		$95.00	$110.00	$125.00	$175.00
Pitcher	½ gal.	75.00	95.00	140.00	150.00

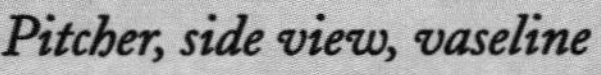

Pitcher, side view, vaseline

FINE CUT AND BLOCK

OMN: King Nr 25.

Manufactured by: King, Son and Company, ca 1885. The cake stand has a scalloped gallery. This pattern has been reproduced, but not the cake stand.

Item	Size	Crystal	Solid Colors	Amber Blocks
Cake stand	8"	$75.00	$120.00	$300.00
	9"	85.00	140.00	325.00
	10"	95.00	150.00	350.00
	11"	120.00	175.00	
	12"	150.00	200.00	

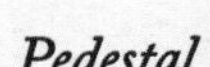

Pedestal

Top view of cake stand

FINE CUT AND PANEL

OMN: Bryce Nr 260 – Russian; AKA: Button and Oval Medallion, Finecut and Panel, Fine Cut with Panels, Nailhead and Panel.

Manufactured by: Jones, Cavitt and Company, 1886; Bryce Brothers, ca. 1889. This cake stand is square with scallops. However, there is a ¼" round raised edge to accommodate a round cake. Crystal cake stand courtesy of Marian Smith.

Item	Size	Crystal	Amber	Blue	Vaseline
Cake stand	9"	$85.00	$100.00	$120.00	$160.00
	10"	95.00	120.00	150.00	190.00

Stacked cake stands

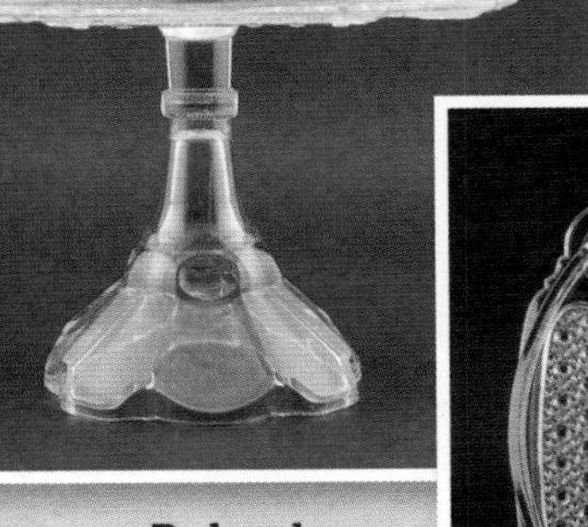

Pedestal

Top view of cake stand, vaseline

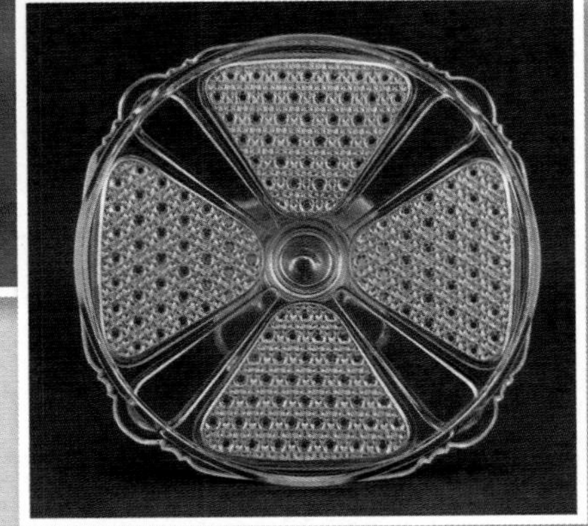

Top view of cake stand, clear

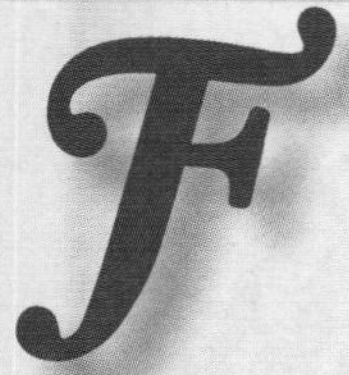

FINE CUT STAR AND FAN

AKA: Fine Cut Fan.

Manufactured by: Bryce, Higbee and Company, 1903; and J. B. Higbee Glass Company, 1910. There is a scalloped gallery and the pattern is repeated on the pedestal and base.

Item	Size	Crystal
Cake stand	9"	$60.00

Top view of cake stand

Pedestal

FISHSCALE

OMN: Coral.

Manufactured by: Bryce Brothers, Pittsburgh, Pennsylvania, 1888. This pattern is well named. There is a small gallery and the pattern is repeated on the base.

Item	Size	Crystal
Cake stand	9"	$65.00
	10"	75.00
	10½"	90.00
	11"	110.00
Creamer		60.00

Top view of cake stand

Pedestal

Creamer

FLATTENED DIAMOND AND SUNBURST

Manufactured by: Westmoreland Specialty Glass Company, 1880s. There is a gallery and a scalloped edge that extends beyond the edge of the gallery. The design is repeated on the pedestal.

Item	Size	Crystal
Cake stand	9½"	$75.00
Nappy		20.00

Pedestal

Top view of cake stand

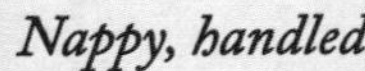

Nappy, handled

FLEUR-DE-LIS AND DRAPE

OMN: United States Glass Nr 15009; AKA: Fleur-de-lis and Tassel.

Manufactured by: United States Glass Company, Pittsburgh, Pennsylvania, Factory "A," 1891. This is an impressive cake stand with a dainty scalloped gallery and beaded bottom rim. The pedestal has beaded panels and is hollow.

Item	Size	Crystal	Emerald Green
Cake stand	9"	$90.00	$135.00
	10"	120.00	150.00
Spooner	5" x 3½"	50.00	70.00
Celery	6¾" x 3¾"	65.00	85.00

Spooner and celery

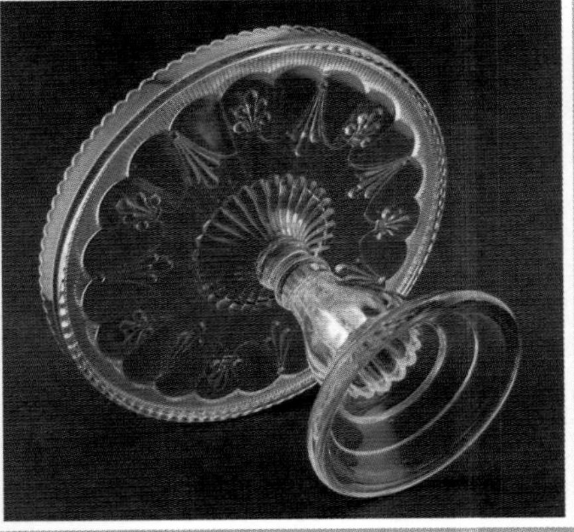

Pedestal

Top view of cake stand

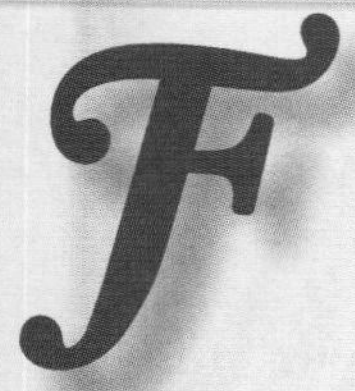

FLORAL OVAL

AKA: Banner, Cane and Sprig, Pittsburgh Daisy, and Spray and Cane.

Manufactured by: John F. Higbee Glass Company, 1910; and New Martinsville Glass Company, 1916. This pattern is readily available to the collector.

Item	Size	Crystal
Cake stand	9" x 4¾"	$60.00

Top view of cake stand

Pedestal

FLORIDA

OMN: United States Glass Nr 15056 – Florida; AKA: Emerald Green Herringbone (emerald green only), Paneled Herringbone (crystal only), Prism and Herringbone.

Manufactured by: United States Glass Company, Pittsburgh, Pennsylvania, Factory "B," 1898. This was the tenth state pattern made by U. S. Glass. Since retiring to sunny Florida (away from snow and ice), this is one of my favorite patterns, especially in green. Note the gallery, and the scallops that extend beyond the edge of the plate. The herringbone is continued down the pedestal.

Item	Description	Size	Crystal	Green
Cake stand		9¾" x 6½"	$110.00	$225.00
Bowl	Round, flat	9"	35.00	50.00
Pitcher	Water	½ gal.	50.00	90.00

Top view of cake stand

Pedestal

Bowl and pitcher

FLORIDA

AKA: Sunken Primrose.

Manufactured by: Greensburg Glass Company, 1893. Although this has the same name as a state, it is not a state pattern. At almost 11½", this is one of the largest cake stands. The pattern is continued on the base.

Item	Size	Crystal
Cake stand	11⅜" x 6¼"	$175.00

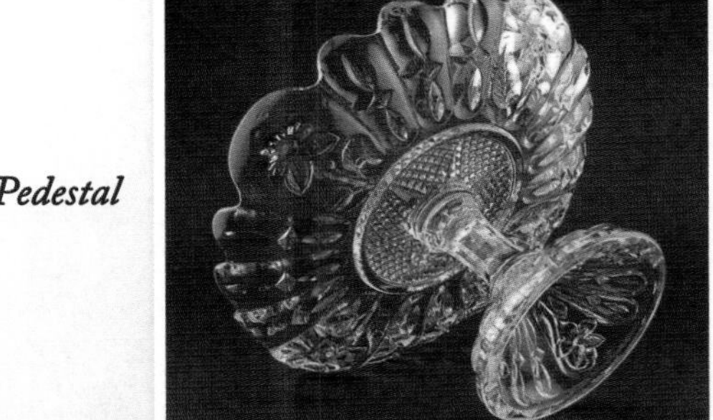

Pedestal

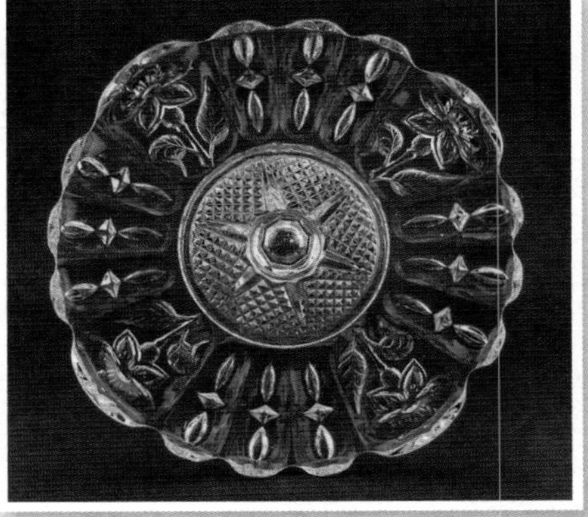

Top view of cake stand

FLORIDA PALM

AKA: Perfection, Tidal.

Manufactured by: Bryce, Higbee and Company, 1900.

Item	Size	Crystal
Cake stand	9"	$65.00

Pedestal

Top view of cake stand

FLOWER BAND

AKA: Bird Finial, Frosted Flower Band.

Manufactured by: Unknown, 1870s.

Item	Description	Crystal
Compote	Covered	$450.00

Compote

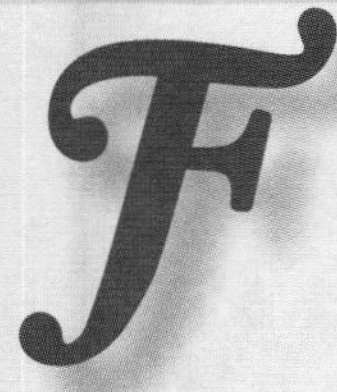

FLOWER POT

AKA: Flower Plant, Potted Plant.

Manufactured by: Unknown, ca late 1870s – early 1880s. Easily identified by the design, a pot of flowers. Occasionally pieces are found in amber and vaseline.

Item	Description	Size	Crystal
Cake stand		10½"	$225.00
Compote	Open		75.00
	Covered		125.00
Bowl	Berry, footed, square		25.00

Top view of cake stand

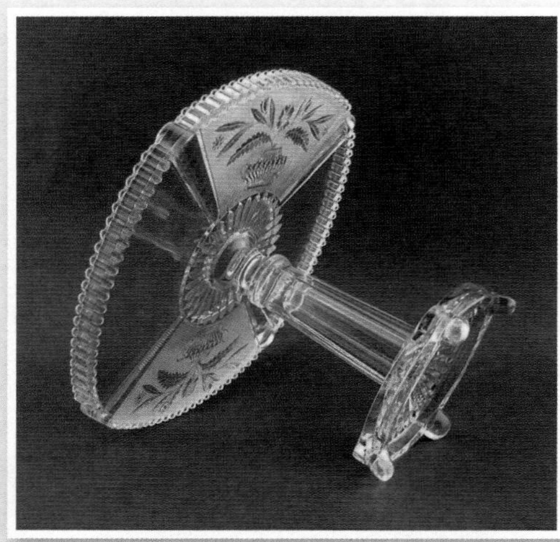

Pedestal

Compote, open

Close-up of pattern

Compote and berry bowls

F

FOSTORIA'S ATLANTA

OMN: Fostoria Nr 500 – Atlanta; AKA: Crystal Lion Head, Frosted Atlanta, Late Lion, Square Lion, Square Lion Heads.

Manufactured by: Fostoria Glass Company, Moundsville, West Virginia, 1895. This non-flint glass is easily identified by the lions on the corners of the item and on the handles of the sugar bowl and butter dish lid. All pieces in the pattern seen by the authors are square.

Item	Description	Size	Crystal	Crystal/Frosted
Cake stand	Square	9¼"	$250.00	$300.00
		10"	275.00	350.00
Compote	Square, scalloped	4¾"	90.00	100.00
Creamer		6" x 5"	125.00	175.00

Pedestal

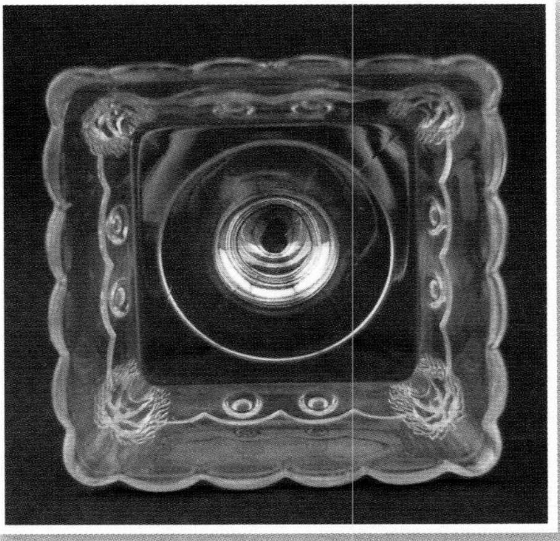

Compote, interior

Creamer

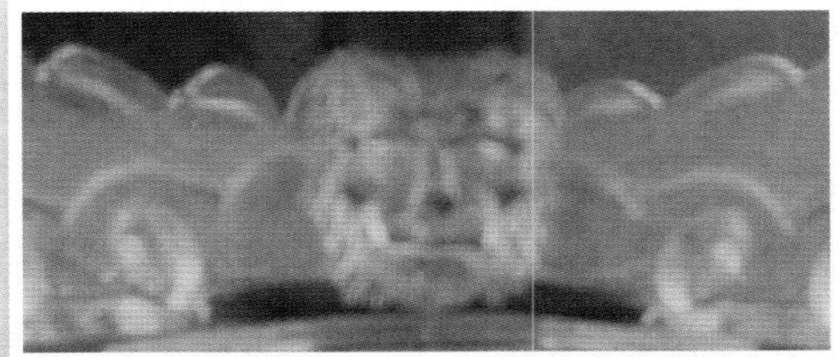

Close-up of pattern

FRISCO

OMN: Fostoria Nr 1229.

Manufactured by: Fostoria Glass Company, 1904. A square cake stand is being reproduced in blue and rose. A high standard compote was made in this pattern, so it can be presumed that a cake stand was originally made.

Item	Size	Crystal
Cake stand		$95.00
Creamer	4¾" x 5"	40.00

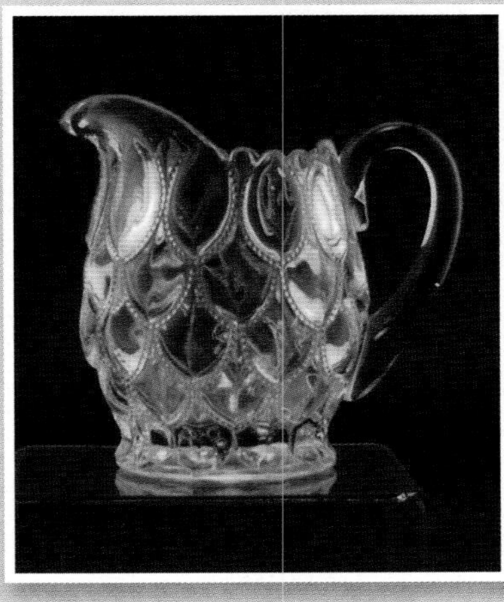

Creamer

FRONTIER

OMN: New Martinsville Nr 718; AKA: Colonial and Mitre.
Manufactured by: New Martinsville Glass Manufacturing Company, ca. 1911.

Item	Size	Crystal w/Gilding
Cake stand	12"	$110.00
Pitcher		170.00
Spooner		45.00
Tumbler		40.00

Pitcher and tumblers

Spooner

FROSTED CIRCLE

OMN: United States Glass Nr 15007 – Horn of Plenty; AKA: Crystal Circle (without the frosting).
Manufactured by: United States Glass Company, Pittsburgh, Pennsylvania, after 1891. This cake stand has a scalloped gallery. Cake stand, crystal, courtesy of Carolyn Crozier.

Item	Size	Crystal	Crystal w/Frosting
Cake stand	8"	$80.00	$125.00
	9"	100.00	140.00
	9½"	120.00	170.00
	10"	140.00	200.00

Clear and frosted cake stands

Top view of cake stand, crystal with frosted circles

Cake stand pedestal, frosted top

F

FROSTED MEDALLION

AKA: Sunburst Rosette.

Manufactured by: Unknown late 1880s. Small and large medallions decorate the top, pedestal, and base; there is a scalloped gallery. This pattern is similar to Rosette, manufactured by Bryce Brothers.

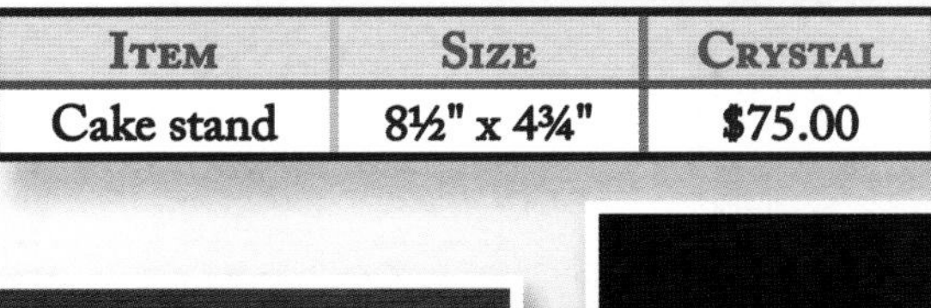

Item	Size	Crystal
Cake stand	8½" x 4¾"	$75.00

Pedestal

Cake stand

FULTON

AKA: Martha's Tears.

Manufactured by: Brilliant and Greensburg Glass Company, 1889. The design is featured on the plate and base. There is a scalloped gallery.

Item	Crystal
Cake stand	$60.00

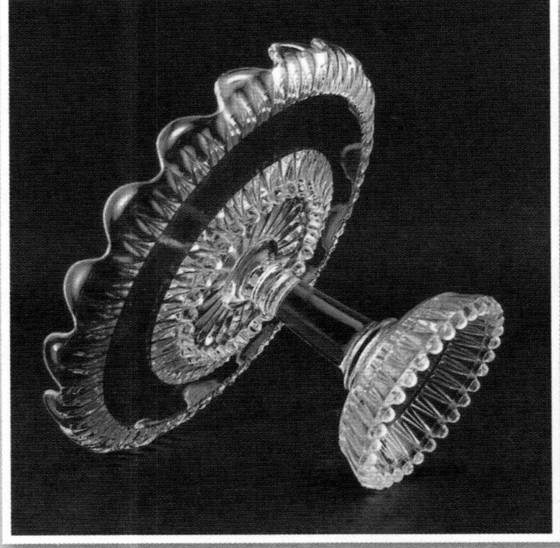

Pedestal

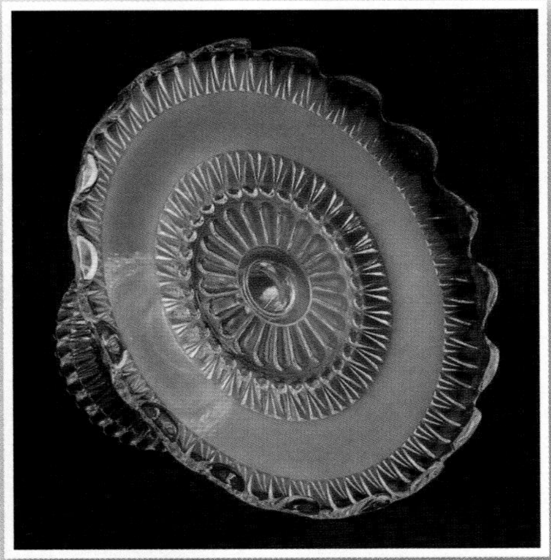

Top view of cake stand

GALA

AKA: Daisy with X Band, Hawaiian Lei.

Manufactured by: J. B. Higbee Company, 1913; and Jefferson Glass Company, Toronto, Canada, after 1913. The design appears on both the plate and base. There are deep scallops on the plate that turn inward.

Top view of cake stand

Item	Size	Crystal
Cake stand	6"	$55.00
	8"	60.00
	9"	75.00
	9⅜"	80.00

Pedestal

GALLOWAY

OMN: United States Glass Nr 15086 – Mirror, Jefferson Nr 15061; AKA: Mirror Plate, U. S. Mirror, Virginia, Woodrow.

Manufactured by: United States Glass Company, Pittsburgh, Pennsylvania, ca 1904; and Jefferson Glass, Toronto, Canada, ca 1900 – 1925. This cake stand has a large, scalloped, sawtooth gallery. The base on the cake stand and compote are different. The bottom of the sauce dish is the same as the compote base.

Item	Size	Crystal	Crystal w/Rose Stain
Cake stand	8½"	$130.00	$375.00
	9½"	145.00	425.00
	10"	170.00	475.00
Compote	6½" x 4¼"	40.00	70.00
Sauce dish		10.00	25.00

Top view of cake stand

Pedestal

Compote pedestal

Compote interior

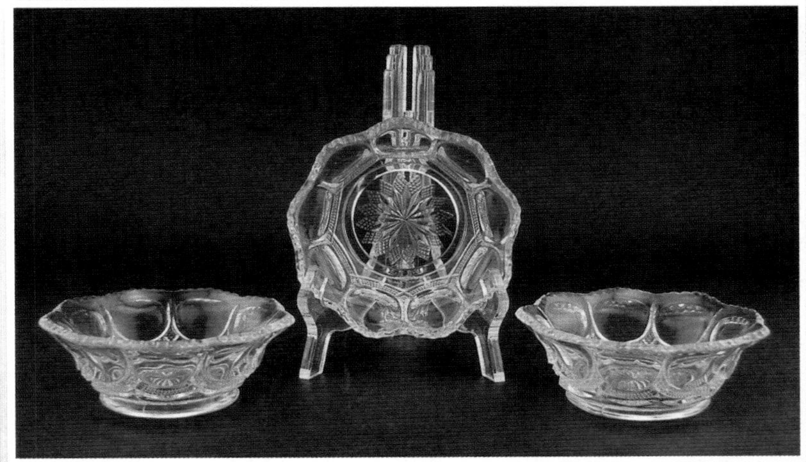

Sauce dishes

GARDEN OF EDEN

AKA: Fish, Lotus, Lotus and Serpent, Lotus with Serpent, Turtle.

Manufactured by: Unknown, 1870s – 1880s. This is not a particularly pretty pattern; the pedestal resembles a knotted tree trunk; there is a scalloped gallery. Some items have a serpent on the stem (see butter dish and mug).

Item	Size	Crystal
Cake stand	11" x 6¼"	$135.00
Mug	4" x 3½"	50.00
Butter dish	6½" x 5¾"	75.00

Butter dish

Mug

Pedestal

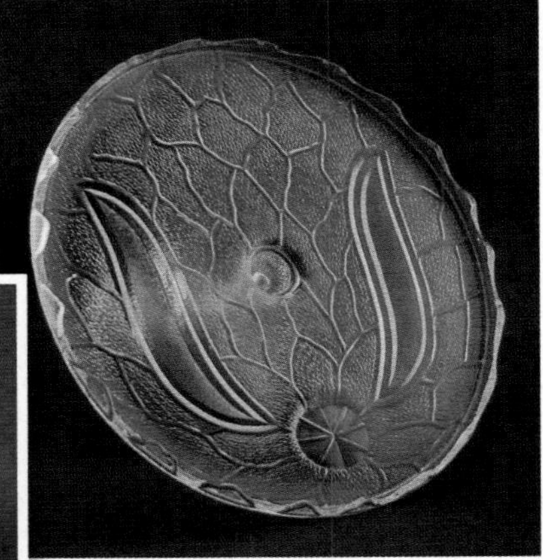

Top view of cake stand

GARDEN PINK

AKA: Indiana Nr 167.

Manufactured by: Indiana Glass Company, 1913. Courtesy of Kelly and Jeff Fugle.

Item	Size	Crystal
Cake stand	9"	$75.00

Top view of cake stand

Cake stands

GARFIELD DRAPE

AKA: Canadian Drape.

Manufactured by: Attributed to Adams and Company, 1880s. This non-flint ware was issued after the assassination of President Garfield. The base of the pedestal is completely different from the cake stand. Usually the pedestal either matches the top of the plate or is plain. Dainty flowers are inside the drapes, as well as in between the drapes; hard to see on the cake stand but more prominent on the creamer and sauce dishes. There is a small, plain gallery.

Item	Description	Size	Crystal
Cake stand		9½"	$225.00
Creamer	Pressed handle		65.00
Bowl	Sauce, flat		10.00
	Footed	3½"	15.00

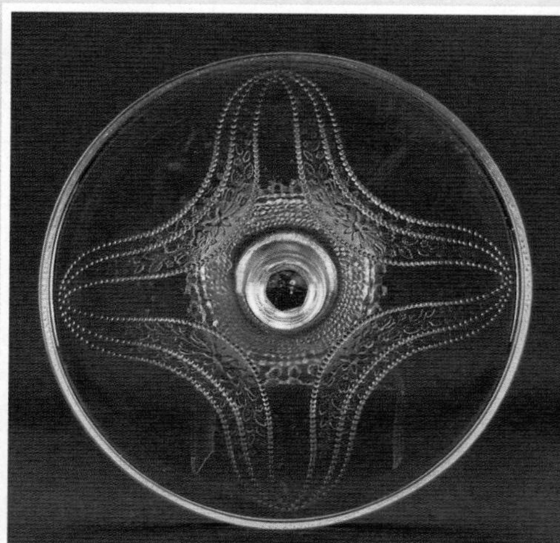

Top view of cake stand

Creamer and sauce bowls, footed

Pedestal

GEM

AKA: Nailhead.

Manufactured by: Bryce, Higbee and Company, Pittsburgh, Pennsylvania, ca. 1885. The pattern is only on the plate; pedestal and base are plain; and there is a scalloped gallery.

Item	Size	Crystal
Cake stand	8¾"	$65.00
	9½"	70.00

Stacked cake stands

GEORGIA

OMN: United States Glass Nr 15076 – Georgia; AKA: Peacock Eye, Peacock Feather(s).

Manufactured by: United States Glass Company, at Factory "E," ca 1902. This is part of the "state series" patterns, the tweny-ninth issued by U. S. Glass. Blue or any other color would be considered rare. There is a small scalloped gallery. The peacock feather is featured on both the plate and pedestal, which is hollow. Note: Pedestal on the compote is different from the cake stand. Cake stand and bowl courtesy of Ashton Marie and Ethan Turner James. Compote and cruet courtesy of Logan Michael and Garett Marshall Poillucci.

Item	Size	Crystal
Cake stand	8½"	$65.00
	9"	75.00
	10"	90.00
	11"	135.00
Bowl		15.00
Compote	5"	20.00
Cruet w/original stopper	8¼"	75.00

Top view of cake stand

Pedestal

Compote

Cruet

Bowl

GIANT BULL'S EYE

OMN: Bellaire Nr 151, United States Glass Nr 157; AKA: Bull's Eye and Spearhead, Bull's Eye Variation, Concave Circle, Excelsior.

Manufactured by: Bellaire Goblet Company, 1889; Model Flint Glass Company, 1891; United States Glass Company, 1898. Cruet is courtesy of Carolyn Crozier.

Item	Size	Crystal
Cake stand		$135.00
Cruet w/original stopper	2¼" x 6¾"	75.00

Cruet

GLADIATOR

Manufactured by: McKee Brothers, 1897.

Item	Description	Size	Crystal
Cake stand			$65.00
Bowl	Oval	10" x 6"	35.00

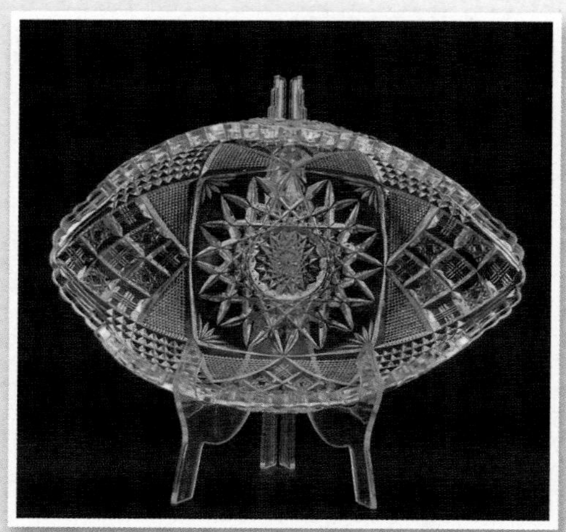

Bowl

GLOBE AND STAR

Manufactured by: Unknown, ca 1870 – 1900. This is a very ornate cake stand with a scalloped gallery and scalloped pedestal base.

Item	Size	Crystal
Cake stand	9" x 6"	$200.00

Top view of cake stand

Pedestal

G

GOOD LUCK

AKA: Horseshoe, Prayer Mat, and Prayer Rug.

Manufactured by: Adams and Company, Pittsburgh, Pennsylvania, 1891. This pattern has both the horseshoes (hence the name "Good Luck") and prayer rugs. Beads are on the underside of the rim of the cake plate and the pedestal base rests on tiny beads.

Item	Size	Crystal
Cake stand	8"	$275.00
	9"	165.00
	10"	180.00
Relish		20.00
Spooner	3¾" d x 4¾" h	40.00

Stacked cake stands

Top view of cake stand

Spooner

Relish

GRAND

OMN: New Grand; AKA: Diamond Medallion, Fine Cut and Diamond, Fine Cut Medallion.

Manufactured by: Bryce, Higbee and Company, Pittsburgh, Pennsylvania, ca 1885. These cake stands differ in that one has a plain gallery and the other has a scalloped ½" gallery. Note: Pedestals are also different.

Item	Size	Crystal
Cake stand	8"	$60.00
	9"	75.00
	10"	90.00

Top view of cake stand, plain edge

Pedestal

Pedestal

Top view of cake stand, scalloped edge

G

GRATED DIAMOND AND SUNBURST

OMN: Duncan Nr 20.

Manufactured by: George Duncan and Sons, Pittsburgh, Pennsylvania, ca 1895. This is a very ornate cake stand with a scalloped gallery. The pedestal is unusual because it is swirled down to the scallops on the base.

Item	Size	Crystal
Cake stand	10½"	$75.00

Pedestal

Top view of cake stand

GRENADE

AKA: Grenada.

Attributed to Model Flint Company, Albany, Indiana, dates unknown.

Item	Size	Crystal
Cake stand		$85.00
Bowl	8½"	45.00

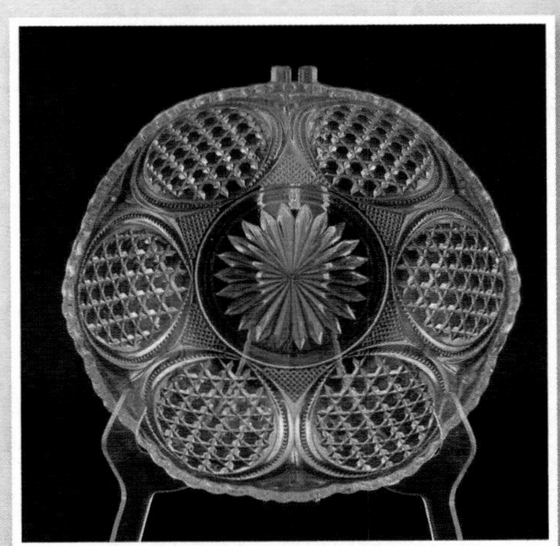

Bowl

GROUP THUMBPRINT

AKA: Panelled Thumbprint.

Manufactured by: West Virginia Glass Company, 1895.

Item	Description	Size	Crystal
Cake stand		8" x 4½"	$65.00
Bowl	Gold trimmed	9½" x 5¼"	35.00

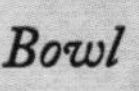

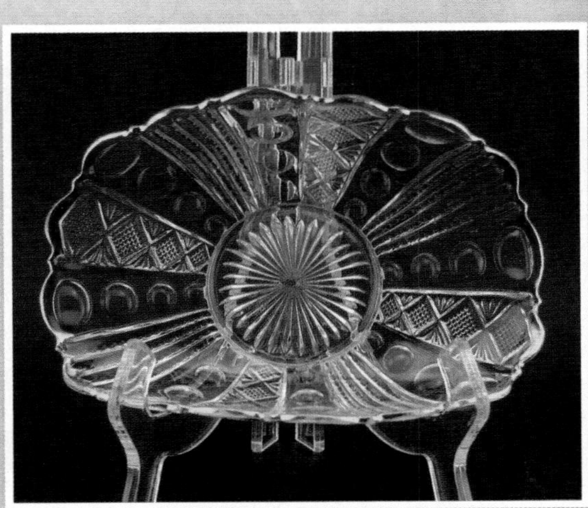

Bowl

HANOVER

AKA: Blockhouse, Block with Stars, Hanover Star.

Manufactured by: Richards and Hartley Glass Company, Tarentum, Pennsylvania, ca 1888. This is truly an impressive cake stand, made of very clear glass, and sparkling like cut crystal. The pattern is repeated on the pedestal, which is hollow.

Item	Size	Crystal	Blue	Amber	Vaseline
Cake stand	10¼" x 6"	$125.00	$150.00	$125.00	$175.00

Top view of cake stand

Pedestal

HARTLEY

OMN: Richard's and Hartley Nr 900; AKA: Daisy and Button with Oval Panels, Paneled Diamond Cut and Fan.

Manufactured by: Richards and Hartley, Tarentum, Pennsylvania, ca 1887. The panels are repeated on the pedestal with a single row around the base.

Item	Description	Size	Crystal	Amber	Blue	Canary
Cake stand		10"	$80.00	$90.00	$125.00	$150.00
Compote	Open	8"	35.00	40.00	50.00	65.00
Bowl		8"	40.00	45.00	50.00	75.00

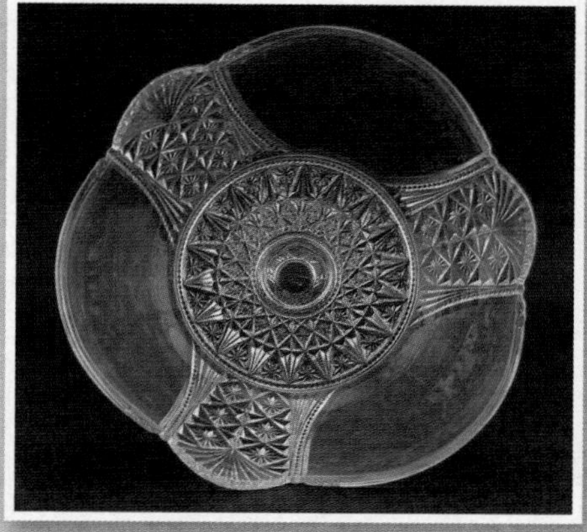

Compote interior

Pedestal

Bowl

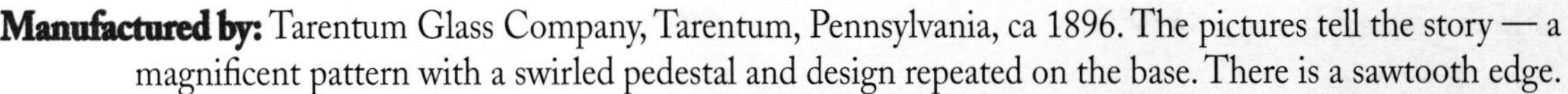

HARVARD YARD

AKA: Tarentum's Harvard.

Manufactured by: Tarentum Glass Company, Tarentum, Pennsylvania, ca 1896. The pictures tell the story — a magnificent pattern with a swirled pedestal and design repeated on the base. There is a sawtooth edge.

Item	Size	Crystal
Cake stand	9¼"	$100.00

Pedestal

Top view of cake stand

HEART STEM

Manufactured by: Unknown, believed to be in 1880s. The pedestal is flat, where normally it is round or square, which has three perforations: two hearts and a modified club.

Item	Size	Crystal
Cake stand		$175.00
Compote	8" x 12"	145.00

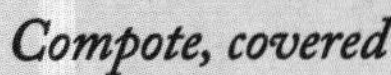

Compote, covered

HEART WITH THUMBPRINT

OMN: Tarentum's Hartford; AKA: Bull's Eye in Heart, Columbia, Columbian, Heart and Thumbprint.

Manufactured by: Tarentum Glass Company, Tarentum, Pennsylvania, ca 1898. This is a particularly appealing pattern. One sold in December 2002 for $1,224; one was listed for sale in January 2008 but was removed with no bids in a few hours. The top of the cake stand has six hearts with thumbprints, divided by arrow shaped designs. The pattern is repeated on the pedestal, and the base is decorated with thumb prints divided by slashes.

Item	Description	Size	Crystal	Crystal w/Ruby	Crystal w/Gold
Cake stand		9" x 5¹⁄₁₆"	$700.00	$1,500.00	$850.00
Bowl		8"	45.00	175.00	65.00
Nappy	Handled		45.00	75.00	55.00
Card tray			25.00	65.00	45.00

Top view of cake stand

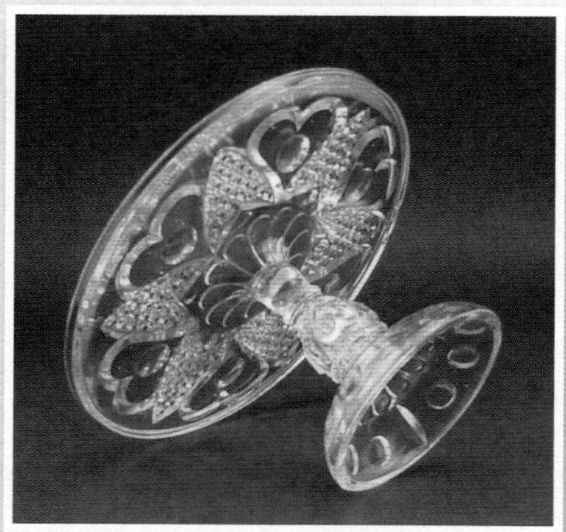

Pedestal

Card tray, crystal with gilding, and nappy

Bowl, crystal with gilding

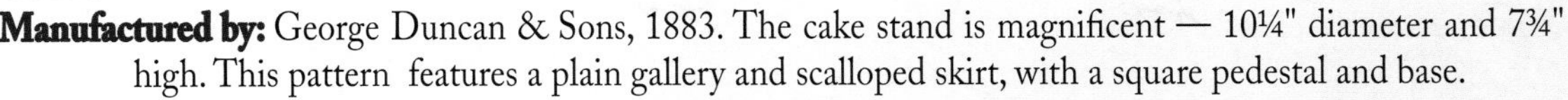

HEAVY FINECUT

OMN: Duncan Nr 800.

Manufactured by: George Duncan & Sons, 1883. The cake stand is magnificent — 10¼" diameter and 7¾" high. This pattern features a plain gallery and scalloped skirt, with a square pedestal and base.

Item	Size	Crystal	Vaseline
Cake stand	10¼" x 7¾"	$150.00	$275.00
Water tray		125.00	250.00

Pedestal

Top view of cake stand

HEAVY GOTHIC

OMN: United States Glass Nr 15014; AKA: Whitton.

Manufactured by: United States Glass Company, Pittsburgh, Pennsylvania, 1891.

Item	Size	Crystal	Crystal w/Ruby
Cake stand	9"	$95.00	$240.00
	10"	120.00	275.00
Creamer	5½" x 4¾"	45.00	65.00
Sugar	6½" x 4¼"	65.00	100.00

Creamer and sugar

HECK

AKA: Double Prism, Teardrop Row.

Manufactured by: Model Flint Glass Company, 1893. This is a massive, brilliant pattern and one of the most popular made by Model Flint. Six prisms comprise the pedestal which is very similar to the Chandelier pattern. The plate portion has a very deep brandy well, and prisms radiate from the center. There is a 1½" prismed skirt and a ½" gallery.

Item	Crystal
Cake salver	$175.00

Top view of cake salver

Pedestal

HERO

AKA: Ruby Rosette.

Manufactured by: Elson Glass Company, Martins Ferry, Ohio, 1891; and West Virginia Glass Company, Martins Ferry, Ohio, ca 1893. This pattern is similar to Pillow Encircled.

Item	Size	Crystal
Cake stand		$175.00
Butter dish	7½" x 7"	90.00

Butter dish, open

HEXAGONAL BULL'S-EYE

AKA: Creased Hexagon Block, Double Red Block (red stained).

Manufactured by: Dalzell, Gilmore and Leighton, Findlay, Ohio, 1888 – 1902. This cake stand has a pointed scalloped gallery and skirt.

Item	Size	Crystal
Cake stand	9"	$150.00

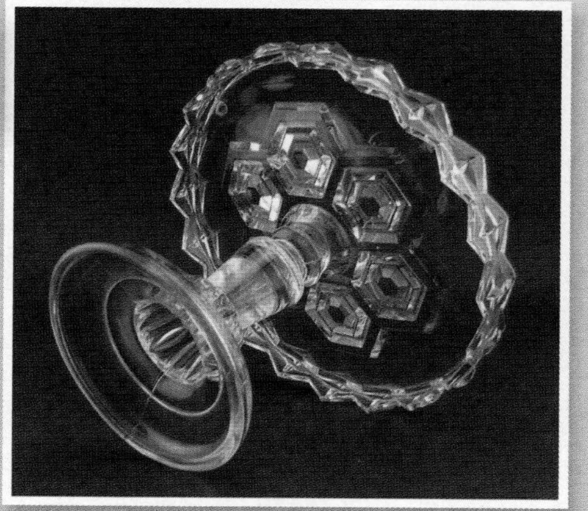

Pedestal

Top view of cake stand

HICKMAN

AKA: Empire, Jubilee Nr 1, LaClede.

Manufactured by: McKee and Brothers, Jeannette, Pennsylvania, ca 1888 – 1900; and Federal Glass, 1914.

These cake stands differ in that the 9" cake stand has a scalloped gallery, while the 10½" has the same pattern but with a sawtooth skirt. The 10½" cake stand has a small square in the center, and the 9" one has a large square with alternating oval and six-sided design surrounding the square. The skirt has fine points in each scallop with a straight line in between the points. The mustard jar has underplate attached. Made in crystal and green.

Item	Size	Crystal
Cake stand	7"	$75.00
	9"	65.00
	10½"	80.00
Bowl	7"	35.00
Mustard		65.00
Olive dish		15.00
Salt shaker		35.00

Stacked cake stands

Top view of cake stand

Bowl, olive dish, salt shaker, and mustard

Cake stands, side by side

HIDALGO

OMN: Adams Nr 5; AKA: Frosted Waffle; Waffle – Red Top.
Manufactured by: Adams and Company, Pittsburgh, Pennsylvania, 1880.

Item	Description	Size	Crystal
Cake stand			$95.00
Compote	With cover	6⅜" x 6¾"	85.00

Interior of compote

Side view

HIGH HOB

OMN: Westmoreland Nr 550.
Manufactured by: Westmoreland Glass Company, Grapeville, Pennsylvania, 1915.

Item	Size	Crystal
Cake stand		$45.00
Bowl	9"	35.00
Pitcher		55.00

Bowl and pitcher

HOBNAIL

Manufactured by: Columbia Glass Company, ca. 1870 – 1880. Easy to see why this was named; hobnails appear on the plate surface, pedestal, and base. The gallery and skirt of this cake stand are comprised of hobnails.

Item	Description	Size	Crystal
Cake stand	Crystal	10"	$250.00

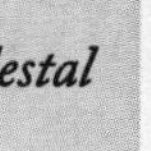

Pedestal

Top view of cake stand

HOBSTAR AND TASSEL

OMN: Imperial Nr 334½ D.
Manufactured by: Imperial Glass Company 1909. At first glance the tassels look like serpents.

Item	Description	Size	Crystal
Cake plate			$55.00
Bowl	Gold trim	6"	30.00

Bowl

HOLLY

Attributed to the Boston and Sandwich Glass Company, Sandwich, Massachusetts. This cake stand with roping on the gallery is embellished with sprigs of holly and berries on the top; a truly festive cake stand especially for the holidays. The pedestal and base are plain.

Top view of cake stand

Item	Size	Crystal
Cake stand	8½"	$250.00
	9½"	285.00
	10⅝" x 5¼"	350.00
	12¼"	575.00

Pedestal

HONEYCOMB

OMN: Bellaire Nr 40, Cape Cod Nr 96, Central Nr 136, Cincinnati, Cincinnati Honeycomb, Doyle Nr 500, New York, O'Hara Nr 3, Vernon; AKA: Honeycomb External, Midget New York, Thousand Faces.

Manufactured by: Bakewell, Pears and Company, 1875; Bellaire Goblet Company, 1889 – 1890; Boston Silver and Glass Company, 1869; and Doyle and Company, ca. 1880s.

Compote

Item	Description	Size	Crystal
Cake stand		8"	$110.00
		9½"	175.00
		10½"	225.00
		11¼"	250.00
Celery	Scalloped rim		45.00
Compote		8½"	50.00
Sugar	No lid		80.00
Wine			25.00
Shaker			25.00
Spooner	Scalloped rim		35.00

Celery, sugar, spooner, wine, shaker

HORN OF PLENTY

OMN: Comet; AKA: Peacock Tail.

Manufactured by: Boston and Sandwich Glass Company; Bryce Brothers; McKee and Brothers, ca 1830s – 1850s. Compote courtesy of Carolyn Crozier.

Item	Size	Crystal
Cake stand		$2,800.00
Compote	9¼" x 9½"	175.00

Interior view of compote

Side view of compote

I

HORSESHOE STEM

Manufactured by: O'Hara Glass Company, ca 1880. The pattern derives its name from the pedestal. This is truly a magnificent cake stand, one of the biggest seen. It has a plain plate and gallery with a scalloped skirt. No record of this gigantic (12" x 10") size has been found in any reference books.

Item	Size	Crystal
Cake stand	7½"	$270.00
	8½"	290.00
	9½"	340.00
	12" x 10"	475.00

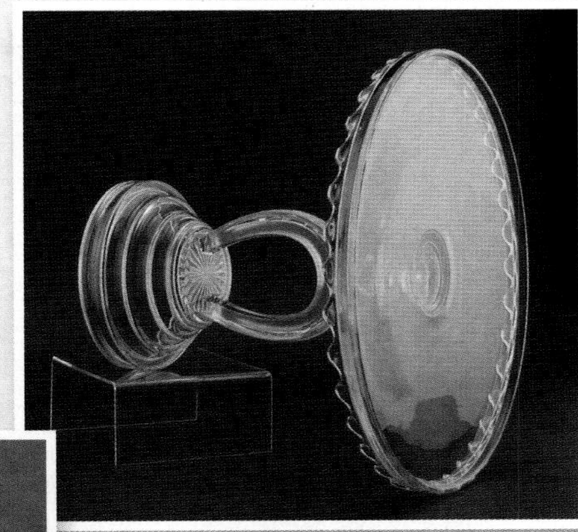

Top view of cake stand

Pedestal

ILLINOIS

OMN: United States Glass Nr 15052; AKA: Clarissa, Star of the East.

Manufactured by: United States Glass Company, Pittsburgh, Pennsylvania, at Factory "G" and Factory "P," ca. 1897. This is the sixth pattern in the "state series" and is mostly found in crystal but in rare instances can be found in crystal with ruby stain, emerald green, and possibly other colors. The cake stand in this pattern is square, with a square pedestal base. Reference *Pennsylvania Glassware 1870 – 1904*, The American Historical Catalog Collection.

Item	Size	Crystal	Green
Cake stand		$200.00	
Toothpick		40.00	
Pitcher	1 pt.	100.00	
	1½ pt.	120.00	
	½ gal.	175.00	$225.00

Toothpick

Pitcher

INDIANA

OMN: Model Flint Glass Nr 808; AKA: Eight-O-Eight.

Manufactured by: Model Flint Glass Company, 1896. This pattern is very similar to Kansas, which has oval and round circles. There is a sawtooth edge around the circles and the plain panels. There is a scalloped edge that extends beyond the rim of the plain gallery.

Item	Size	Crystal
Cake stand	10½"	$90.00

Top view of cake stand

Pedestal

INDIANA

OMN: United States Glass Nr 15029; AKA: Prison Window(s).

Manufactured by: United States Glass Company, Factory "U," Gas City, Indiana, ca 1897. This is first of the "states series" patterns.

Item	Description	Size	Crystal	Crystal w/Gold
Cake stand			$65.00	$75.00
Bowl	Gold trimmed	6½"	25.00	30.00

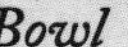

Bowl

INDIANA NR 156

AKA: Horsemint.

Manufactured by: Indiana Glass Company, Dunkirk, Indiana, ca 1913. This plate features a scalloped gallery. This pattern has been reissued.

Item	Size	Crystal
Cake stand	9¼" x 3¾"	$80.00

Pedestal

Top view of cake stand

INDIANA NR 168

AKA: Creole and Gaelic.

Manufactured by: Indiana Glass Company, Dunkirk, Indiana, 1908. The pattern consists of four panels containing a flower with seven petals. Two panels have flowers with six leaves and opposing panels have stems with five leaves. There is a scalloped gallery.

Sugar

Item	Size	Crystal
Cake stand	7½"	$55.00
	9½" x 3½"	65.00
Sugar (no lid shown)		45.00

Top view of cake stand

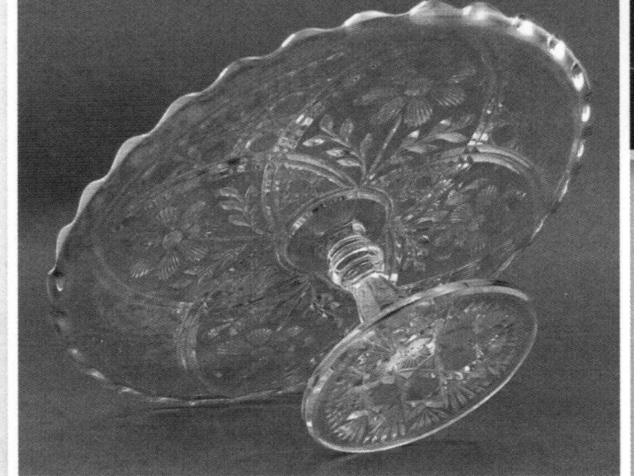

Pedestal

INVERTED FEATHER

AKA: Nearcut Nr 2651.

Manufactured by: Cambridge Glass Company, 1906. Appropriately named, this cake stand features a small scalloped gallery and a plain pedestal with a sawtooth edge on the base of the pedestal.

Item	Size	Crystal
Cake stand	10" x 5"	$75.00

Top view of cake stand

Pedestal

IRIS

AKA: Paden City Nr 206, Pineapple.

Manufactured by: J. B. Higbee Glass Company, 1917; and Paden City, 1918. On the plate surface are four pineapples with fans separating them; the gallery is scalloped. The pedestal is plain with a lined base.

Top view of cake stand

Item	Size	Crystal
Cake stand	6"	$60.00
	9"	70.00

Pedestal

IVANHOE

OMN: Dalzell Nr 65D.

Manufactured by: Dalzell, Gilmore and Leighton, 1890.

Item	Crystal
Cake stand	$110.00
Butter dish	80.00
Sugar	40.00

Butter dish

IVY IN SNOW

OMN: Forest; AKA: Forest Ware, Ivy in Snow-Red Leaves (ruby stained).

Manufactured by: Cooperative Flint Glass Company, Beaver Falls, Pennsylvania, 1898. Several pieces in this pattern have been reissued by Kemple Glass Works, East Palestine, Ohio, and Kenova, West Virginia, and Phoenix Glass Company, Monaca, Pennsylvania. This plate features four stems with leaves and buds on a stippled background. There is a plain gallery.

Pedestal

Top view of cake stand

Item	Size	Crystal Round	Crystal Square
Cake stand	8" x 4¼"	$135.00	$150.00
	10"	150.00	175.00

JACOB'S LADDER

OMN: Imperial – Bryce; AKA: Maltese.
Manufactured by: Bryce, Walter and Company, 1876.

Item	Description	Size	Crystal
Cake stand		8"	$75.00
		9"	90.00
		11"	120.00
		12"	175.00
Compote (lid not shown)		7½" x 7½"	175.00
	With Maltese Cross finial	8½" x 10½"	225.00

Compotes, side by side

Compote

Compote, interior

JAPANESE

AKA: Bird in Ring, Butterfly and Fan, Grace, Japanese Fan.
Manufactured by: George Duncan and Sons Glass Company, Pittsburgh, Pennsylvania, 1880. The three different scenes are shown.

Item	Description	Size	Crystal
Cake stand			$225.00
Sugar	Covered	9"	155.00

Sugar, ⅓ pattern

Sugar, ⅓ pattern

Sugar, ⅓ pattern

JASPER

AKA: Belt Buckle, Late Buckle.

Manufactured by: Bryce Brothers, Pittsburgh, Pennsylvania, ca 1880. The 9" cake stand was reproduced.

Item	Size	Crystal
Cake stand	8"	$55.00
	9"	75.00
	11"	85.00
	12"	115.00
Spooner	4" x 6"	45.00

Spooner

JERSEY SWIRL

OMN: Windsor Swirl; AKA: Swirl, Swirl and Diamonds, Windsor.

Manufactured by: Windsor Glass Company, ca. 1886. The gallery on this plate is plain, but there is a sawtooth skirt, which extends beyond the base of the gallery. The pattern is repeated on the pedestal and base. Buyer beware, this elegant pattern was widely reproduced in the 1960s and 1970s (ashtray, 4" bowl, 6½" compote, goblet, salt dip, sauce, and wine). The cake stand *was not* reproduced.

Item	Size	Crystal	Amber	Blue	Canary
Cake stand	8¾"	$90.00	$100.00	$130.00	$150.00
Compote	9½" x 9½"	105.00	105.00	125.00	150.00

Top view of cake stand

Compote and cake stand

Pedestal

JEWELED MOON AND STARS

OMN: Imperial; AKA: Late Moon and Star, Moon and Star Variant, Moon and Star Variation, Moon and Star with Waffle Stem.

Manufactured by: Cooperative Flint Glass Company, Beaver Falls, Pennsylvania, 1896. This is a spectacular cake stand which features amber and blue stain and has a skirt with the pattern repeated on the base. Cake stand courtesy of Tom Neale.

Item	Description	Size	Crystal	Crystal w/Frosting	Crystal w/Color Stain
Cake stand		9"	$120.00	$145.00	$250.00
		10"	135.00	170.00	300.00
Bowl	Round, covered	7"	80.00	100.00	160.00

Bowl

Cake stand

JUBILEE

AKA: Isis, Nellie, Radiant Daisy and Button.

Manufactured by: McKee Glass Company, ca. 1894. This cake stand features a plain gallery, ribbed column pedestal, and the pattern is repeated on the base.

Item	Description	Size	Crystal
Cake stand		9½"	$75.00
Pitcher	Water		85.00

Pedestal

Water pitcher

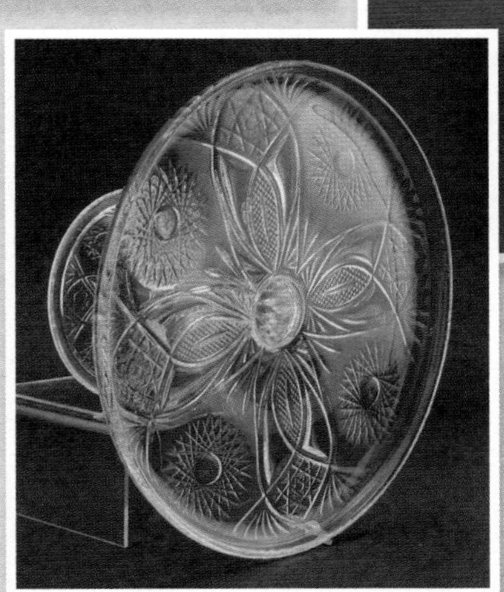

Top view of cake stand

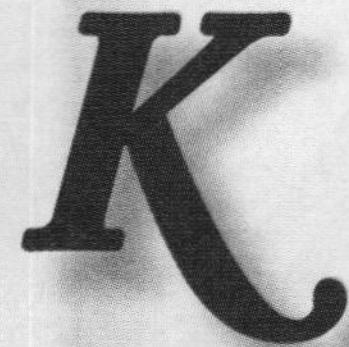

KALONYAL

OMN: Heisey Nr 1776.

Manufactured by: A. H. Heisey and Company, Newark, Ohio, 1906. This is a very plain cake stand with a chain-like deep, scalloped skirt. Cake stand courtesy of Carolyn Crozier.

Item	Size	Crystal
Cake stand	9" x 7"	$300.00

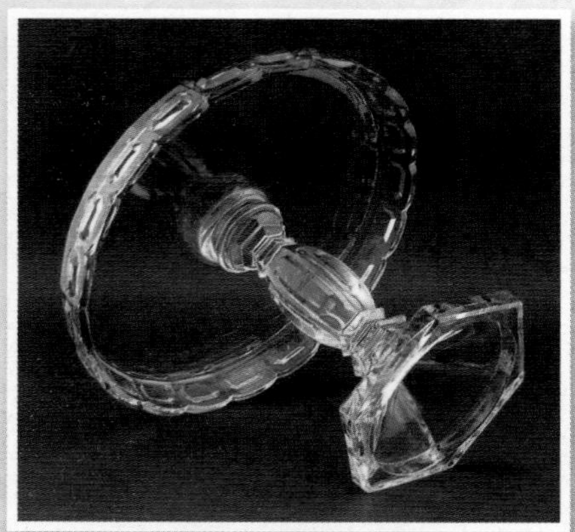

Cake stand

Pedestal

KANSAS

OMN: United States Glass Nr 15072 – Kansas; AKA: Jewel and/with Dewdrop, Jewel with Dewdrop(s), Kokomo Nr 8.

Manufactured by: United States Glass Company, Pittsburgh, Pennsylvania, 1901; Kokomo Glass Manufacturing Company, Kokomo, Indiana, ca. 1903; and Federal Glass Company, Columbus, Ohio, ca 1914. This is another one of the very popular "state series" patterns, twenty-fifth issued, which is very pretty with the stained jewels and gilding. The top of the cake plate has alternating beaded panels; one plain and one with beaded circles and ovals. This pattern has a deep scalloped gallery; the pedestal consists of plain panels with beaded edges down to the beaded base. The combination of stained jewels with gold trim is very rare. This pattern is very similar to Indiana by Model Flint Glass. Cake stand courtesy of Joanne Yarnall; pitcher courtesy of Sue Edelmon.

Item	Description	Size	Crystal	Crystal w/Stained Jewels
Cake stand	High standard	8"	$90.00	$150.00
		9" or 9½"	120.00	200.00
		10"	150.00	250.00
	Low standard	8"	70.00	115.00
		9" or 9½"	90.00	150.00
		10"	100.00	175.00
Pitcher	Water	½ gal.	85.00	150.00

Top view of cake stand

Top view of cake stand, crystal with stained jewels

K

Pitcheer

Pedestal

KAYAK

OMN: Imperial Nr 2.

Manufactured by: Imperial Glass Company, 1904. It is easy to see how this pattern received its name. Beads decorate the gallery and base of the plate. Kayaks appear on the pedestal, with another half of a kayak on the base.

Item	Size	Crystal
Cake stand	7¾" x 5¼"	$65.00
	9¾" x 5½"	90.00

Pedestal

Top view of cake stand

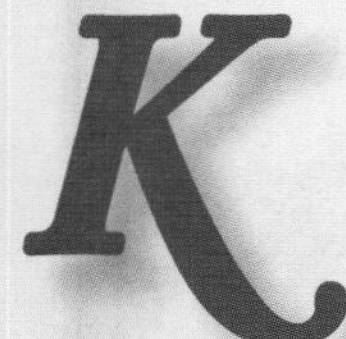

KENTUCKY

OMN: United States Glass Nr 15051 – Kentucky.

Manufactured by: United States Glass Company, Pittsburgh, Pennsylvania. This pattern is very similar to Millard; the difference being that the "petals" in Kentucky are stippled and plain in Millard. There is a scalloped gallery with the pattern repeated on the base. This was the fifth in the "state series" patterns.

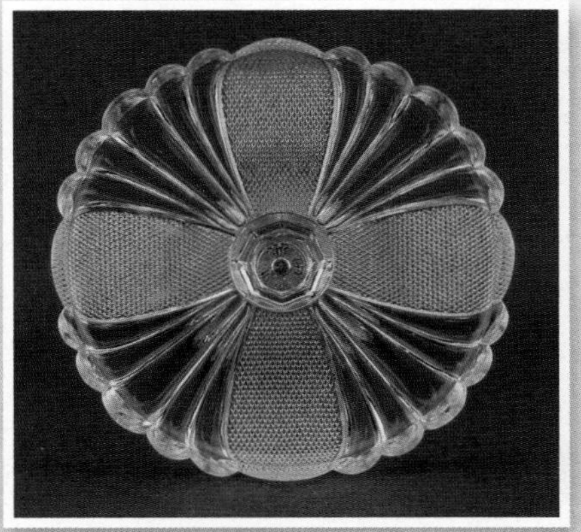

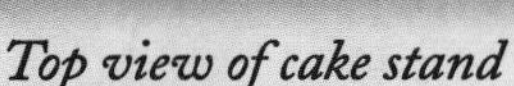

Top view of cake stand

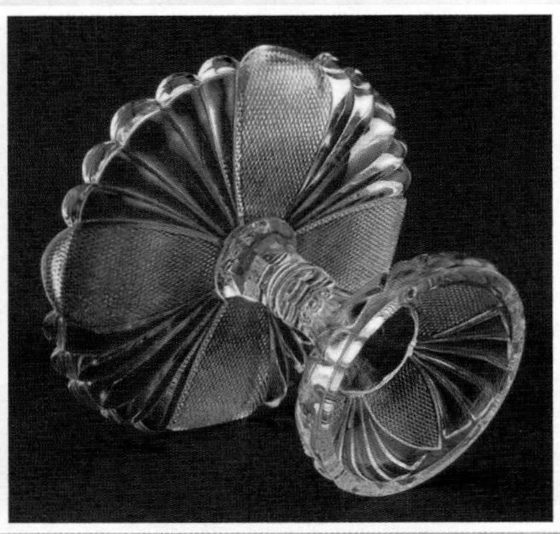

Pedestal

Item	Size	Crystal
Cake stand	9½"	$100.00
	10½"	125.00
Plate	9"	45.00

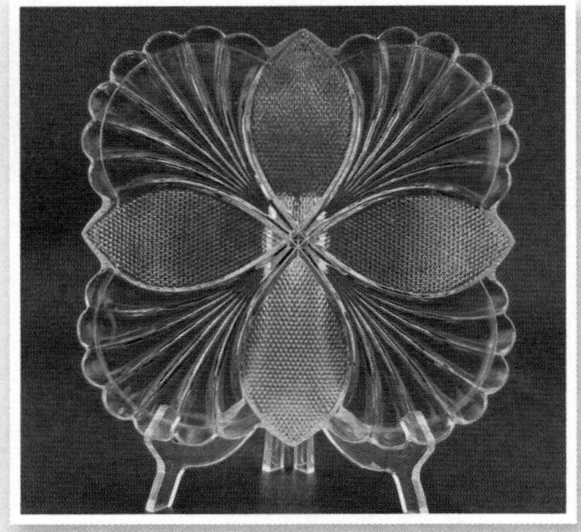

Plate

KING ARTHUR

OMN: Duncan Nr 68.

Manufactured by: Duncan and Miller Glass Company, 1905. The panels on the top of the plate extend down to an unusually generous skirt that is gilded. There is a small plain gallery.

Item	Size	Crystal	Crystal w/Gold
Cake stand	9½"	$120.00	$175.00

Top view of cake stand

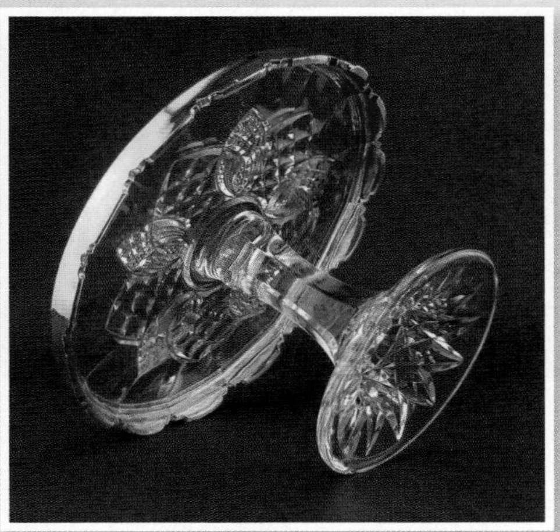

Pedestal

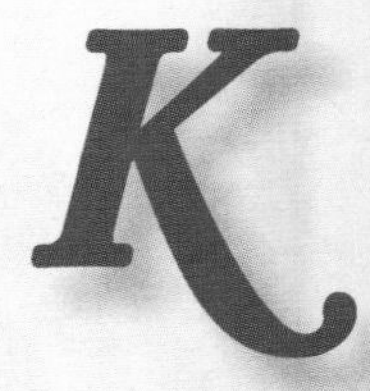

KING'S CROWN

OMN: Excelsior, XLCR; AKA: Blue Thumbprint and Ruby Thumbprint.

Manufactured by: Adams and Company, 1890, and U. S. Glass, 1891. Although King's Crown is heavily reproduced, the cake stands found to be reproduced are the 12" and 12½" low standard ones without a gallery. This pattern has a sawtooth gallery and skirt. The design is repeated on the base.

Item	Description	Size	Crystal	Crystal w/Ruby Stain
Cake stand		9"	$125.00	$450.00
		10¼" x 7¼"	150.00	550.00
		12¾"		125.00
Compote		7"	35.00	45.00
Nappy	Handled		35.00	45.00

Pedestal

Top view of cake stand, crystal

Nappy, handled

Compote

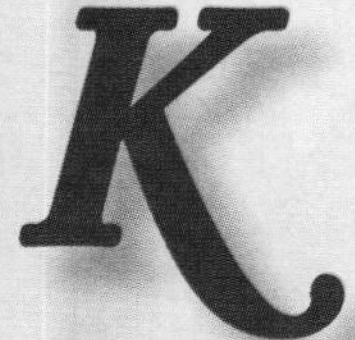

KING'S CURTAIN

Manufactured by: Unknown, reportedly made ca 1880. This cake stand is made of very clear glass and at 6½" tall is quite impressive. There is a small, plain gallery. The pedestal consists of two rings and six plain panels; the base is perfectly plain.

ITEM	SIZE	CRYSTAL
Cake stand	9½" x 6½"	$75.00

Top view of cake stand

Pedestal

KLONDIKE

OMN: Amberette, Dalzell Nrs 75 and 75D; AKA: English Hobnail Cross, Frosted Amberette, Klondyke.
Manufactured by: Dalzell, Gilmore and Leighton, 1898. The butter dish bottom is pictured to show the design on the cake stand.

ITEM	DESCRIPTION	SIZE	CRYSTAL	CRYSTAL W/AMBER	CRYSTAL FROSTED W/ AMBER
Cake stand	Square	8"	$150.00	$395.00	$850.00
Butter dish		5⅞" x 7"	110.00	225.00	400.00

Butter dish

Butter dish bottom

KOKOMO

OMN: Richards and Hartley Nr 190; AKA: Bar and Diamond, Jenkins Nr 623, Richards and Hartley Swirl Band. (On some pieces the swirl is reversed.)

Manufactured by: Richards and Hartley Glass Company, ca. 1885; and later Kokomo Glass Company (Jenkins), ca. 1901.

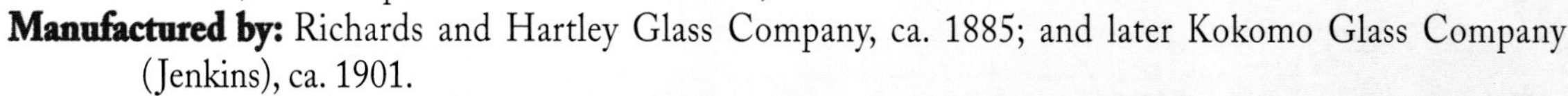

Item	Description	Size	Crystal	Crystal w/Ruby
Cake stand			$95.00	$400.00
Compote	Low standard	8" x 7¼"	55.00	125.00
	Open	7¼" x 3¾"	35.00	75.00
Pitcher	Water	½ gal.	80.00	215.00
Goblet		6"	35.00	85.00

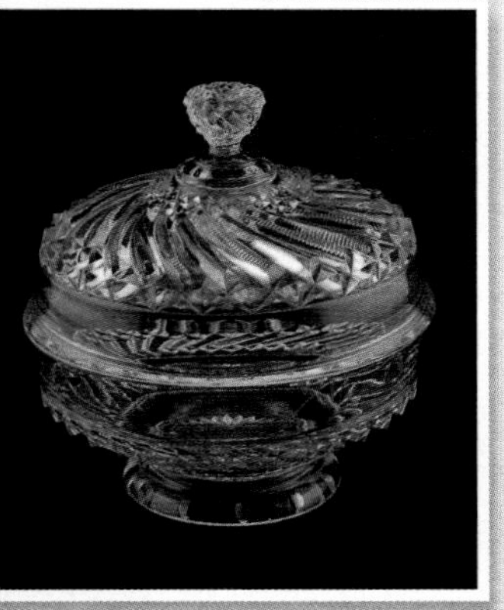

Compote

Pitcher and goblets

Compote, ruby stain

LACY DAISY

OMN: United States Glass Nr 9525; AKA: Daisy.

Manufactured by: United States Glass Company, ca. 1918.

Item	Size	Crystal
Cake plate		$65.00
Bowl	7¾"	35.00
Sugar	4½" x 5"	65.00

Bowl

Sugar, covered

LACY DEWDROP

AKA: Beaded Drop, Beaded Jewel, Co-Op Nr 1902, Lace Dewdrop, and Phoenix Nr 800.

Manufactured by: Cooperative Flint Glass Company, ca. 1902; Phoenix Glass, 1937; and Kemple Glass, 1944. This was not originally made in amber; the pitcher is a re-issue.

Item	Size	Crystal Plain	Crystal Gallery	Amber
Cake stand	8"	$65.00	$85.00	
	9"	75.00	95.00	
	10"	85.00	110.00	
Pitcher		85.00		$75.00

Pitcher, amber

LADDER WITH DIAMOND

AKA: Fine Cut and Ribbon Bars.

Manufactured by: Tarentum Glass Company, Tarentum, Pennsylvania, 1903.

Item	Size	Crystal
Cake stand		$110.00
Bowl	9"	45.00

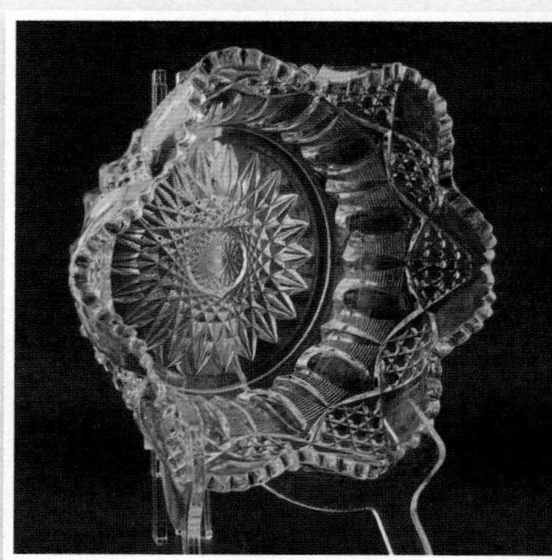

Bowl

LATE THISTLE

AKA: Inverted Thistle.

Manufactured by: Cambridge Glass Company, 1906. Cake stand pictured is a reproduction by Mosser Glass Company. This is a pretty pattern with thistles and leaves. The rim is scalloped. A gift from Lorraine Dolezal.

Item	Description	Size	Crystal	Pink
Cake stand	Reproduction	11⅛" x 5⅞"	$65.00	$45.00

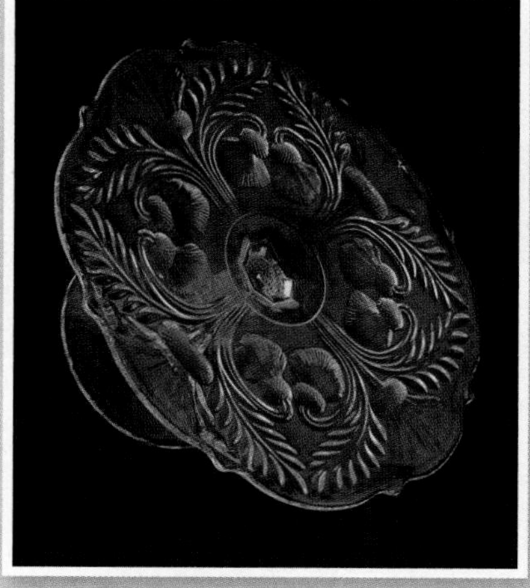

Top view of cake stand

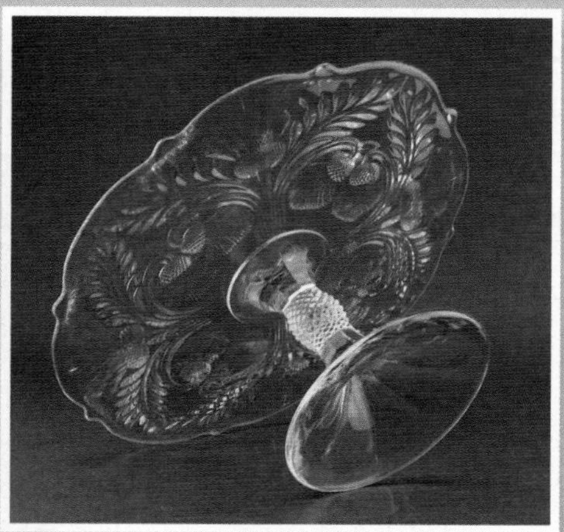

Pedestal

LATTICE

AKA: Diamond Bar.
Manufactured by: King and Son, 1880.

Item	Size	Crystal
Cake stand		$125.00
Compote (no lid shown)	8¼" x 8"	75.00
	9" x 9¼"	85.00

Compote, interior

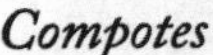

Compotes

LATTICE THUMBPRINT

OMN: Central Nr 796; AKA: Rope and Thumbprint.
Manufactured by: Central Glass Company, ca. late 1800s. There is a scalloped gallery. The center design on the plate is repeated on the base. The pedestal is a bulbous column.

Item	Size	Crystal	Vaseline	Amber	Blue
Cake stand	8"	$75.00	$135.00	$75.00	$115.00
	9"	85.00	150.00	90.00	135.00
	10"	110.00	170.00	115.00	150.00

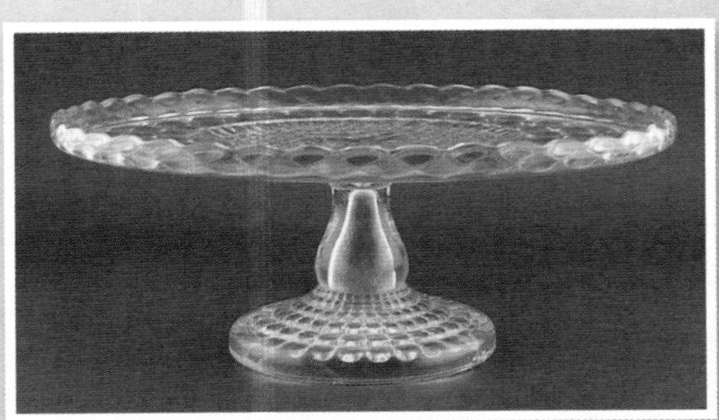

Pedestal

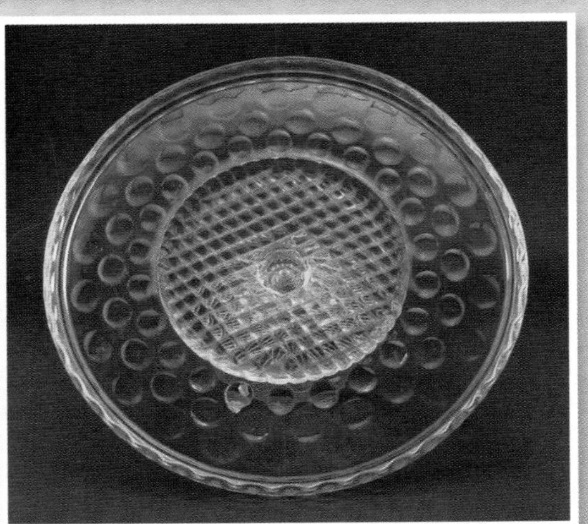

Top view of cake stand

LAVERNE

AKA: La Verne, Leverne, Star in Honeycomb.
Manufactured by: Bryce Brothers, ca. 1880s. This pattern features a small scalloped gallery with an octagon base.

Item	Size	Crystal
Cake stand	9½" x 5½"	$85.00

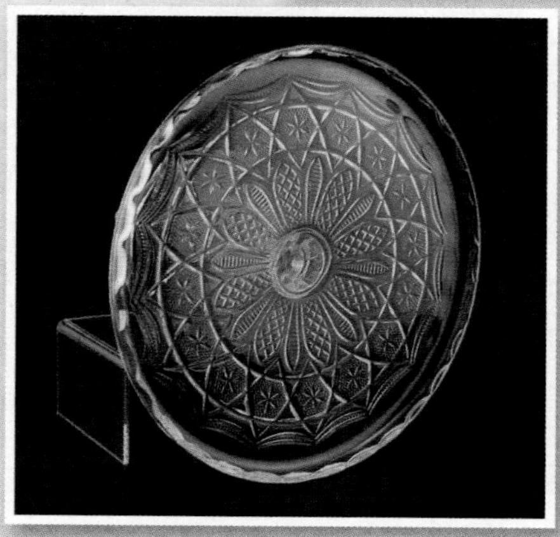

Top view of cake stand

Pedestal

LEAF

AKA: Concordia Maple Leaf, Maple Leaf, Maple Leaf on Trunk.
Manufactured by: Unknown.

Item	Crystal	Amber	Vaseline	Green/Blue
Cake stand	$45.00	$70.00	$130.00	$90.00
Double relish	35.00	40.00	75.00	55.00

Double relish

LION

AKA: Frosted Lion.
Manufactured by: Gillander and Sons, Philadelphia, Pennsylvania, 1877. Three lion heads on the tree trunk pedestal easily identify this pattern. Note the lion resting on the collared base of the oval compote. The finials on covered pieces are sitting lions.

Item	Description	Size	Crystal w/Frosting
Cake stand			$175.00
Compote	Covered	7" x 11" h	250.00
	Covered, oval	8¾" x 8½" h	225.00
Sugar		5" x 9"	160.00
Celery		8½" x 4"	110.00

L

Compote

Celery

Oval compote covered

Pedestal

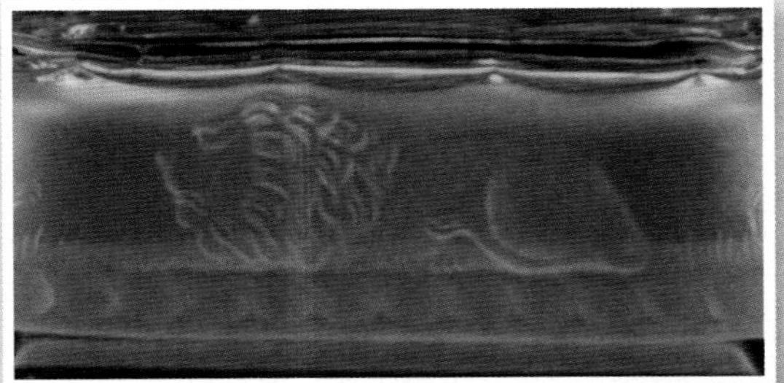

Close-up of base

Finial

Sugar

LION AND CABLE

OMN: Richards and Hartley Nr 525 – Proud Lion; AKA: Tiny Lion.
Manufactured by: Unknown. Tiny lions perched on the tops of the handles easily identify this pattern.

Item	Description	Size	Crystal
Cake stand			$175.00
Sugar (lid not shown)		6"	135.00
Pitcher	Milk		150.00

Pitcher and sugar

LITTLE BO PEEP

Manufactured by: Unknown. Written on this child's plate is the nursery rhyme: "Little Bo Peep has Lost Her Sheep and Can't Tell Where to Find Them." Dancing bears are on the edge of the plate.

Child's plate

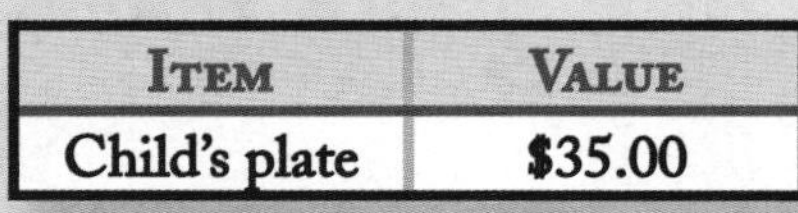

Item	Value
Child's plate	$35.00

LOOP AND JEWEL

AKA: Jewel and Festoon, Queen's Necklace, Venus.
Manufactured by: National Glass Company, 1903; and Indiana Glass Company, 1906.

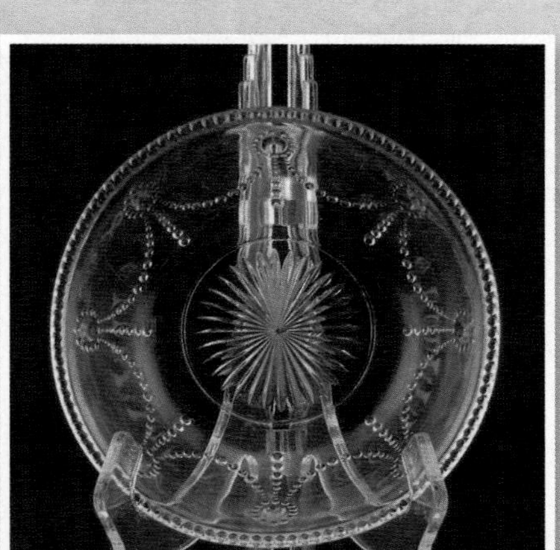

Bowl

Item	Crystal
Cake stand	$75.00
Bowl	35.00

LOOP WITH DEWDROP(S)

OMN: United States Glass Nr 15028.
Manufactured by: United States Glass Company, ca. 1892.

Item	Size	Crystal
Cake stand	9"	$85.00
	10"	95.00
Creamer		40.00

Creamer

LOUISE

OMN: Fostoria Nr 1121; AKA: Starred Jewel, Sunk Jewel.
Manufactured by: Fostoria Glass Company, Moundsville, West Virginia, ca. 1901. This scalloped rim cake plate is flat with no skirt or gallery; the pattern is repeated on the pedestal base.

Top view of cake stand

Item	Size	Crystal
Cake stand	10"	$90.00
	11"	100.00

Pedestal

LOUISIANA

OMN: United States Glass Nr 15053 – Louisiana; AKA: Granby, Sharp Oval and Diamond.
Manufactured by: United States Glass Company, Pittsburgh, Pennsylvania, at Factory "B," ca. 1898. Louisiana was the seventh in the "state series" patterns. There is a beaded gallery and the pattern is repeated on the pedestal base. If you have collected a frosted piece in this "state series," add an additional 25 – 30%.

Item	Description	Size	Crystal
Cake plate		7"	$100.00
		9"	95.00
		10"	110.00
Compote	Covered	12" x 8½"	125.00

Top view of cake stand

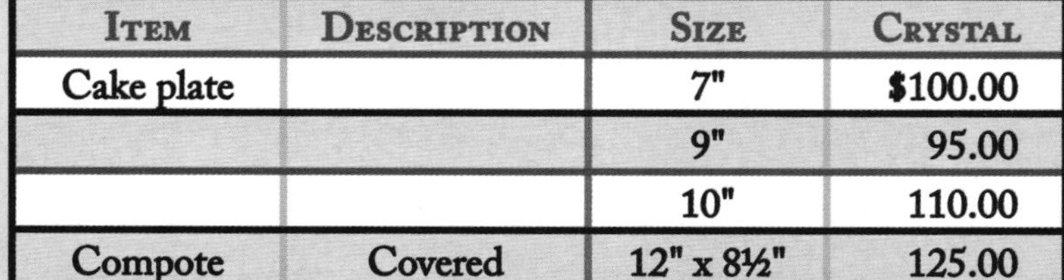

Pedestal

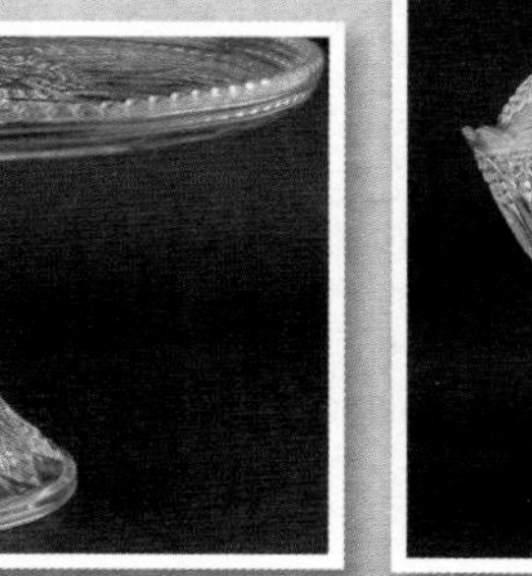

Compote

MADORA

AKA: Arrowhead and Oval(s), Beaded Oval and Fan Nr 2, Medallion(s) and Fan(s), Ramona, and Style.

Manufactured by: Bryce, Higbee and Company, 1905; John B. Higbee Glass Company, 1907; New Martinsville Glass Manufacturing Company, 1915. There is a scalloped gallery with a plain pedestal and flat base.

Item	Size	Crystal
Cake stand	9½" x 4½"	$60.00

Top view of cake stand

Stacked cake stands

MAGNA

Manufactured by: Co-Operative Flint Glass Company, ca. 1898. Two different styles of cake stands are pictured individually and side-by-side. The first cake stand pictured has a scalloped gallery with the pattern repeated on the pedestal and base. The second cake stand has a scalloped edge on the plate, with the pattern again repeated on the pedestal and base.

Item	Size	Crystal
Cake stand	10"	$75.00
	11"	95.00

Top view of cake stand

Pedestal

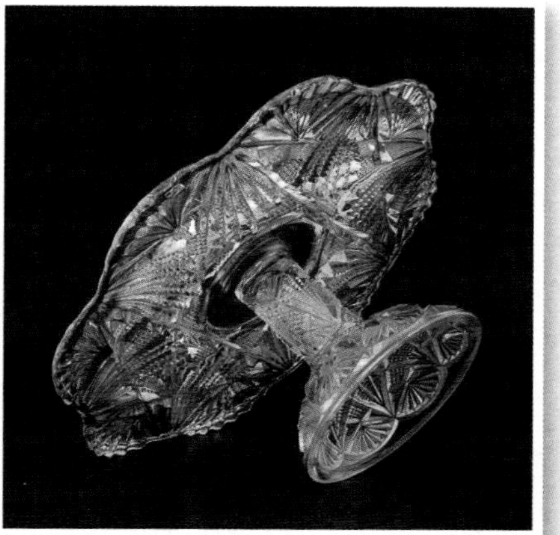
Pedestal

Top view of cake stand

Cake stands side by side

MAGNOLIA

AKA: Clear Magnolia, Frosted Magnolia, Frosted Water Lily, Magnolia Blossom, Water Lily.
Manufactured by: Dalzell, Gilmore and Leighton, 1891. There is a plain gallery, with a sawtooth edge on the bottom of the plate. The pedestal is comprised of several rings stacked on top of one another, resting on a lined base.

Item	Size	Crystal	Crystal w/Frosting
Cake stand	9½"	$200.00	$375.00

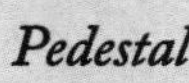
Pedestal

Top view of cake stand

MAINE

OMN: United States Glass Nr 15066; AKA: Panelled Flower, Panelled Stippled Flower, Stippled Panelled Flower, Stippled Primrose.

Manufactured by: United States Glass Company, Pittsburgh, Pennsylvania, 1899. A compote is pictured. This is the nineteenth in the "state series" patterns.

Item	Size	Crystal	Green
Cake stand	8"	$75.00	$100.00
	9"	85.00	110.00
	10"	100.00	125.00
	11"	125.00	175.00
Compote	8¼"	60.00	75.00

Compote interior

Pedestal

MAJESTIC

AKA: Cube and/with Double Fan, Divided Block with Sunburst – Variant, Pilgrim.

Manufactured by: Cambridge Glass Company, 1903; and McKee Brothers Glass Company, 1893. This pattern has the gallery and the skirt with a connecting pattern between the two. Normally the gallery and skirt are different. The pattern is repeated on the pedestal and base.

Item	Description	Size	Crystal
Cake stand		8½" x 4"	$85.00
		9¼" x 6¼"	95.00

Top view of cake stand

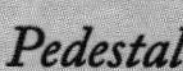

Pedestal

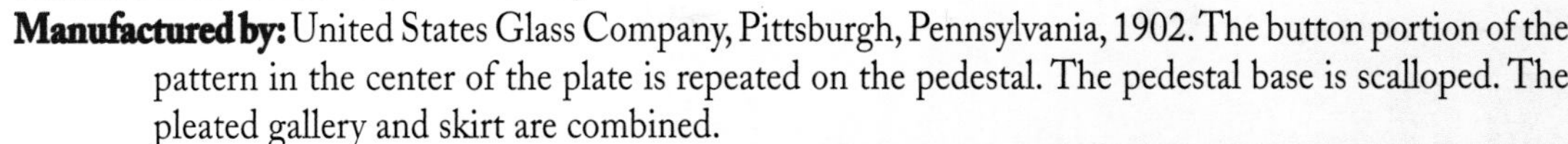

MANHATTAN

OMN: United States Glass Nr 15078; AKA: New York.

Manufactured by: United States Glass Company, Pittsburgh, Pennsylvania, 1902. The button portion of the pattern in the center of the plate is repeated on the pedestal. The pedestal base is scalloped. The pleated gallery and skirt are combined.

Item	Size	Crystal	Crystal w/Rose Stain
Cake stand	8½"	$125.00	$300.00
	9"	145.00	325.00
	10"	170.00	350.00

Pedestal

Top view of cake stand

Stacked cake stands

Top view of cake stand

Pedestal

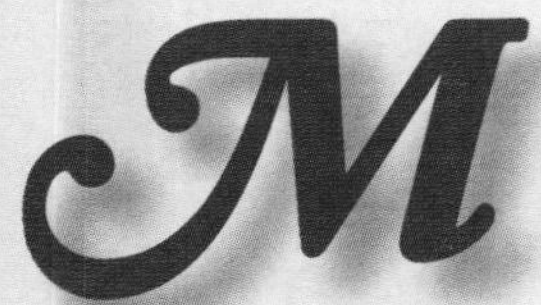

MARDI GRAS

OMN: Duncan Nr 42; AKA: Empire, Panelled English Hobnail with Prisms, Siamese Necklace.

Manufactured by: George Duncan's Sons and Company, Washington, Pennsylvania, ca. 1899; Duncan and Miller Glass Company, ca. 1900. The cake stand is a high standard with a slight plain gallery and flared scalloped skirt. The pattern is repeated on the pedestal base.

Item	Size	Crystal	Crystal w/Ruby
Cake stand	9¼"	$110.00	$300.00
	10"	140.00	350.00
	11¾"	170.00	400.00
Toothpick		40.00	140.00

Top view of cake stand

Pedestal

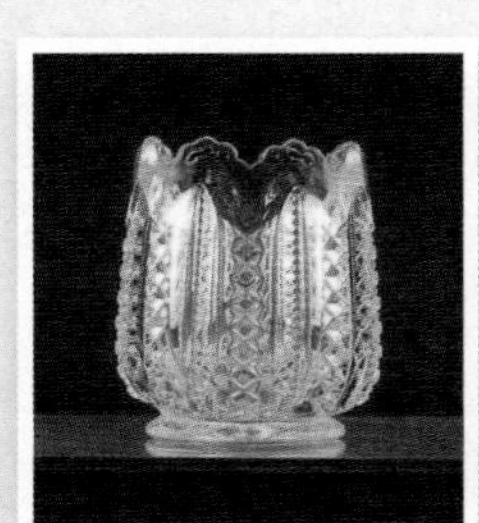

Toothpick

MARLBORO

OMN: United States Glass Nr 15105; AKA: Heart Plume.

Manufactured by: United States Glass Company, Pittsburgh, Pennsylvania, Factory "B," ca 1907.

Item	Crystal
Cake stand	$75.00
Pitcher	55.00

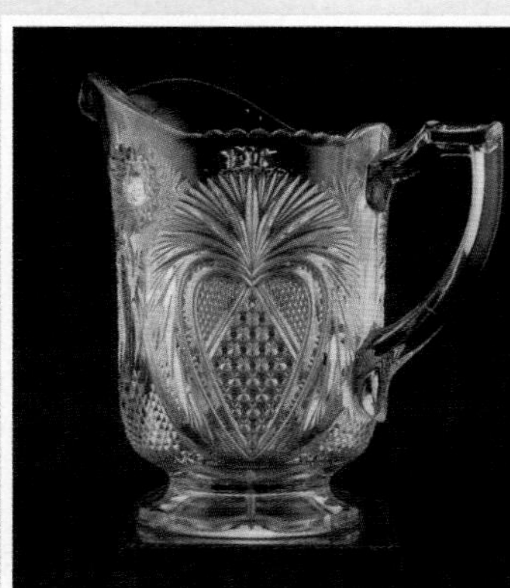

Pitcher

MARSH FERN

OMN: Riverside Nr 327.

Manufactured by: Riverside Glass Works, Wellsburg, West Virginia, ca. 1889. There is a plain gallery with a pleated skirt. The pattern is repeated on the base.

Item	Size	Crystal
Cake stand	9¼"	$85.00

Pedestal

Top view of cake stand

MARSH PINK

AKA: Dahlia, Square Fuchsia.
Manufactured by: Unknown, ca. 1880s.

Item	Size	Crystal
Cake stand		$85.00
Plate	10"	45.00

Plate

MARYLAND

OMN: United States Glass Nr 15049; AKA: Inverted Loop(s) and Fan(s), Loop and Diamond, Loop(s) and Fan(s).
Manufactured by: United States Glass Company, Pittsburgh, Pennsylvania, at Factory "B," ca. 1897. This is the third in the "state series" pattern found in crystal and crystal with ruby stain. There is a scalloped gallery, with a portion of the pattern repeated on the base. The cake stands are courtesy of Tanya and Mike Poillucci and Laura and Curtis Marshall; spooner is courtesy of Riley Shay Hoch.

Item	Size	Crystal	Crystal w/Ruby
Cake stand	8"	$60.00	$250.00
	9"	75.00	300.00
	10"	95.00	350.00
Spooner		70.00	125.00

Top view of cake stand

Pedestal

Cake stands

Spooner

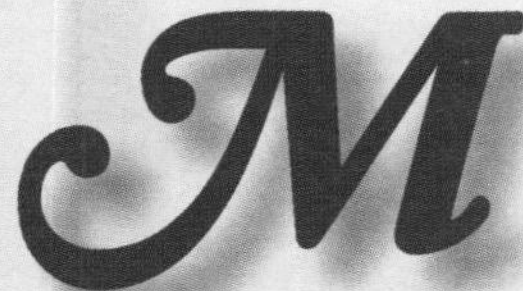

MASCOTTE

AKA: Dominion, Etched Fern and Waffle, Minor Block.

Manufactured by: Ripley and Company, Pittsburgh, Pennsylvania, 1884. The skirt and gallery are plain, with the pattern only in the center of the plate. The pattern is repeated half way up the side of the basket. The handle is nickel plated.

Item	Description	Size	Crystal	Crystal w/Etching
Cake stand	Non-flint	8"	$70.00	$100.00
		9"	90.00	125.00
		10½"	100.00	140.00
		12"	125.00	170.00
Cake basket			125.00	175.00

Top view of cake stand

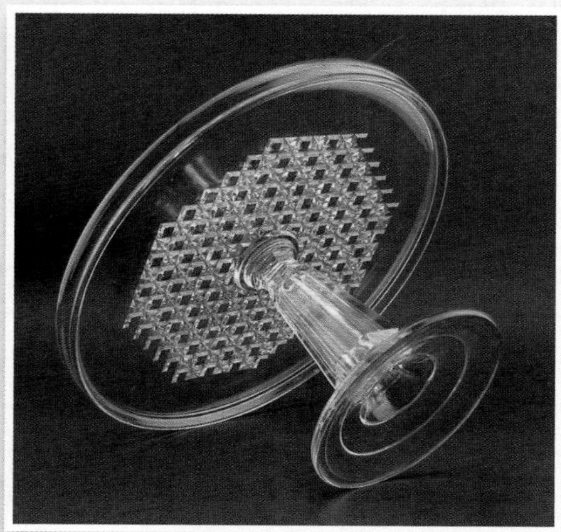

Pedestal

Cake basket

Pedestal

MASONIC VARIANT

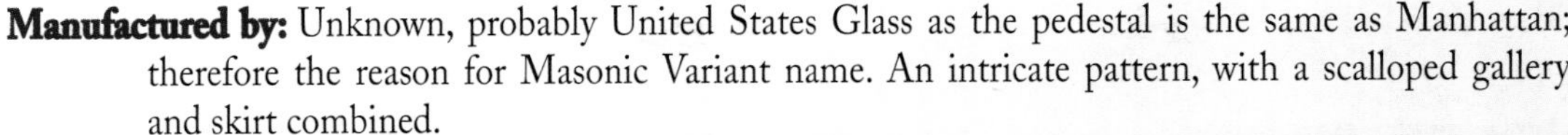

AKA: Inverted Prism with Double Block Band.

Manufactured by: Unknown, probably United States Glass as the pedestal is the same as Manhattan; therefore the reason for Masonic Variant name. An intricate pattern, with a scalloped gallery and skirt combined.

Item	Size	Crystal
Cake stand	9"	$65.00
	10"	80.00
Butter dish	5½" x 7¼"	65.00

Top view of cake stand

Butter dish

Pedestal

MASSACHUSETTS

OMN: United States Glass Nr 15054 – Massachusetts; AKA: Arched Diamond Point(s), Cane Variant, Geneva, Star and Diamonds.

Manufactured by: United States Glass Company, Pittsburgh, Pennsylvania, at Factory "K," ca 1898. This is the eighth in the "state series" patterns.

Item	Size	Crystal	Crystal w/Gold
Cake stand		$125.00	$200.00
Relish	7" x 5¼"	30.00	35.00

Relish

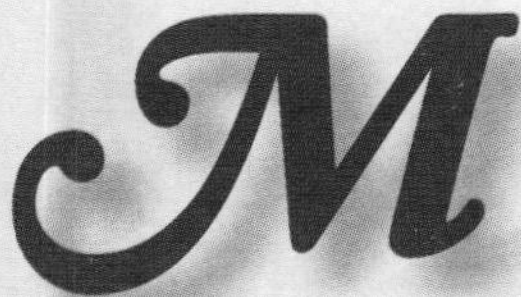

McKEE'S SUNBURST

AKA: Aztec Sunburst, Sunburst.

Manufactured by: McKee-Jeannette Glass Company, ca. 1905. There is a scalloped gallery; the pedestal is plain with a rayed base.

Top view of cake stand

Item	Size	Crystal
Cake stand	9"	$55.00
	12"	85.00
Bowl	6"	20.00
Compote		30.00

Compote and bowl

Pedestal

MEDALLION

AKA: Hearts and Spades, Spades.

Manufactured by: Unknown, ca. 1885 – 1895. This is one of the most unusual cake stands made; the shape is unique. There is a plain gallery. The plate portion is round, with an extended edge which is larger on two sides. The base is the same shape as the top. The base on the pitcher matches the base on the cake stand.

Item	Description	Size	Crystal	Amber	Apple Green	Blue	Canary/ Yellow
Cake stand	Non-flint	9¼"	$95.00	$100.00	$225.00	$150.00	$240.00
Pitcher	Water, pressed handle	½ gal.	50.00	60.00	150.00	110.00	160.00

Pedestal

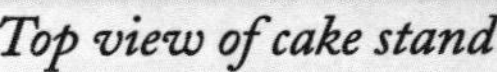

Top view of cake stand

Pitcher

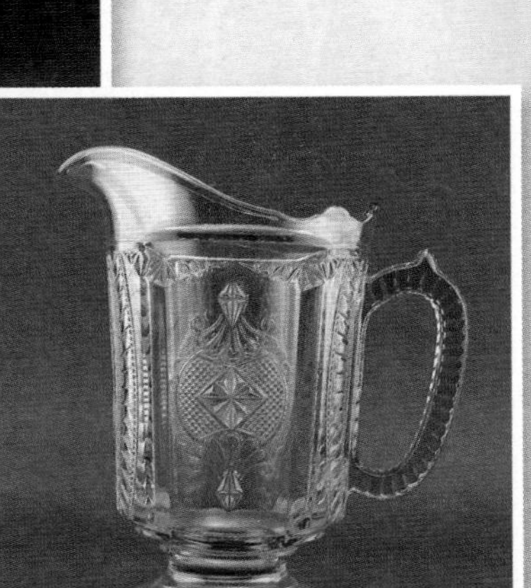

MEDALLION SUNBURST

AKA: Banquet.

Manufactured by: Bryce, Higbee and Company, ca. 1905. There is a scalloped gallery. Portions of the pattern are repeated on the pedestal and base.

Item	Size	Crystal
Cake stand	9"	$75.00
	9½"	75.00

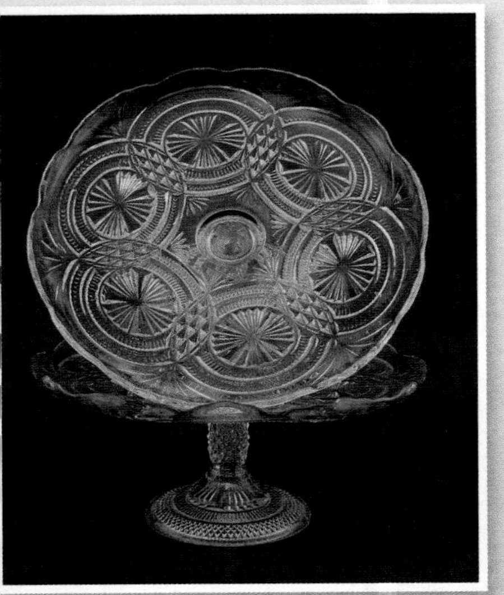

Stacked cake stands

Top view of cake stand

Pedestal

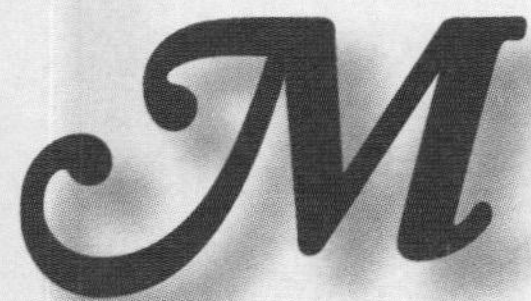

MELROSE

AKA: Diamond Beaded Band.

Manufactured by: Brilliant Glass Works, Brilliant, Ohio, ca. 1887 – 1888; Greensburg Glass Company, Greensburg, Pennsylvania, ca. 1889; McKee Brothers, Jeannette, Pennsylvania (chocolate items), ca. 1901; John B. Higbee Glass Company, Bridgeville, Pennsylvania, ca. 1907; New Martinsville Glass Manufacturing Company, New Martinsville, West Virginia, ca. 1916; and Dugan Glass Company (Diamond Glassware Company), Indiana, Pennsylvania, ca. 1915. There is a plain gallery; the pattern is repeated on the pedestal and base. Colors are crystal and crystal with ruby stain.

Item	Size	Crystal	Crystal w/Ruby
Cake stand	9"	$85.00	$135.00
Compote	8¼" x 6¾"	45.00	90.00

Top view of cake stand

Pedestal

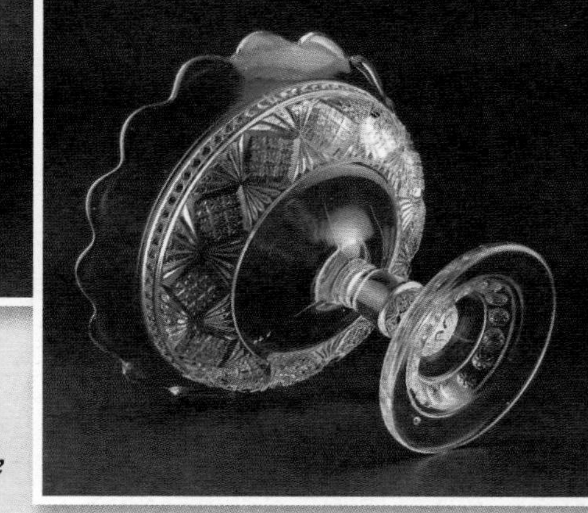

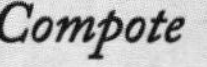

Compote

MICHIGAN

OMN: United States Glass Nr 15077 – Michigan; AKA: Loop and Pillar, Loop with Pillar, Panelled Jewel.

Manufactured by: United States Glass Company, Pittsburgh, Pennsylvania, Factory "G." This is the thirtieth in the "state series."

Item	Description	Size	Crystal	Rose Blush
Bride basket	In silver plate holder		$100.00	$225.00
Butter dish		5¾" x 8"	$95.00	225.00

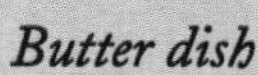

Butter dish

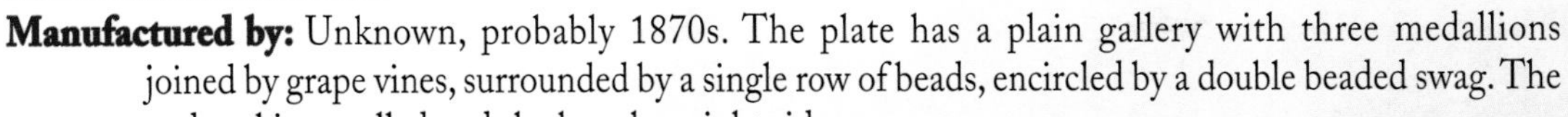

MINERVA

AKA: Roman Medallion.

Manufactured by: Unknown, probably 1870s. The plate has a plain gallery with three medallions joined by grape vines, surrounded by a single row of beads, encircled by a double beaded swag. The pedestal is panelled and the base has eight sides.

Item	Description	Size	Crystal
Cake stand		8"	$125.00
		9"	140.00
		10"	160.00
		10½"	170.00
		11"	300.00
Compote (lid not shown)	Covered	8"	185.00

Top view of cake stand

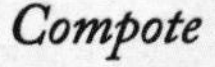

Compote

Pedestal

MINNESOTA

OMN: United States Glass Nr 15055 – Minnesota; AKA: Muchness (Unitt).

Manufactured by: United States Glass Company, Pittsburgh, Pennsylvania, at Factory "F" (Ripley and Company) and Factory "G" (Gillander and Sons), Greensburg, Pennsylvania, ca. 1898. This is ninth in the "state series" pattern with no known reproductions. The only record found, indicating a cake stand exists, is one pictured in the *U. S. Glass, The States Patterns, Identification and Value Guide*, 1998.

Item	Description	Size	Crystal	Crystal w/Gold
Cake stand			$125.00	$140.00
Compote	Open	7¾" x 6½"	55.00	60.00
Lemonade cup			35.00	40.00

Top view of cake stand

Pedestal

Lemonade cup

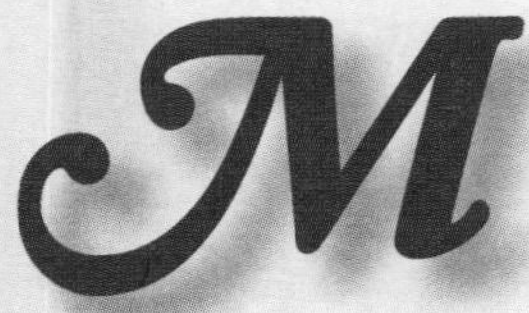

MISSOURI

OMN: United States Glass Nr 15058 – Missouri; AKA: Palm and Scroll, Palm Leaf and Scroll.

Manufactured by: United States Glass Company, ca. 1899. This is the twelveth pattern in the "state series" and is found in high and low standard. The scalloped pattern on the gallery is repeated on the base. The palm leaf pattern is repeated on the pedestal.

Top view of cake stand, high standard

Item	Description	Size	Crystal	Green
Cake stand	High standard	6"	$70.00	$100.00
		8"	65.00	80.00
		9½"	70.00	90.00
		10"	80.00	100.00
		11"	125.00	200.00
	Low standard	8"	50.00	60.00
		10"	60.00	70.00

Pedestal

Stacked cake stands

MOON AND STAR

OMN: Palace; AKA: Bull's Eye and Star, Star and Punty.

Manufactured by: Adams and Company, Pittsburgh, Pennsylvania, 1888. The Moon and Star pattern is found in crystal and crystal with frosting or ruby stain, which was decorated by the Pioneer Glass Company in Pittsburgh, Pennsylvania. There is a sawtooth gallery and scalloped skirt. The pattern is repeated on the pedestal and base. Watch out for the numerous reproductions including the piece shown in amber that has the pedestal joined to the plate with glue, rather than a glass wafer, as in the originals. Note that the pedestal is different on the amber piece.

Item	Description	Size	Crystal	Crystal w/Frosting	Crystal w/Ruby	Amber
Cake stand		9"	$125.00	$170.00	$350.00	
		10⅛"	150.00	190.00	375.00	
	Reproduction	10½"				$50.00
Bowl		7¼"	35.00	65.00	125.00	

Pedestal

Top view of cake stand

Pedestal

Top view of cake stand

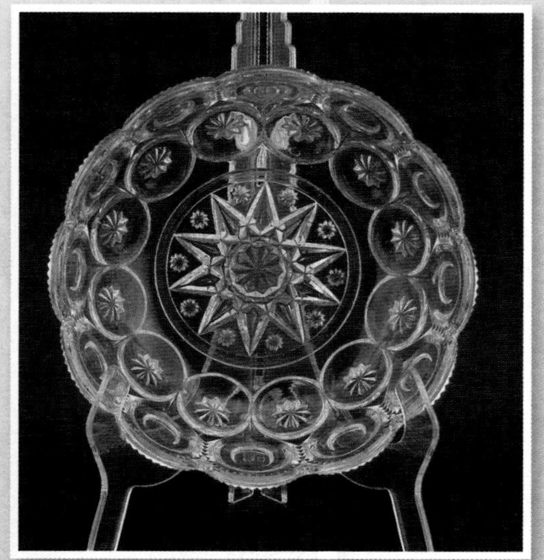

Bowl

NAIL

OMN: United States Glass Nr 15002; AKA: Recessed Pillar – Red Top, Recessed Pillar – Thumbprint Band.

Manufactured by: United States Glass Company, Pittsburgh, Pennsylvania, 1891. This is a very impressive cake stand that is aptly named with the nails in the design. There is a scalloped gallery. The pedestal is four-sided and the base is larger than normal at 5¾". The top is etched with leaves and vines.

Item	Description	Size	Crystal	Etched	Crystal w/Ruby
Cake stand	w/Frosting	9½" x 7"	$150.00	$175.00	$400.00
Sauce dish	Footed		15.00	20.00	35.00

Top view of cake stand

Sauce dishes

Pedestal

NELLY

AKA: Florence, Strigal, Sylvan.

Manufactured by: McKee Glass Company, 1892. Although a cake stand is not available to be photographed, a picture seen in a cookbook of this eight-sided piece shows that it is square with corners removed. The skirted edge has pointed prisms — very ornate. The Nelly cake stand has a similar shape to Nr 1883. However, the base of the pedestal on Nelly is round, not square. The pattern can easily be confused with Wellsburg.

Item	Crystal
Cake stand	$100.00
Pitcher	45.00

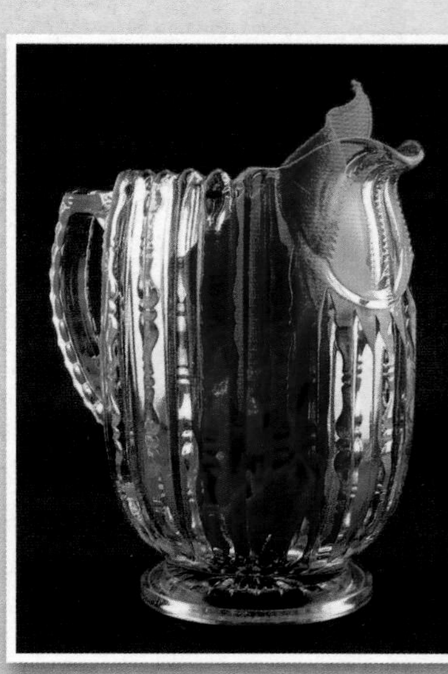

Pitcher

N

NEVADA

OMN: United States Glass Nr 15075 – Nevada.

Manufactured by: United States Glass Company, 1902. This "state series" pattern is difficult to identify because it is so plain. This is the twenty-eighth pattern in the "state series" by U. S. Glass.

Item	Size	Crystal	Crystal w/ Decorations
Cake stand	10"	$75.00	$125.00
Compote	8" x 8½"	45.00	75.00

Compote

NEW CRESCENT

Manufactured by: J. B. Higbee Glass Company, ca. 1898. There is a scalloped gallery; the pattern is repeated on the pedestal base.

Item	Size	Crystal
Cake stand	9½"	$60.00

Top view of cake stand

Stacked cake stands

Pedestal

NEW ERA

AKA: Yoke and Circle.

Manufactured by: J. B Higbee Glass Company, 1912. This pattern is easily identified by the eight-pointed star in the center of the plate and the intertwined loops around the perimeter. There is a scalloped gallery with plain pedestal and a portion of the design is repeated on the base. Cake stand courtesy of Eunice Stearns Crow.

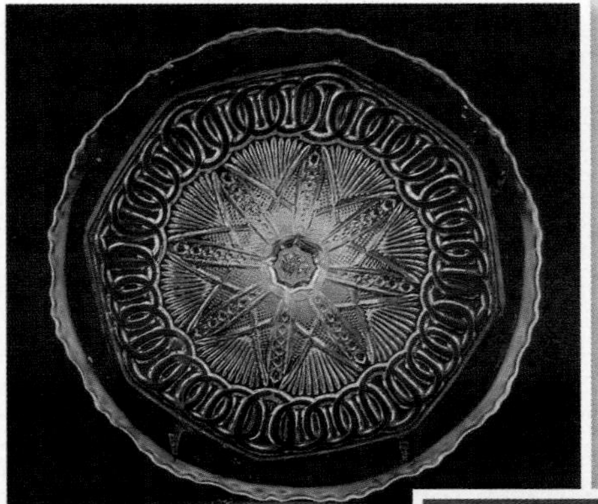

Item	Size	Crystal
Cake stand	9¾" x 4½"	$65.00
Celery	10" x 6¼"	25.00

Top view of cake stand

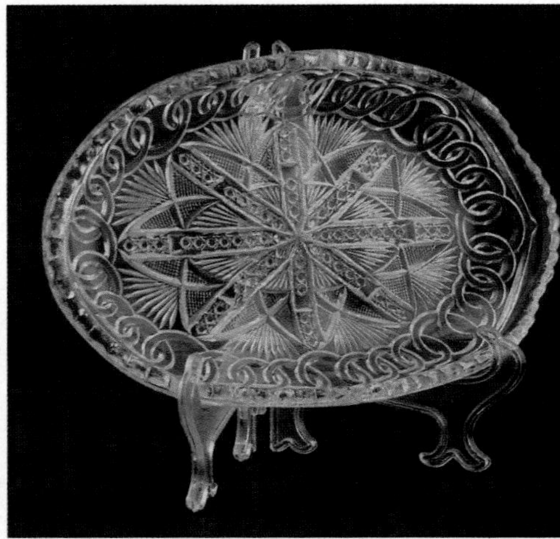

Pedestal

Celery

NEW HAMPSHIRE

OMN: United States Glass Nr 15084 – New Hampshire; AKA: Bent Buckle, Maiden's Blush, Modiste, Red Loop and Fine Cut.

Manufactured by: United States Glass Company, Pittsburgh, Pennsylvania, ca. 1903. This is the thirty-fifth pattern in the "state series" patterns.

Item	Size	Crystal	Crystal w/ Rose Stain
Cake stand	9"	$125.00	$300.00
Creamer	5¼" x 5"	75.00	125.00

Creamer

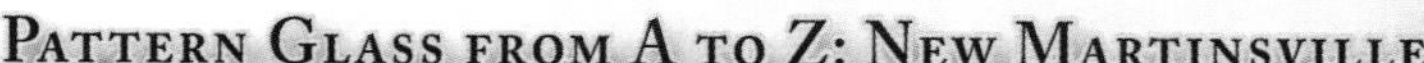

NEW JERSEY

OMN: United States Glass Nr 15070 – New Jersey; AKA: Loop(s) and Drop(s), Red Loop and Fine Cut (Millard).

Manufactured by: United States Glass Company, Pittsburgh, Pennsylvania, at Factories "G" (Gillander and Sons, Greensburg, Pennsylvania), "P" (Doyle and Company, Pittsburgh, Pennsylvania), and "D" (George Duncan and Sons, Pittsburgh, Pennsylvania), ca. 1900 – 1908. This is the twenty-third in the "state series" patterns. The pattern consists of a series of connecting loops; the exterior loops are plain and the interior loops have a grated-type design. There is a scalloped gallery.

Item	Description	Size	Crystal	Crystal w/Ruby
Cake stand	High standard	8"	$125.00	$375.00
Cake plate		11"	50.00	125.00
Bowl	Berry, master	8½" x 4"	45.00	80.00
	Individual	4¼" x 2"	20.00	40.00
Olive dish			20.00	40.00

Bowls

Cake plate

NEW MARTINSVILLE

OMN: New Martinsville Nr 727.

Manufactured by: New Martinsville Glass Manufacturing Company, ca. 1920. This style with metal ring (band) was patented by New Martinsville. The pedestal could be removed from the plate so more pieces could be packed in a barrel, which saved tremendously on shipping costs. Plate and pedestal are both marked "patented." The picture of the pedestal shows the patented metal ring. This is a plain cake stand with a plain gallery; the only distinguishing features are the metal band and panelled pedestal base.

Top view of cake stand

Item	Size	Crystal
Cake stand	9"	$45.00

Pedestal

NIAGARA FALLS

Manufactured by: Unknown. A beautiful depiction of one of our treasured natural formations. The lighthouse is pictured and two passengers can be seen in the canoe.

Item	Size	Crystal
Water tray	11½" x 16"	$175.00

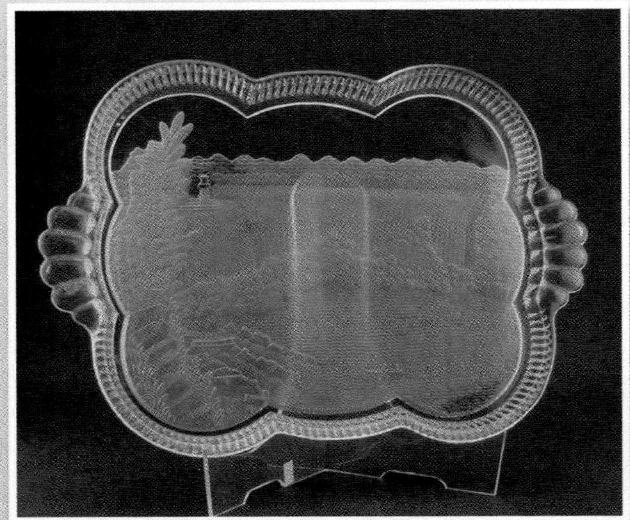

Water tray

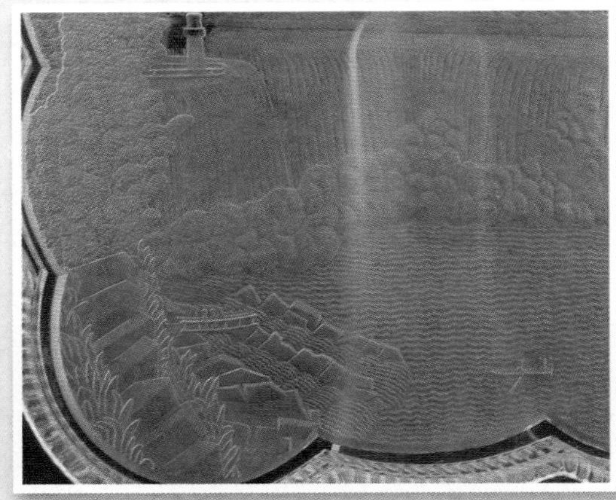

Close-up of pattern

NUGGETT – LATE

Manufactured by: Diamond Glass Company, Montreal, Canada, 1902. (Reference *Collecting Glass Volume 2* by William Heacock, 1985.) The pattern around the slightly raised gallery of the plate is repeated on the base. There is a thumb print design around the exterior of the gallery. The shell ends on this pattern are pointed while those on Shell and Jewel are more rounded. See cake stand and pitcher listed under Shell and Jewel.

Item	Size	Crystal
Cake stand	9¾" x 5"	$115.00
	10¾" x 5½"	150.00
Compote (no cover shown)	8¼" x 8½"	85.00

Top view of cake stand

Stacked cake stands

Compote

NR 33 SALVER

AKA: Crocheted Skirt, Lace Edge with Skirt.

Manufactured by: Cooperative Flint Glass, ca. 1920. This pattern is popularly referred to as Lace Edge with Skirt on internet auctions. It is interesting that Nr 33 has a heavier, hollow stem pedestal — different from the one pictured in the catalog.

Item	Size	Crystal
Cake stand	10¼"	$65.00

Pedestal

Top view of cake stand

NR 44 SALVER

AKA: Crocheted Edge, Lace Edge (Raised).

Manufactured by: Cooperative Flint Glass, ca. 1920. This cake salver is commonly referred to as Lace Edge, Raised, on the internet auctions. (See note about the pedestal on Nr 33.) The first picture shows Nrs 33 and 44 side by side.

Item	Size	Crystal
Cake stand	10¼"	$65.00

Nrs 33 and 44 side by side

Top view of cake stand

Pedestal

NR 75 – SQUARE

Manufactured by: Adams and Company, Pittsburgh, Pennsylvania, 1882 – 1887. A most unusual pattern because it is both round and square. There is a plain round gallery. This cake stand was evidently a difficult pattern to remove from the mold, as the bottom of the round portion is heavily chipped yet there is no damage to the square bottom, which is scalloped. Normally there would be no wear in this area. The square pedestal is hollow and rests on four feet. The small, footed compote has a design in the center of the bowl, which is a variation of the design on the pedestal base of the cake stand and large compote. This same design is featured on the bread plate in this pattern.

Item	Description	Size	Crystal	Etched
Cake stand		10" x 7"	$195.00	$220.00
Compote	Square, etched	13¾" x 7½"	175.00	195.00
		8½" x 7½"	85.00	95.00

Top view of cake stand

Pedestal

Compote

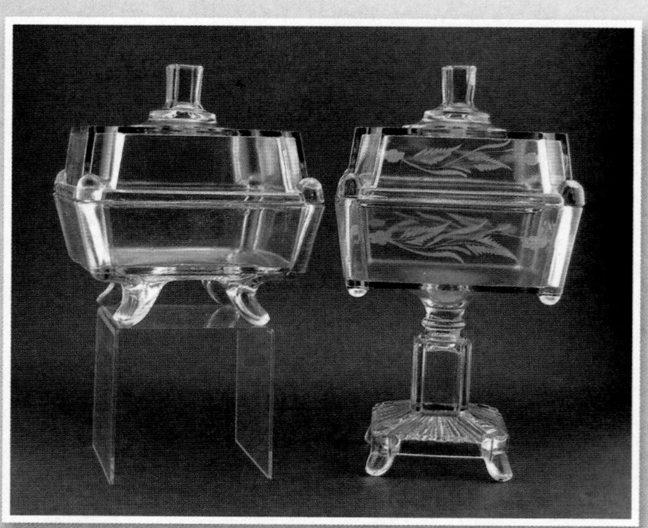

Compotes side by side

NR 120

Manufactured by: Adams and Company, 1884. This is a very rare cake stand, the only reference and picture for it is found in EAPG *The Glass Club Bulletin* 1990 – 1991, from *Adams & Company, A Closer Look*, by Jane Shadel Spillman. This is an absolutely outstanding piece as it is a double oval with diamonds. Although the cake stand is oval, there is a round center (with a ½" gallery) for displaying a round cake. The base of the pedestal is rectangular, 6" x 4½", and rests on four feet, one at each corner.

Item	Size	Crystal
Cake stand	12" x 7"	$375.00
Compote	9¾" x 7½" x 8"	120.00

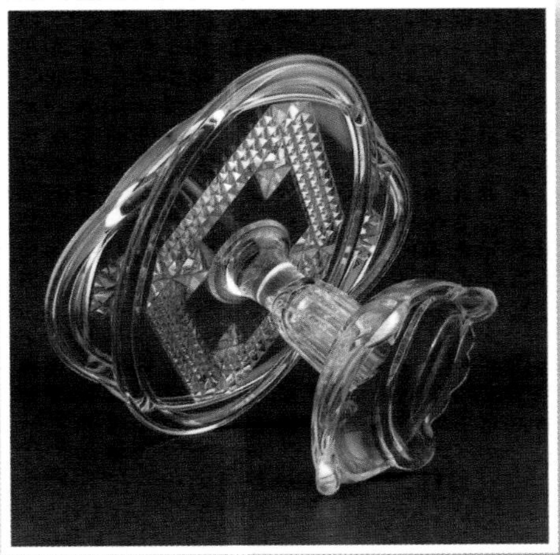

Pedestal

Top view of cake stand

Compote side view

Compote interior

NR 331 BLOCK

AKA: Late Block.

Manufactured by: George Duncan and Sons, 1889.

Item	Size	Crystal
Biscuit/cracker	6" x 9½"	$85.00

Biscuit/cracker

NR 474

OMN: Arch Foot and Daisy, Floral and Hobstar, Hobstar and Flower, Imperial Nr 474.

Manufactured by: Imperial Glass Company, 1915; Indiana Glass Company, 1915. The butter dish is a reproduction from the late 1960s.

Item	Size	Crystal
Cake stand		$55.00
Butter dish	7" x 5½"	35.00

Butter dish

NR 1641

AKA: Sovereign.

Manufactured by: Fostoria Glass Company, 1909 – 1913. This pattern was re-introduced as Sovereign in 1969, without a brandy well, supposedly as prizes for Avon top sellers. The pedestal in the Sovereign pattern is glued to the plate, and in time the glue turns yellow, and may separate. The scalloped gallery and skirt are combined. The swirled pattern is repeated on the pedestal base. This cake stand is one of the originals, and it glows beautifully under a black light.

Item	Size	Crystal
Cake stand	10" x 7½"	$225.00

Pedestal

Top view of cake stand

NR 1883

OMN: 1883 Pattern.

Manufactured by: Diamond Glass Company. There is a plain gallery. The top and base have eight sides. The two clear bars are obvious in the crystal and blue cake stands; however, this is not the case with the cranberry stained cake stand as the two bars are covered with stain and less apparent. This pattern is similar to Hobnail with Bars. The Hobnail with Bars has a raised panel on all four corners on the pedestal base; this pattern does not.

Item	Size	Crystal	Blue	Crystal w/Cranberry Stain	Vaseline
Cake stand	10"	$150.00	$225.00	$250.00	$275.00

Top view of cake stand, blue

Top view of cake stand, clear

Pedestal

Top view of cake stand, clear with cranberry (red) stain

Pedestal

OESTERLING, JOHN, SALVER, PLAIN

AKA: Baker's Stand.

Manufactured by: Central Glass Company, ca. 1880s. This cake stand is attributed to John Oesterling who, with other employees, left Hobbs-Barnes Factory to form Central Glass Company in 1863.

Item	Size	Green
Cake stand	10½" x 8"	$145.00

Cake stand

O'HARA DIAMOND

OMN: O'Hara's Diamond, United States Glass Nr 15001; AKA: Ruby Star, Sawtooth and Star.

Manufactured by: United States Glass Company, Pittsburgh, Pennsylvania, at Factory "L," ca. 1891. This cake stand has a scalloped gallery and skirt. The plain diamonds on the plate are repeated on the pedestal base.

Item	Size	Crystal	Crystal w/Ruby
Cake stand	9"	$95.00	$275.00
	10"	125.00	350.00

Pedestal

Top view of cake stand

O'HARA'S CRYSTAL WEDDING

AKA: Box Pleat, Corinthian.

Manufactured by: O'Hara Glass Company, 1875. This is a very plain pattern with the rim of the compote scalloped. The finial, which is in the shape of a diamond with a rod through it, rests on a cross. The base of the pedestal has four feet with swirls.

Item	Description	Size	Crystal
Cake stand		10¼" x 7¾"	$90.00
Compote	Covered	11" x 7½"	95.00

Compote

O

O'HARA'S CRYSTAL WEDDING VARIANT

Manufactured by: Unknown.

Item	Crystal
Cake stand	$90.00

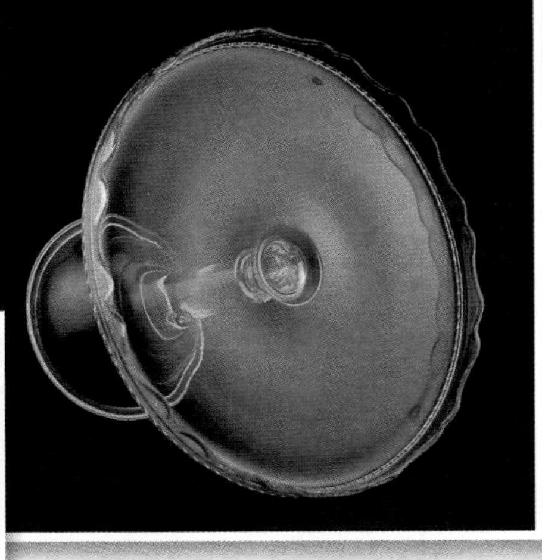

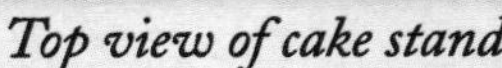

Top view of cake stand

Pedestal

OKAY

AKA: Snowflake Base.

Manufactured by: Indiana Glass Company, 1907. The design is in the center of the plate, which is comprised of nine panels. The hollow pedestal has eight panels with a plain base.

Item	Size	Crystal
Cake stand	9" x 4½"	$50.00
Sugar (no lid shown)		15.00

Top view of cake stand

Sugar

Pedestal

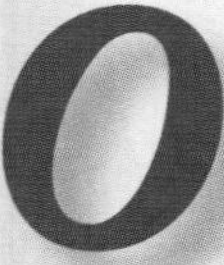

OMNIBUS

OMN: United States Glass Nr 15124; AKA: Hobstar, Keystone, Late Pathfinder, Pathfinder.

Manufactured by: United States Glass Company, 1910. This pattern has been reproduced by Imperial Glass Company. There is a scalloped edge. The blue cake stand is a reproduction. The crystal cake stand is courtesy of Carolyn Crozier.

Item	Description	Size	Crystal
Cake stand		9¾" x 4"	$75.00
Celery		6½" x 6½"	45.00

Top view of cake stand

Pedestal

Celery

O

ONEATA

AKA: Chimo.
Manufactured by: Riverside Glass Works, Wellsburg, West Virginia, 1907.

Item	Size	Crystal	Crystal w/Rose Blush
Cake salver		$100.00	$175.00
Butter dish	4¾" x 7¼"	90.00	125.00

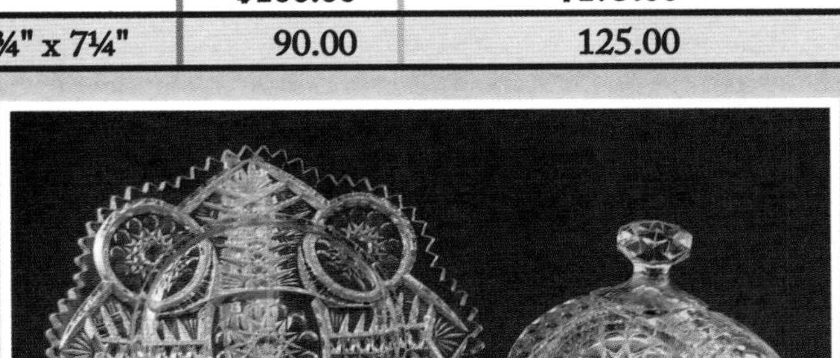
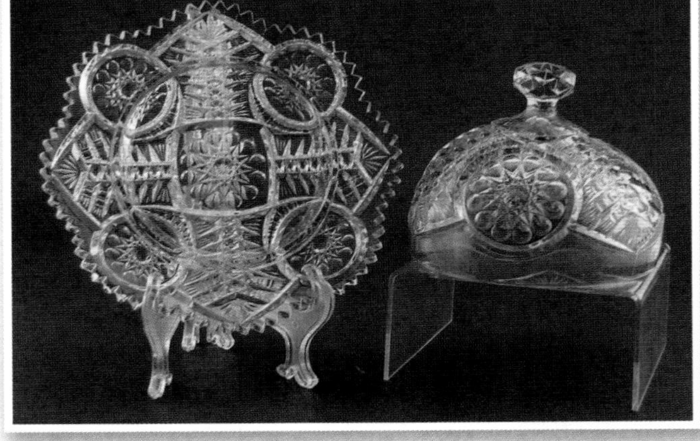
Butter dish

ONE-O-ONE

AKA: Beaded 101, One Hundred and One, 1-0-1.
Manufactured by: George Duncan and Sons, ca. 1885.

Item	Description	Size	Crystal
Cake stand		9"	$190.00
Bread plate	Round, scalloped rim	11"	40.00

Bread plate

OPEN BASKETWEAVE

OMN: Central Nr 861; AKA: Open Plaid, Plaid.
Manufactured by: Central Glass Company, 1880s.

Item	Description	Size	Crystal
Cake stand			$90.00
Compote	Covered	7" x 10½"	75.00

Compote

OPEN ROSE

AKA: Moss Rose.
Manufactured by: Unknown, ca 1870s.

Item	Size	Crystal
Cake stand		$190.00
Spooner	3" x 5¾"	40.00

Spooner, footed

OPPOSING PYRAMIDS

AKA: Flora, Truncated Prisms.
Manufactured by: Bryce, Higbee and Company, 1890s. This pattern is appropriately named, as opposing pyramids appear on the top, bowl, and base of the compote.

Item	Size	Crystal
Cake stand		$125.00
Compote	8" x 12"	95.00

Compote

OREGON

OMN: United States Glass Nr 15073 – Oregon; AKA: Beaded Loop(s), Beaded Ovals.
Manufactured by: United States Glass Company, Pittsburgh, Pennsylvania, ca. 1901. This is the twenty-sixth of the "state series" patterns and may be found in crystal and ruby flashed. The "ovals" in the pattern are repeated on the pedestal. There is a scalloped gallery.

Item	Size	Crystal
Cake stand	6"	$75.00
	7½"	55.00
	8"	65.00
	8½"	75.00
	9"	95.00
	10"	115.00

Top view of cake stand

Pedestal

O

ORNATE STAR

AKA: Ladders and Diamonds with Star, Tarentum's Star.

Manufactured by: Tarentum Glass Company, Tarentum, Pennsylvania, ca. 1907. This is a very ornate pattern, and the gilding makes it even more special.

Item	Size	Crystal
Cake stand		$75.00
Cake plate	10" x 1½"	45.00

Cake plate

OVAL MEDALLION

AKA: Argyle, Beaded Oval Window(s), Maltese Cross, Variant.

Manufactured by: Bryce Brothers, 1885. Even though the pattern name has "oval" in it, the cake stand is actually oval, with what appear to be railroad tracks in the design. The base is rectangular. There is a plain gallery. Note that the finial on the butter dish is a Maltese Cross. The Maltese Cross is imprinted in the center bottom of the butter dish, which is handled. Photographs of the blue cake stand are courtesy of Cindy Johnson.

Item	Description	Size	Crystal	Vaseline	Blue	Amber	Etched
Cake stand		10¼"	$225.00	$355.00	$340.00	$250.00	$285.00
Compote (no lid shown)	Covered	9" x 8"	175.00	300.00	250.00	190.00	215.00
Butter dish		6½" x 7¾"	100.00	275.00	200.00	125.00	140.00

Top view of cake stand, blue

Pedestal

Top view of cake stand, crystal

Pedestal

Compote

Butter dish

Butter dish, open

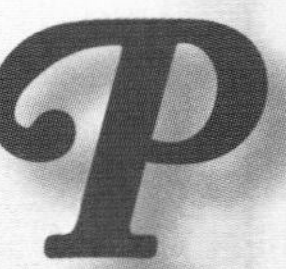

OVAL PANEL

Manufactured by: Unknown.

Item	Crystal
Cake stand	$45.00
Condiment holder	25.00

Condiment holder

PADDLEWHEEL

AKA: Fernwheel.

Manufactured by: Westmoreland Specialty Glass Company, 1912. The rim of the plate is scalloped.

Item	Size	Crystal
Cake plate	10¼"	$45.00

Cake plate

PALMETTE

AKA: Hearts and Spades, Spades.

Manufactured by: Unknown. Courtesy of Carolyn Crozier.

Item	Size	Crystal
Cake stand		$85.00
Syrup	4⅜" x 7⅞"	175.00

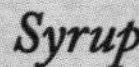
Syrup

PALM LEAF FAN

Manufactured by: Bryce, Higbee Glass Company, ca. 1905. There is a scalloped gallery and the pattern is repeated on the base. The pitcher is recognized by one large palm leaf covering the entire side. This pattern may be found in carnival colors.

Item	Description	Size	Crystal
Cake stand		9" x 4"	$70.00
Pitcher	Milk		80.00

Top view of cake stand

Pedestal

Pitcher

PANAMA

OMN: United States Glass Nr 15088; AKA: Fine Cut Bar, Viking.

Manufactured by: United States Glass Company, 1904. A beautiful cake stand with scalloped gallery and alternating pointed panels with diamonds and slashes. This pattern was named in recognition of the new Republic of Panama.

Item	Size	Crystal
Cake stand	9½"	$65.00
Biscuit/cracker jar		75.00
Nappy		20.00

Top view of cake stand

Pedestal

Nappy

Biscuit

PANELED DAISY

OMN: Brazil; AKA: Daisy and Panel.
Manufactured by: Bryce Brothers, Pittsburgh, Pennsylvania, ca 1888.

Compote

Item	Size	Crystal
Cake stand	8"	$75.00
	9"	85.00
	10"	95.00
	11"	140.00
Compote	8½" x 5¼"	65.00

Pedestal

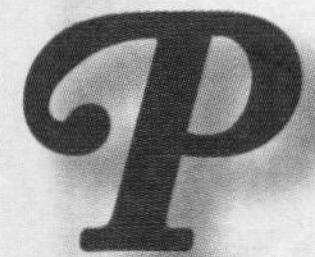

PANELED THISTLE

OMN: Delta; AKA: Canadian Thistle.

Manufactured by: J. B. Higbee Company, Bridgeville, Pennsylvania, ca. 1908; and Jefferson Glass Company, Toronto, Canada, ca. 1920. This design has a scalloped gallery with alternating panels of thistle and sunburst design with stars. The eight panel dividers descend down the pedestal and onto the base.

Item	Size	Crystal
Cake stand	6"	$110.00
Cake tray	9"	65.00
	10"	95.00

Top view of cake stand

Pedestal

PANELLED DIAMOND BLOCK(S)

OMN: Duncan Nr 24; AKA: Quartered Block, Quartered Diamond.

Manufactured by: Duncan and Sons and Company, 1894. This cake stand has a scalloped gallery, and the pattern is repeated on the base.

Item	Size	Crystal
Cake stand	9½" x 5"	$100.00
Creamer		40.00

Creamer

Pedestal

Top view of cake stand

PANELLED ENGLISH HOBNAIL

AKA: Narrow Panelled English Hobnail, Notched Finecut, Panelled Star and Square.
Manufactured by: Tarentum Glass Company, Tarentum, Pennsylvania, 1907.

Item	Description	Size	Crystal
Bowl	Sauce	4¾"	$20.00

Bowl

PANELLED FORGET-ME-NOT

OMN: Bryce Regal.
Manufactured by: Bryce Brothers, ca. 1875. As the name suggests, forget-me-nots alternate with clear panels and panels with diamonds. There is a slightly scalloped gallery.

Item	Size	Crystal	Amber	Blue
Cake stand	8"	$60.00	$80.00	$140.00
	9"	70.00	90.00	165.00
	10"	80.00	100.00	190.00
	11"	115.00	120.00	225.00
	12"	125.00	150.00	275.00

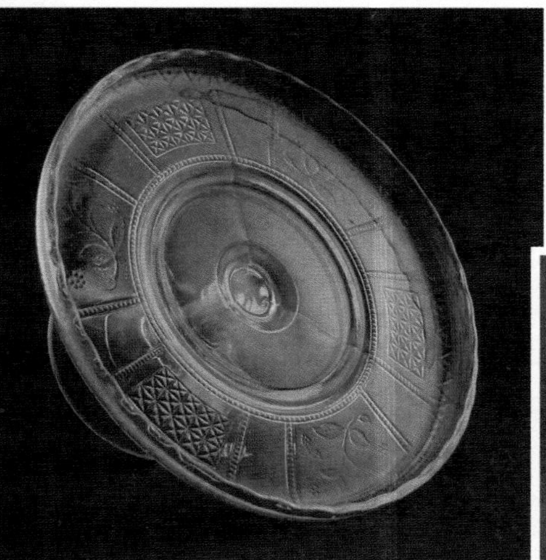

Top view of cake stand

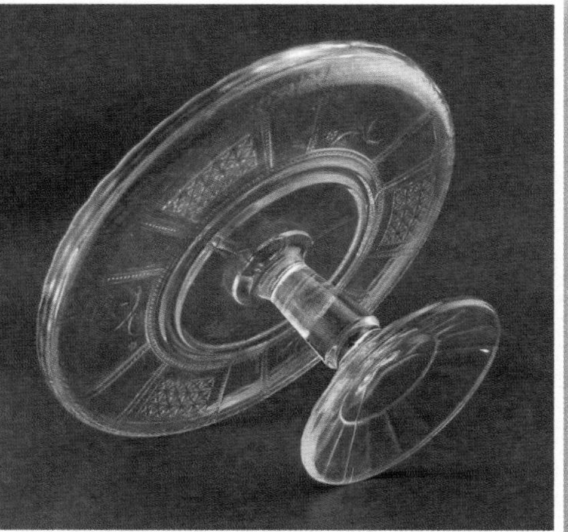

Pedestal

PANELLED HEATHER

OMN: Indiana Nr 126.

Manufactured by: Indiana Glass Company, 1911. This is a very dainty pattern alternating heather with plain panels featuring a scalloped gallery.

Item	Size	Crystal	Crystal w/Stain
Cake stand	9"	$75.00	$125.00

Stacked cake stands

Top view of cake stand

PANELLED PALM

OMN: United States Glass Nr 15095; AKA: Brilliant.

Manufactured by: United States Glass Company, 1906.

Item	Size	Crystal	Crystal w/Gold
Cake stand		$75.00	$85.00
Spooner	4⅛" x 3⅝"	20.00	25.00
Sugar	4⅝" x 6"	35.00	40.00

Sugar and spooner

PANELLED SUNFLOWER

AKA: Panelled Wild Daisy.

Manufactured by: Unknown. Creamer courtesy of Carolyn Crozier.

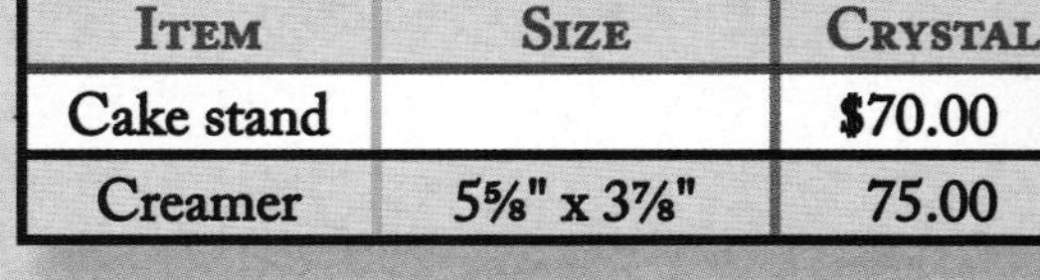

Item	Size	Crystal
Cake stand		$70.00
Creamer	5⅝" x 3⅞"	75.00

Creamer

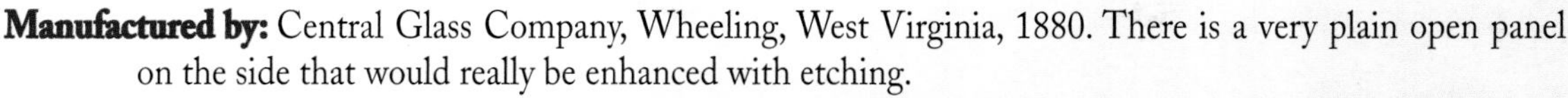

P

PANEL RIB AND SHELL

OMN: Central Nr 730.

Manufactured by: Central Glass Company, Wheeling, West Virginia, 1880. There is a very plain open panel on the side that would really be enhanced with etching.

Item	Size	Crystal
Cake stand		$135.00
Compote	7¾" x 5¼"	65.00

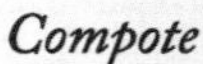

Compote

PATTEE CROSS

OMN: United States Glass Nr 15112.

Manufactured by: United States Glass Company, Factory "E," Tarentum, Pennsylvania, and Factory "B," Pittsburgh, Pennsylvania, ca. 1909. This pattern can easily be confused with Pillow and Sunburst. The pattern is also very similar to Sydney. The Pattee Cross pattern was listed in the Sears Catalog as Gloria. There is a scalloped gallery and the pattern is repeated on the base, which is scalloped.

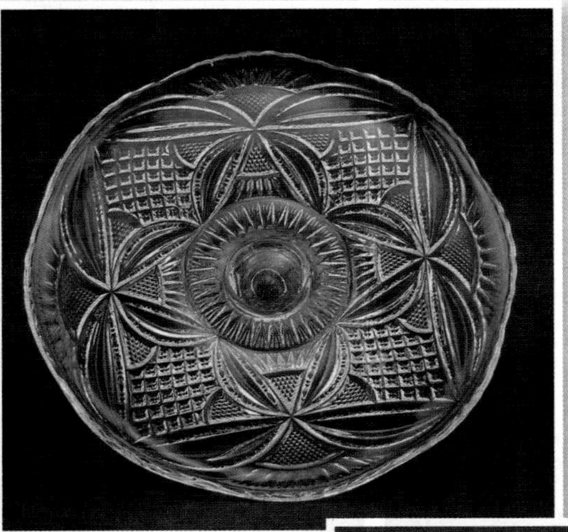

Item	Size	Crystal	Crystal w/Ruby Stain
Cake stand	9"	$75.00	$140.00
Creamer		40.00	50.00

Top view of cake stand

Creamer

Pedestal

PAVONIA

AKA: Pineapple Stem.

Manufactured by: Ripley and Company, ca. 1885. The pedestal is in the shape of a pineapple, which rests on a plain round base. This cake stand features a plain gallery with a scalloped skirt. The design around the cake plate edge is repeated inside the compote.

Item	Description	Size	Crystal	Crystal w/Etching	Crystal w/Ruby
Cake stand	High standard, non-flint	8"	$110.00	$140.00	$175.00
		9"	125.00	175.00	225.00
		10"	150.00	200.00	265.00
Cake plate		10"	35.00	45.00	55.00
Compote		8"	40.00	55.00	85.00

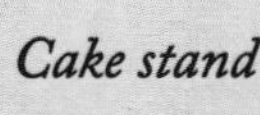

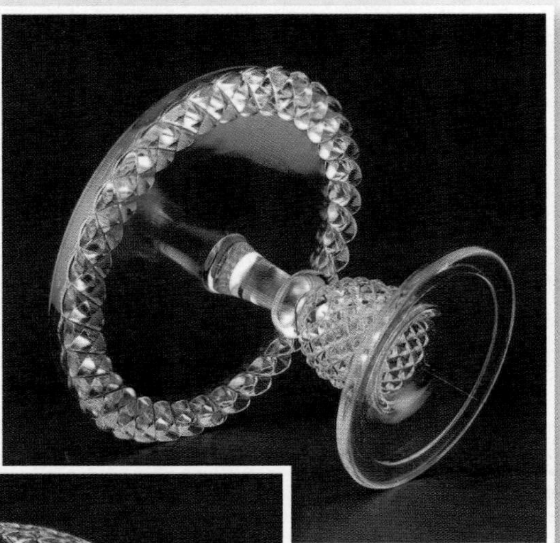

Cake stand

Pedestal

Top view of cake stand, etched

Compote pedestal

Compote interior

P

PEERLESS (HEISEY)

OMN: Heisey Nr 300, 300½.

Manufactured by: A. H. Heisey Glass Company, 1899. This is a beautiful cake stand with a small scalloped edge. The panels are repeated on the pedestal and base. The bottom of the base is ribbed.

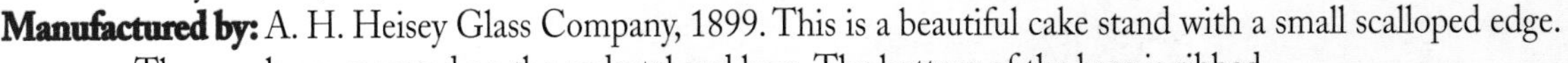

Item	Size	Crystal
Cake stand	9"	$90.00
	10"	100.00
Compote	9" x 7¾"	90.00

Pedestal

Top view of cake stand

Compote pedestal

Compote interior

PEERLESS (MODEL)

AKA: Sunburst Diamond.

Manufactured by: Model Flint Glass Company, Albany, Indiana, 1898. This impressive cake salver is very large with a ruffled gallery. The pedestal base has the same design as the plate surface.

Item	Description	Size	Crystal
Cake salver		11¼" x 6¼"	$125.00
Cup	Punch		30.00

Pedestal

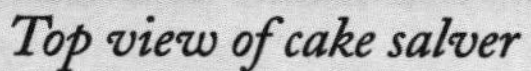

Top view of cake salver

Cups

PENNSYLVANIA

OMN: United States Glass Nrs 15048 and 15048½ – Pennsylvania; AKA: Balder, Hand, Kamoni.

Manufactured by: United States Glass Company, Pittsburgh, Pennsylvania, 1898 – 1912. This is the second in the "states series" patterns.

Item	Description	Crystal
Cake stand		$125.00
Decanter	w/Original stopper	110.00

Decanter with original stopper

PERKINS

AKA: Fortuna, Higbee's Fashion.

Manufactured by: J. B. Higbee Company, 1915; and later New Martinsville, 1918. One of the more common patterns, it is readily available on internet auctions. It has a scalloped gallery, with alternating tiny and large scallops.

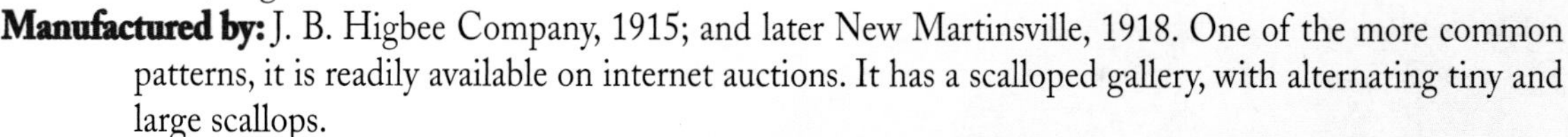

Item	Description	Size	Crystal
Cake stand		6"	$50.00
		9½"	75.00
Cake plate	Handled	11"	50.00
Celery vase	Handled		35.00

Top view of cake stand

Celery vase

Pedestal

PETTICOAT

AKA: Riverside's National.

Manufactured by: Riverside Glass Company, ca. 1901. This is a classy pattern with alternating rows of diamonds near the base, which is comprised of gilded scallops. The rim of the pitcher is also scalloped.

Pitcher

Item	Crystal	Vaseline
Cake stand	$125.00	$375.00
Pitcher	190.00	350.00

PILLOW AND SUNBURST

AKA: Elite.

Manufactured by: Westmoreland Specialty Glass Company, Grapeville, Pennsylvania, ca 1897. Westmoreland made this pattern with covers on the sugar and creamer, which were used to ship powdered (dry) mustard. The lids are interchangeable.

Item	Description	Crystal
Cake stand		$75.00
Sugar		75.00
Creamer (no lid shown)		75.00
Sugar	Two handles	80.00

Sugar and creamer

Covered sugar

PILLOW ENCIRCLED

OMN: Model Nr 857; AKA: Midway.

Manufactured by: Model Flint Glass Company, ca. 1889; and Cambridge Glass Company, 1901. Found in Montgomery Ward's catalog in 1894. This stand can easily be confused with Starred Block. On close examination, the gallery on Starred Block has a design, whereas the gallery on Pillow Encircled is plain. Both cake stands have "arrows" radiating from the center of the plate; those on Pillow Encircled are curved, while those on Starred Block are straight. Both have deep brandy wells. The pattern, Hero, is also similar.

Item	Size	Crystal
Cake stand	9½"	$175.00

Pedestal

Top view of cake stand

PILLOWS

OMN: Heisey Nr 325.

Manufactured by: A. H. Heisey Glass Company, ca. 1901 – 1910.

Item	Size	Crystal
Cake salver	9"	$200.00
Biscuit/cracker (lid not shown)	6⅞" x 4⅞"	275.00

Biscuit/cracker

PINEAPPLE AND FAN (U. S. GLASS)

OMN: United States Glass Nr 15041; AKA: Cube with Fan, Holbrook.

Manufactured by: United States Glass Company, Pittsburgh, Pennsylvania, Factories "A" and "GP," ca. 1895. There is a small beaded gallery. The pedestal is twisted and the pattern is repeated on the base.

Item	Size	Crystal	Emerald Green	Crystal w/Ruby Stain
Cake stand	10½" x 6½"	$45.00	$75.00	$125.00

Top view of cake stand

Pedestal

PINEAPPLE AND FAN (HEISEY)

OMN: Heisey Nr 1255.

Manufactured by: A. H. Heisey Glass Company, ca. 1898. One of Heisey's prettiest patterns, and especially elegant in emerald. Note that the shape of the compote appears to be round and square. Most pieces in this pattern are not marked with the Diamond H. Courtesy of Carolyn Crozier.

Item	Description	Size	Crystal	Emerald
Cake salver		10"	$155.00	$310.00
		11"	170.00	350.00
Compote	Open	9" x 7½"	145.00	290.00
Creamer	Hotel	4¼" x 3¼"	35.00	70.00
Sugar	Hotel	5¼" x 2⅝"	35.00	70.00

Compote, sugar, creamer

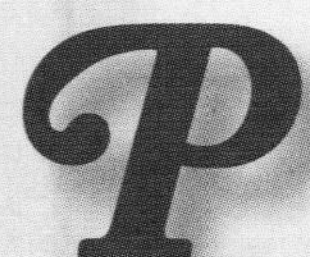

PLAIN BAND

OMN: Heisey Nr 1225.

Manufactured by: A. H. Heisey & Company, Newark, Ohio, 1897. This is a very plain, nondescript pattern, except for the beading on the rim. The pedestal is plain. Not all pieces in this pattern are marked with the Diamond H. Courtesy of Carolyn Crozier.

Banana stand

Item	Size	Crystal
Cake salver	9"	$90.00
	10"	115.00
Banana stand	9"	110.00
	10½"	125.00

PLEAT AND PANEL

OMN: Derby.

Manufactured by: Bryce Brothers, Pittsburgh, Pennsylvania, ca. 1882. This is a very distinctive pattern with eight sides, lines in the four corner panels, and stippling on the four side panels. This cake stand features a plain gallery, pedestal, and a plain base that is eight sided. Note that the sides of the bread tray are scalloped.

Item	Description	Size	Crystal
Cake stand		8"	$100.00
		9"	135.00
		10"	240.00
Bread tray	Open handle		60.00
	Closed handle		40.00
Compote		7"	140.00
		9"	240.00
Creamer		5¾" x 6½"	40.00
Plate		6"	45.00
Pickle dish			25.00
Sauce dish	Square, footed	4"	15.00
Sugar (no lid shown)		4" x 6"	160.00

Top view of cake stand

Pedestal

P

Compotes and bread tray

Sugar and creamer

Bread tray, plate, sauce dish, and pickle

PLEAT BAND

OMN: Indiana Nr 137; AKA: Plain Ware.

Manufactured by: Indiana Tumbler and Goblet Company, ca 1897; National Glass Company, ca 1901; and Indiana Glass Company, ca 1907. Etching is Nr 160. There is a scalloped gallery. The pleat design around the rim of the plate is repeated on the pedestal and base. Courtesy of Carolyn Crozier.

Item	Size	Crystal	Crystal, Etched
Cake stand	10½"	$55.00	$70.00

Top view of cake stand

Top view of cake stands, side by side

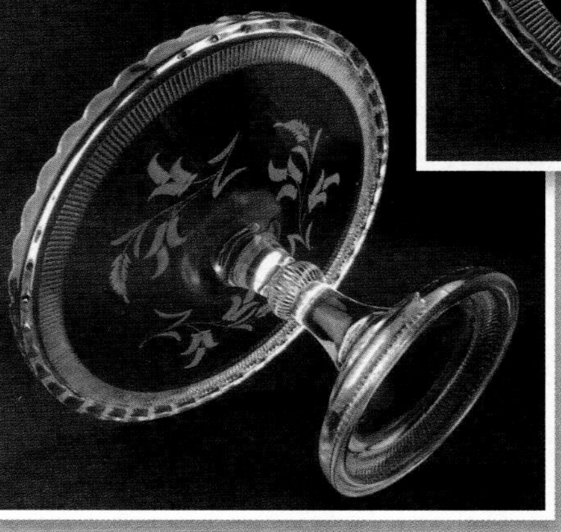
Pedestal

PLEATED MEDALLION

OMN: New Martinsville Nr 713.

Manufactured by: New Martinsville Glass Company, ca 1910.

Item	Description	Size	Crystal
Cake stand			$75.00
Pitcher	Water	½ gal.	65.00

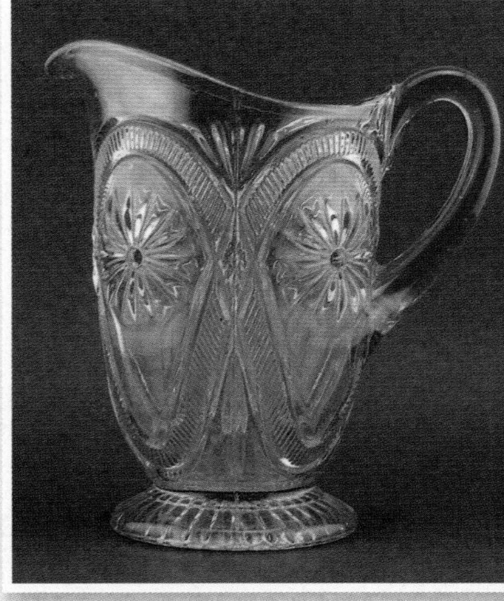

Pitcher

PLUME

OMN: Adams Nr 3.

Manufactured by: Adams and Company, Pittsburgh, Pennsylvania, ca 1874. The plate is enhanced by the plume on the edge, which comprises the gallery and skirt. The plume continues down the pedestal base. Some cake stands are etched, to which 15% should be added to value.

Item	Description	Size	Crystal	Crystal w/Ruby
Cake stand		9"	$135.00	$350.00
		10"	155.00	400.00
Compote	Covered (no lid shown)	9" x 7"	55.00	110.00

Top view of cake stand

Pedestal

Compote

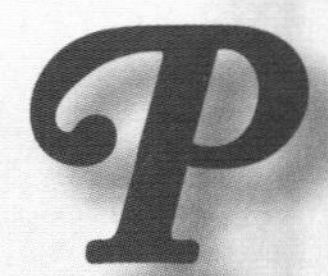

POGO STICK

AKA: Crown.

Manufactured by: Lancaster Glass Company, ca. 1910. There is a plain gallery. Aptly named.

Item	Size	Crystal
Cake stand	10"	$75.00
Bowl	9½"	35.00

Pedestal

Top view of cake stand

POINTED JEWEL

OMN: United States Glass 15006; AKA: Long Diamond, Pointed Jewels, Spear Point.

Manufactured by: United States Glass Company, Pittsburgh, Pennsylvania, at Factories "J" and "N" after 1892.

Sugar

Item	Size	Crystal
Cake stand	10"	$175.00
Sugar	7" x 4½"	80.00

PORTIEUX

Manufactured by: Unknown. The history of this pattern cannot be found. The rim of the plate is scalloped. The pattern is continued down the hollow pedestal base which is scalloped. The name is embossed in the pedestal.

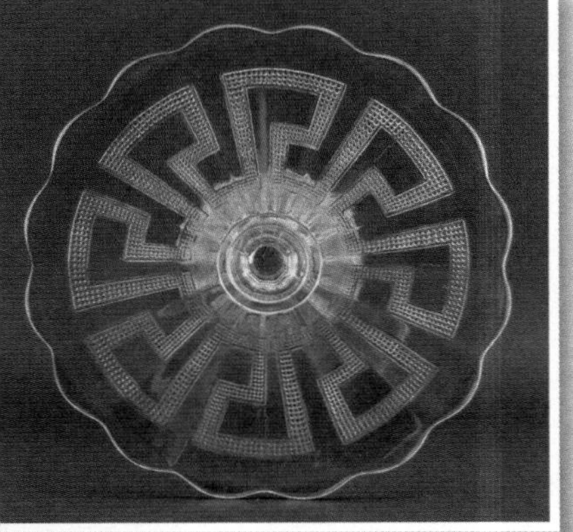

Top view of cake stand

Item	Size	Crystal
Cake stand	9¼"	$65.00

Pedestal

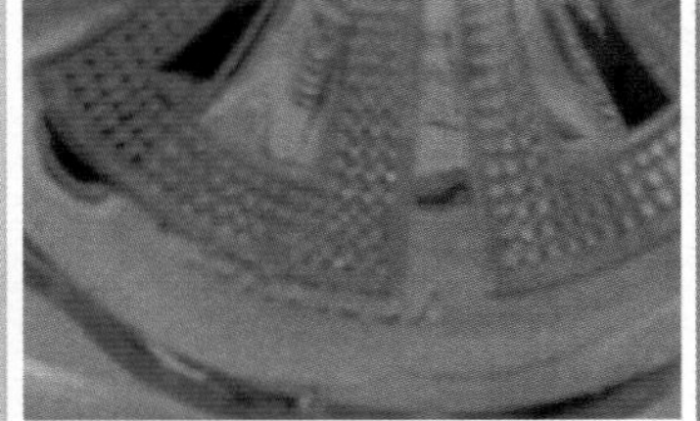

Pedestal base with name

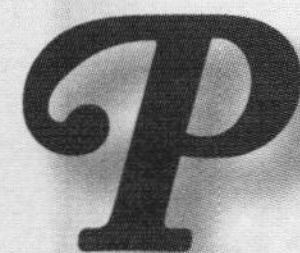

PORTLAND

OMN: United States Glass Nr 15121; AKA: U. S. Portland.
Manufactured by: United States Glass Company, Pittsburgh, Pennsylvania, ca. 1910.

Item	Size	Crystal
Cake stand	10½"	$95.00
Bowl	8½" x 2¼"	35.00
Celery	4½" x 5¾"	60.00

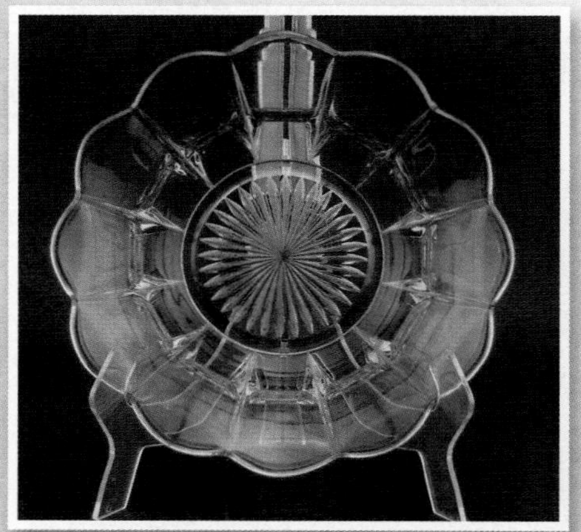

Bowl

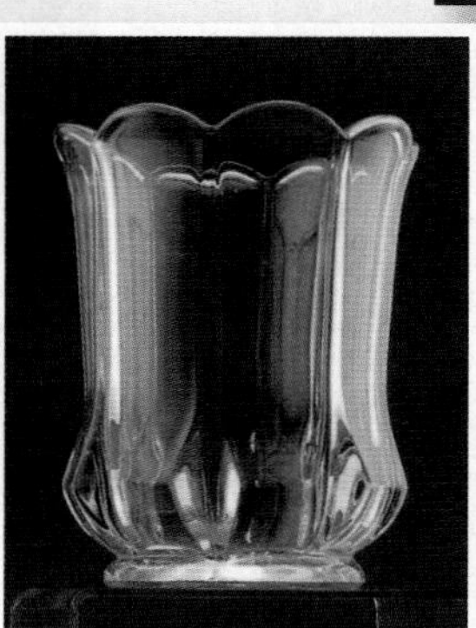

Celery

POST SCRIPT

Manufactured by: Tarentum Glass Company, 1905.

Item	Description	Size	Crystal
Cake stand			$90.00
Card tray	w/Gold trim	5½" x 4"	45.00

Card tray

PRESSED LEAF (N.P.L.)

OMN: New Pressed Leaf "N.P.L."; AKA: New Pressed Leaf.
Manufactured by: McKee Brothers, ca. 1867. A very plain pattern except for the leaf design. Pitcher courtesy of Carolyn Crozier.

Item	Description	Size	Crystal
Cake stand	Non-flint, high standard	10½"	$150.00
	Low standard	6½"	150.00
Goblet		5¾"	30.00
		6"	35.00
Pitcher		8¾" x 8"	180.00

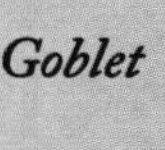

Goblet

Pitcher

PRINCE OF WALES PLUMES

OMN: Heisey Nr 335; AKA: Flambeaux.

Manufactured by: A. H. Heisey Company, ca. 1902. Pieces in this pattern are all marked with the Diamond H. The pattern is repeated on the pedestal base. The cake salver has a small scalloped gallery and skirt. The punch bowl has scallops within scallops on the rim. The gilding on the butter dish enhances an already elegant piece. Cake salver courtesy of Carolyn Crozier.

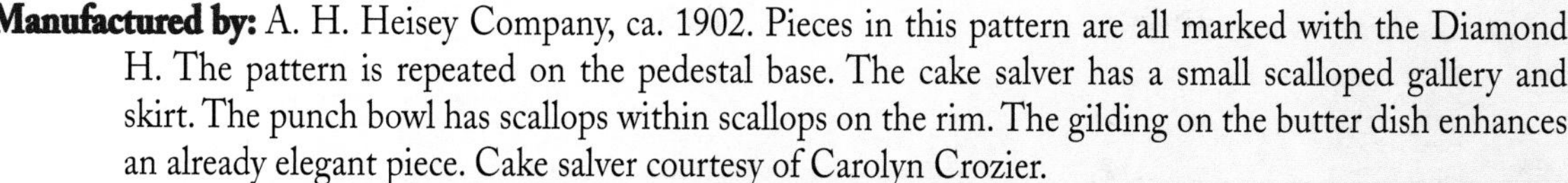

Item	Description	Size	Crystal	Gold Trim
Cake salver		9"	$210.00	$275.00
		10"	225.00	290.00
		12"	250.00	325.00
Cake basket	Crystal	9½" or 10"	210.00	
		12"	230.00	
Butter dish		7 13/16" x 5½"	140.00	175.00
Punch bowl and base		10½"	575.00	
		14"	800.00	

Butter dish

Punch bowl

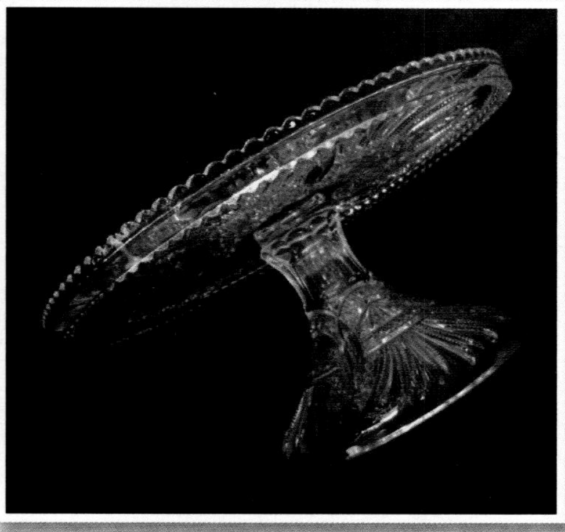

Cake salver

PRINCESS FEATHER

OMN: Rochelle; AKA: Lacy Medallion, Prince's Feather.

Manufactured by: Bakewell, Pears and Company, 1864. Sugar courtesy of Carolyn Crozier.

Item	Description	Size	Crystal
Cake plate	Closed handles	9"	$45.00
Cake stand			175.00
Sugar (no lid shown)		4⅛" x 5⅛"	85.00

Sugar

(THE) PRIZE

AKA: McKee Nr 500, National Nr 500.

Manufactured by: National Glass Company, 1900. This cake stand has deep and shallow scallops on the gallery with a hollow pedestal.

Item	Size	Crystal
Cake stand	9"	$75.00
	10"	85.00

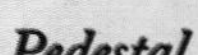

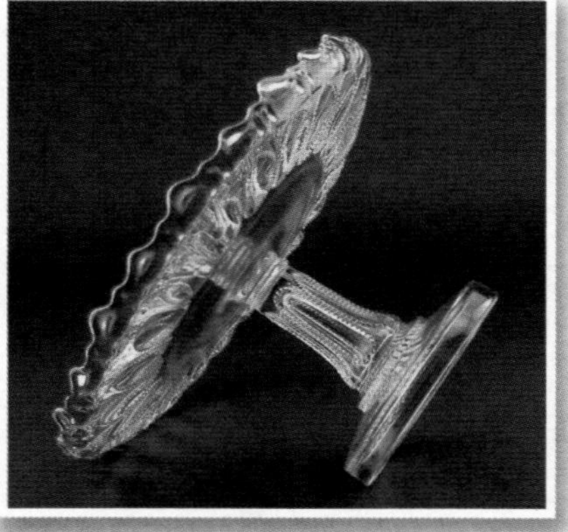

Pedestal

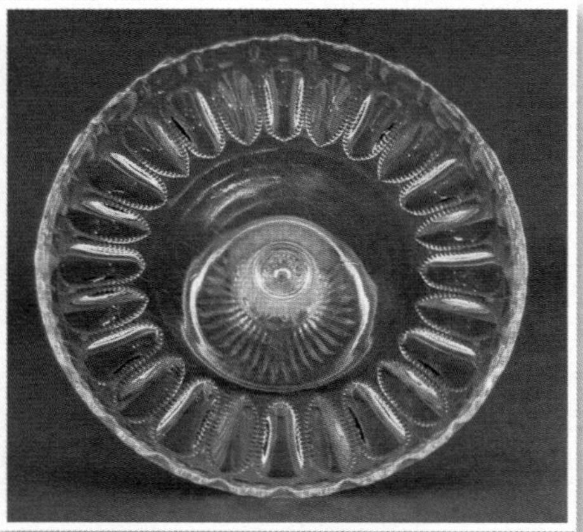

Top view of cake stand

PUNTY BAND

OMN: Heisey Nr 1220.

Manufactured by: A. H. Heisey Company, ca. 1897. The toothpick was made in two styles: scalloped or beaded top. This beaded top toothpick is decorated with ruby stain and is engraved Hutchison.

Toothpick

Item	Size	Crystal	Ruby Stain
Cake salver	9"	$110.00	
	10"	125.00	
Toothpick		60.00	$80.00

PYRAMIDS

AKA: Millard's Pyramid, Mitered Diamond, Sunken Bottoms.

Manufactured by: Unknown. No information is available on the manufacturer. This is a huge cake stand. It does not have a brandy well. The scallops on the gallery are smaller than those on the skirt. The hollow pedestal and base are square with a portion of the pattern repeated on the base.

Item	Size	Crystal	Amber	Blue	Vaseline
Cake stand	10" x 7¾"	$175.00	$210.00	$250.00	$325.00

Pedestal

Top view of cake stand

QUAKER LADY

AKA: Scalloped Prism Band.

Manufactured by: Dalzell, Gilmore and Leighton, 1889. If etched, add 15% to the value. There is pleating between scallops on the top of the plate and scallops on the base. Cake salver courtesy of Tom Patrick O'Brien; compote courtesy of Reece Douglas Fugle.

Pedestal

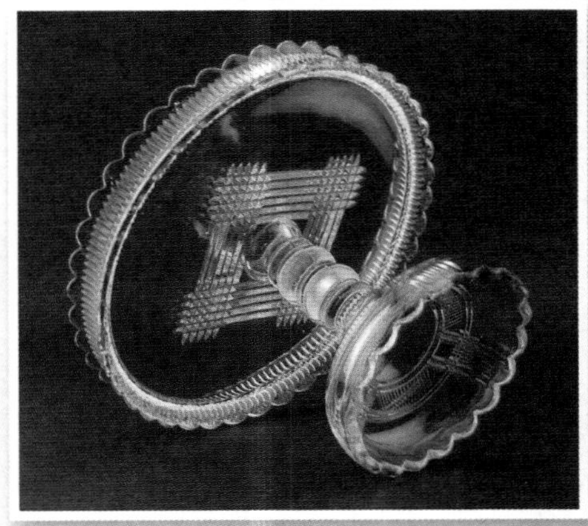

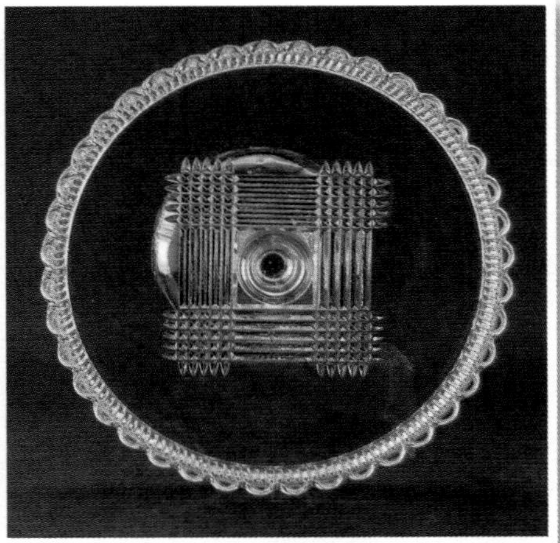

Top view of cake salver

Item	Size	Crystal
Cake salver	9¾" x 6½"	$225.00
Compote	7" x 7¾"	95.00

Cake salver and compote

QUARTERED BLOCK

OMN: Duncan Nr 55.

Manufactured by: Duncan and Miller Glass Company, ca. 1903. There is a small plain gallery; and a pretty triple scalloped skirt. The pattern is continued down the pedestal and base.

Item	Size	Crystal
Cake stand	9½" x 4¾"	$95.00

Pedestal

Top view of cake stand

QUEEN

AKA: Daisy and Button with Pointed Panels, Daisy with Depressed Button, Paneled Daisy and Button, Pointed Panel Daisy and Button, Sunk Daisy and Button.

Manufactured by: McKee Brothers, ca. 1885. Along with other pieces, this non-flint cake stand has been reproduced by L.E. Smith in vaseline and blue. The vaseline reproduction shown is valued at $45.00.

Item	Size	Crystal	Amber	Apple Green	Blue	Canary/Yellow
Cake stand	8"	$50.00	$60.00	$100.00	$90.00	$110.00
	9"	70.00	80.00	125.00	115.00	135.00
	10"	90.00	100.00	140.00	130.00	160.00
Bowl	8"	40.00	45.00	60.00	60.00	75.00

Top view of cake stand, vaseline

Pedestal, vaseline

Top view of cake stand

Pedestal

Bowl

R

QUEEN ANNE

AKA: Bearded Man, Neptune, Old Man, Santa Claus, Viking.

Manufactured by: LaBelle Glass Company, 1880s. A unique pattern with a bearded man pictured on the spout of the creamers. The feet and handles are square.

Item	Size	Crystal	Crystal Etched
Spooner	6"	$60.00	$70.00
Creamer	5"	75.00	85.00

Creamer, etched and plain and spooner, etched

RAILROAD

Manufactured by: Unknown. Marked Engine 330.

Item	Size	Crystal/Frosting
Water tray	12" x 9"	$125.00

Water tray

RAMBLER

OMN: United States Glass Nr 15136.

Manufactured by: United States Glass Company, 1912. The pattern swirls (rambles) around the compote interior. It is interesting that the pedestal does not match the compote bowl.

Item	Description	Size	Crystal
Cake stand		8½"	$60.00
Compote	Open	7½" x 5¾"	35.00

Top view of compote

Pedestal

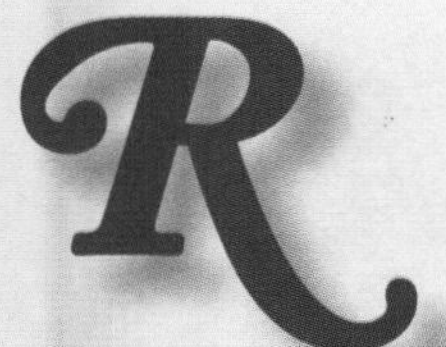

RAYED FLOWER

OMN: Indiana Nr 132.

Manufactured by: Indiana Glass Company, ca. 1920. There is a scalloped gallery and the pattern is repeated on the base.

Item	Size	Crystal
Cake stand	9½" x 4¼"	$65.00

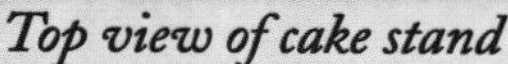

Top view of cake stand

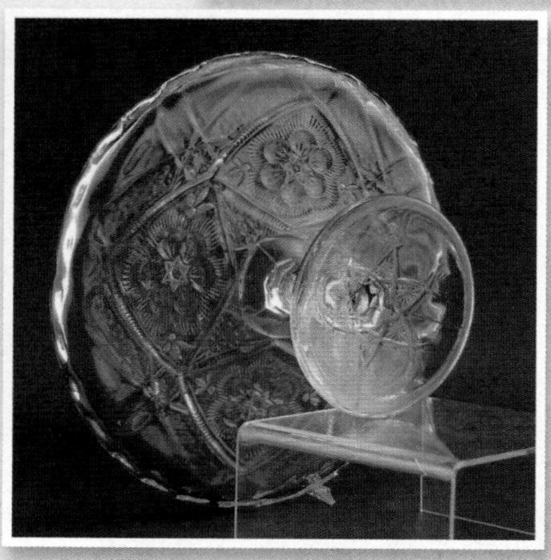

Pedestal

RED BLOCK

OMN: Bryce Nr 175, Captain Kid Nr 150, Central Nr 881, Central Nr 893, Doyle Nr 250, Duncan Nr 328, Eva, Fostoria Nr 140, Pioneer Nr 250, Virginia 140; AKA: Barreled Block, and Clear Block.

Manufactured by: Bryce Brothers, Pittsburgh, Pennsylvania; Central Glass Company, Wheeling, West Virginia; Doyle and Company, Pittsburgh, Pennsylvania, all ca. 1885; Fostoria Glass Company, Fostoria, Ohio, ca. 1890; George Duncan and Sons, Pittsburgh, Pennsylvania; Model Flint Glass Works, Albany, Indiana; Pioneer Glass Works, Pittsburgh, Pennsylvania, ca. 1890. An outstanding pattern with the ruby stain.

Item	Description	Size	Crystal	Crystal w/Ruby
Cake stand		10"	$145.00	$850.00
Sugar	Covered	6¼" x 6½"	65.00	100.00
Goblet			25.00	40.00

Goblet

Sugar

RETICULATED CORD

OMN: O'Hara Nr 600; AKA: Drum.

Manufactured by: O'Hara Glass Company, ca 1885. The handles are closed on the plate.

Item	Size	Crystal
Cake stand		$75.00
Cake plate	10¾"	60.00
Creamer	5¾" x 5"	70.00

Creamer

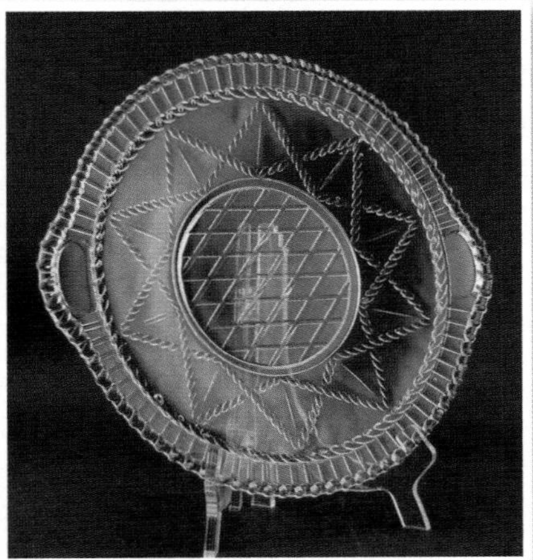

Cake plate

REVERSE TORPEDO

OMN: Dalzell Nr 490D; AKA: Bull's Eye and Cut Diamond Point, Bull's Eye Band, Bull's Eye with Diamond Point, Diamonds and Bull's Eye Band, Pointed Bull's Eye.

Manufactured by: Dalzell, Gilmore and Leighton Glass Company, ca. 1892. An expensive cake stand. The pattern on the skirt is repeated on the base. The open compote has a large scalloped rim.

Item	Description	Size	Crystal
Cake stand	High standard	9¾" x 6⅜"	$225.00
Compote	Open	9"	100.00
	Covered	6"	85.00
Sugar (no lid shown)			110.00

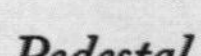
Pedestal

Top view of cake stand

Sugar

Compote, covered

Compote, open

RIBBED ELLIPSE

AKA: Admiral.

Manufactured by: Bryce, Higbee and Company, 1905. J. B. Higbee Glass Company, 1907. One of the more common and available patterns, this cake stand has a scalloped gallery, with the pattern repeated on the base.

Item	Size	Crystal
Cake stand	9¾"	$60.00
Bowl	9"	45.00

Top view of cake stand

Cake stand and bowl

Pedestal

R

RIBBON CANDY

OMN: United States Glass Nr 15010; AKA: Bryce, Double Loop, Figure Eight.

Manufactured by: United States Glass Company, Pittsburgh, Pennsylvania, at Factory "B," ca. 1891. There is a plain gallery, and the ribbon candy pattern is repeated on the pedestal.

Item	Description	Size	Crystal
Cake stand	High standard		$125.00
	Child's miniature	6½"	75.00
	Table size	8"	65.00
		9"	75.00
		10"	85.00

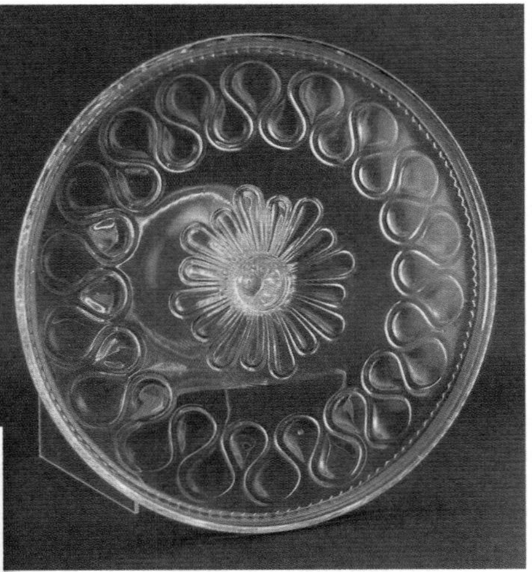

Top view of cake stand

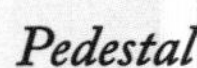

Pedestal

RING AND PETAL NR 1875

Manufactured by: Westmoreland. This square cake stand with rings and petals around the rim has a round pedestal. Courtesy of Bradley A. James.

Item	Description	Size	Milk Glass	Amethyst	Blue
Cake stand	Square	11"	$240.00	$270.00	$85.00
	Round	11½"	130.00	225.00	75.00
Candlesticks			35.00		

Cake stand with candlesticks

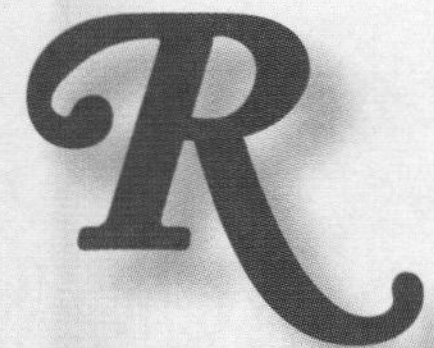

RIPLEY'S NR 10

Manufactured by: Ripley and Company, 1880s. A very distinctive pattern with the design repeated on the pedestal.

Item	Crystal	Engraved
Cake stand	$100.00	$125.00
Cake basket	125.00	150.00

Cake baskets side by side

Cake basket

RISING SUN

OMN: United States Glass Nr 15110 – Sunshine; AKA: Sunrise.

Manufactured by: United States Glass Company, Pittsburgh, Pennsylvania, ca. 1908. It doesn't take much imagination to see how this pattern derived its name. The gilding and red stain on the sunrise make this an outstanding pattern.

Item	Size	Crystal	Crystal w/Green or Rose Stain	Gold trim
Cake stand	10½"	$95.00	$400.00	$425.00
Spooner	6¼" x 3½"	45.00	100.00	125.00

Spooner

RIVERSIDE'S AURORA

Manufactured by: Tygart Valley Glass Company, Grafton, West Virginia, 1908. This item is listed in the Tygart Valley catalog as a "10" footed tray."

Item	Size	Crystal
Cake stand	10" x 2"	$45.00

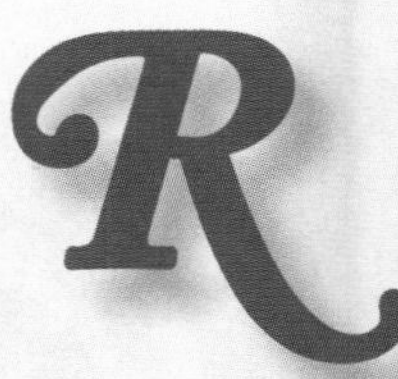

Pedestal

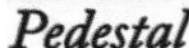

Cake stand

ROANOKE

AKA: Late Sawtooth.

Manufactured by: Ripley and Company, Pittsburgh, Pennsylvania, ca 1889. This elegant cake stand has a scalloped gallery. It stands a lofty 5¾" high. The pedestal is comprised of prism type columns that extend down onto the base. The pattern on the top of the plate is repeated around the base of the pedestal.

Item	Description	Size	Crystal	Crystal w/Ruby Stain
Cake stand	Scalloped rim	6"	$80.00	$135.00
		9"	90.00	200.00
		10½" x 5¾"	100.00	240.00
Bowl	Deep with scalloped rim	7"	25.00	45.00
		8"	25.00	45.00
		9"	40.00	35.00

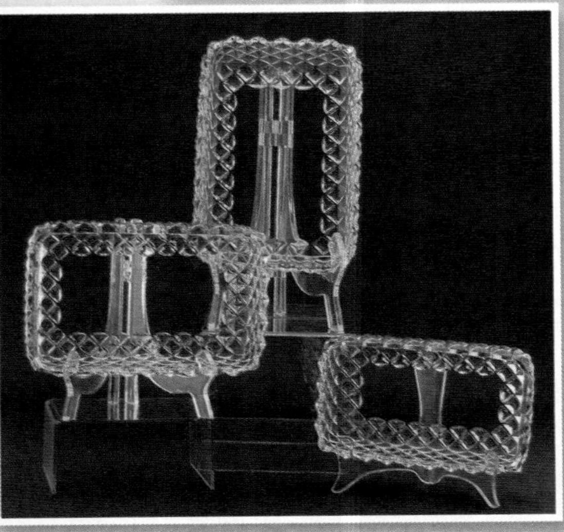

Bowls

Top view of cake stand

Pedestal

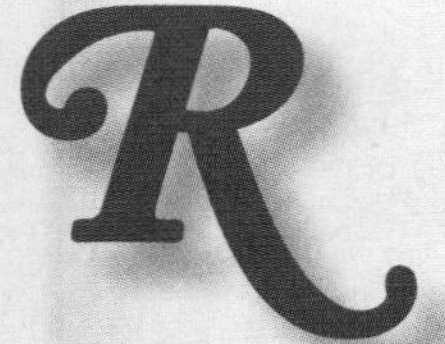

ROBIN HOOD

OMN: Fostoria Nr 603.

Manufactured by: Fostoria Glass Company, Moundsville, West Virginia, ca. 1898. This cake stand is courtesy of my cousin, Eunice Stearns Crow, who has the matching butter dish that belonged to our paternal grandmother.

Item	Description	Size	Crystal
Cake stand		9"	$80.00
		10"	90.00
Syrup (lid not shown)	Original		80.00

Cake stand

Syrup

ROMOLA

Manufactured by: Robinson Glass Company, 1894; and Model Flint Glass, 1901. This is a striking pattern with the six ovals on the top and the scalloped skirt and gallery. The pattern is repeated on the base.

Item	Size	Crystal
Cake stand	8" x 5¾"	$75.00
	10" x 6½"	90.00

Top view of cake stand

Stacked cake stands

ROSE IN SNOW

OMN: Bryce Nr 125; AKA: Rose.

Manufactured by: Bryce Brothers, ca. 1880s. This is a pretty pattern with three stemmed roses pictured in the bowl.

Item	Description	Size	Crystal	Amber	Blue	Canary/ Yellow
Cake stand		9"	$120.00	$160.00	$240.00	$275.00
Compote	Open, low standard	7"	100.00	135.00	175.00	230.00

Compote, side view

Compote, interior

ROSE POINT BAND

OMN: Indiana Nr 153; AKA: Clematis, Waterlily.

Manufactured by: Indiana Glass Company, Dunkirk, Indiana, ca. 1913. This is a dainty cake stand with a band of roses on the border (as the name implies) and flowers and leaves in the center. There is a scalloped gallery with the band repeated on the base of the pedestal.

Item	Size	Crystal
Cake stand	9"	$60.00
	10"	75.00

Pedestal

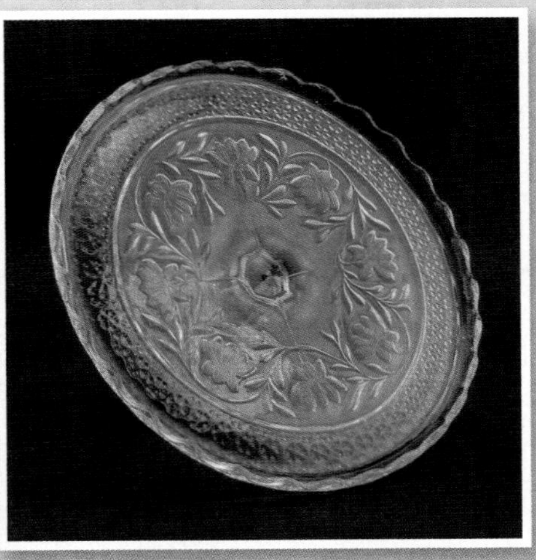

Top view of cake stand

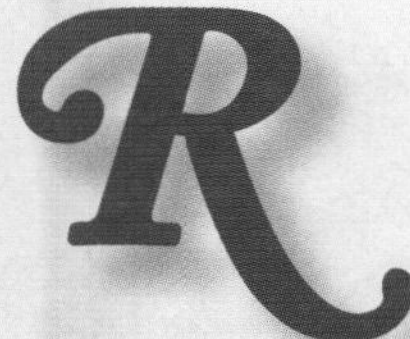

ROSE SPRIG

Manufactured by: Campbell, Jones and Company, 1886. The rose is depicted on the side oval panel of this compote.

Item	Size	Crystal	Amber	Blue	Canary/Yellow
Cake stand	9"	$150.00	$165.00	$200.00	$225.00
Compote	8" x 7½" x 5"	50.00	55.00	65.00	75.00

Compote

ROSETTE

OMN: Magic.

Manufactured by: Bryce Brothers, late 1889. Finding this pattern in amber, blue, or canary is very rare. This is a pretty pattern with the rosettes affixed in panels on the plate surface with double circles and broken lines on the raised rim of the plate and base of the pedestal. The pedestal is twisted. Very clear glass. This pattern is similar to Frosted Medallion.

Item	Description	Size	Crystal
Cake stand	High standard	7"	$65.00
		9"	80.00
		10"	90.00
		11"	125.00
Compote	Covered	6" x 7"	60.00

Top view of cake stand

Pedestal

Compote

R

ROSETTE AND PALMS

Manufactured by: Bryce, Higbee and Company, 1905; and J.B. Higbee Glass Company, ca. 1907. The cake stand has a scalloped gallery, the pedestal and base are plain, the pedestal on the compote has a design. Courtesy of Karen and Sam Ruble.

Item	Description	Size	Crystal
Cake stand		9½"	$60.00
		10" x 5"	65.00
Compote	Covered	7" x 11"	65.00

Cake stand and compote

Stacked cake stands

ROSETTE WITH PINWHEELS

OMN: Indiana Nr 171.

Manufactured by: Indiana Glass Company, late 1920s. This cake stand is relatively easy to find. It has a scalloped gallery with a design on the base.

Item	Size	Crystal
Cake stand	9¾"	$75.00

Pedestal

Top view of cake stand

RUSTIC

AKA: Drapery Variant, Long Tidy, Short Tidy, Stayman, Tidy.

Manufactured by: McKee Brothers, 1880. The unusual design appears on both the top and bottom of the compote. The finial is a log.

Item	Size	Crystal
Cake stand		$150.00
Compote	8¼" x 8"	75.00

Compote

SALVER, PLAIN NR 350 – HEAVY

AKA: Baker's Stand.

Manufactured by: Central Glass Company, ca. 1880s. Basic cake stands were designed to be used for cakes and pastries in bakeries as well as in the home. There are several of these plain salvers with minute differences: one or more rings on the pedestal, bulbous base, and all have a plain gallery.

Item	Size	Crystal
Cake stand	9" x 7¼"	$125.00
	12¼" x 8¾"	200.00

Stacked cake stands

SALVER, PLAIN 350 WARE

Manufactured by: Central Glass Company, patented by John Osterling, 1873. These nameless plain salvers have a ½" gallery. The stems are solid with protruding rings. References have been found for a cover for these plain salvers, and one is pictured on page 28 in *Pennsylvania Glassware, 1870 – 1904*, The American Historical Catalog Collection, 1972. The plain salvers are very similar, with bases and pedestals being slightly different.

Item	Size	Crystal
Salver	9" x 5½"	$125.00

Pedestal

S

SALVER, PLAIN NR F-8313-1

Manufactured by: United States Glass Company, Pittsburgh, Pennsylvania, ca. 1926. The pedestal and base on this salver are completely different from the other plain salvers. See comments on previous page.

Item	Size	Crystal
Salver	10¼" x 8"	$145.00

Cake stand

SCALLOPED SIX POINT

OMN: Duncan Nr 30; AKA: Divided Medallion with Diamond Cut.

Manufactured by: George Duncan and Sons Company, Washington, Pennsylvania, 1897. This pattern actually has eight points, alternating four wide points with diamonds in the center, and four smaller points with slashes. The cake stand has a scalloped gallery. An intricate pattern which is repeated on the pedestal.

Item	Description	Size	Crystal	Crystal w/Gold
Cake stand	Square		$135.00	$150.00
	Round	9½" x 6"	100.00	110.00
Creamer	Individual		12.00	25.00
	Table		50.00	55.00
Sugar bowl w/cover	Individual		15.00	20.00
	Table (no lid)		65.00	75.00
Bowl	Square	8"	45.00	50.00

Sugar and creamer

Top view of cake stand

Bowl, gilded

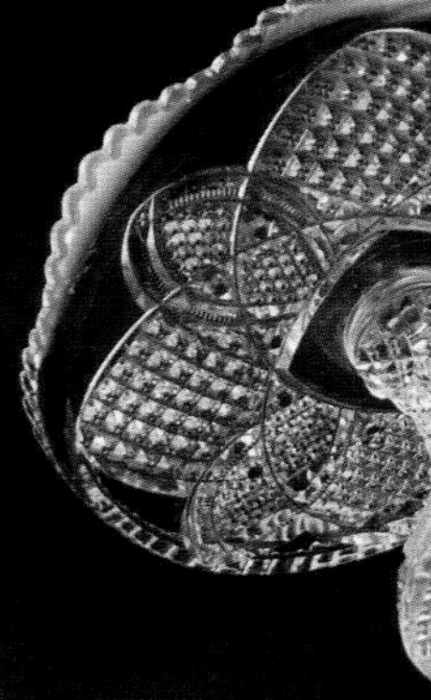

Pedestal

SHELL AND TASSEL

OMN: Duncan Nr 555; AKA: Hedlin Shell, Shell and Spike, Shell and Tassel – Square.

Manufactured by: George A. Duncan and Sons, Pittsburgh, Pennsylvania, 1881. The cake stand in this very elegant pattern is square with shells pictured in the four corners of the cake plate and base. Amber, blue, canary yellow, or any other color would be considered rare.

Top view of cake stand

Item	Size	Crystal
Cake stand	6"	$130.00
	7"	90.00
	8"	100.00
	9½"	120.00
	10"	170.00

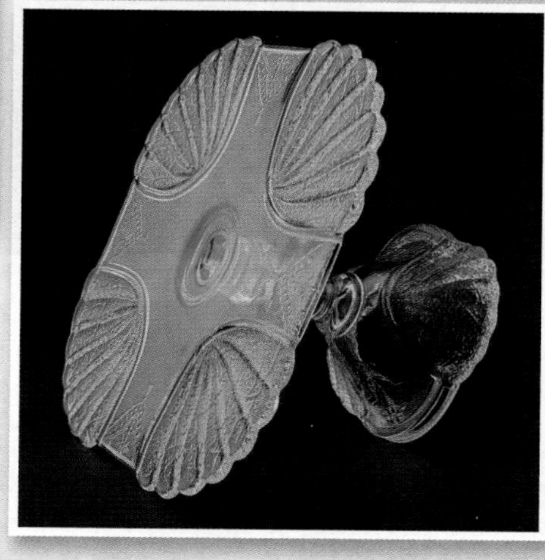

Pedestal

SHERATON

AKA: Ida.

Manufactured by: Bryce, Higbee and Company, Pittsburgh, Pennsylvania, ca.1885. There is a plain gallery with plain pedestal.

Item	Size	Crystal
Cake stand	10¼" x 6"	$70.00

Pedestal

Top view of cake stand

SHOSHONE

OMN: United States Glass Nr 15046 – Victor; AKA: Blazing Pinwheels, Floral Diamond.

Manufactured by: United States Glass Company, Pittsburgh, Pennsylvania, ca. 1895. The plate is slightly curved rather than completely flat like most. The pattern is partially repeated on the top portion of the pedestal base. The cake stand originally came with a cover in the same pattern as the plate, whereas most covers were plain to be interchangeable with any pattern.

Item	Description	Size	Crystal	Green	Crystal w/Ruby	Crystal w/Amber
Cake stand	High standard	9"	$65.00	$85.00	$140.00	$170.00
		10"	75.00	100.00	170.00	200.00
		11"	95.00	125.00	200.00	225.00
Bowl	Flared, with gilding	5½"	25.00	35.00	80.00	90.00

Bowls, crystal with gilding and cake stand

Top view of cake stand

Pedestal

Top view of cake stand, green

SHRINE

OMN: Orient; AKA: Jewelled Moon and Star, Jewel with Moon and Star, Little Shrine, Moon and Star with Waffle.

Manufactured by: Beatty-Brady Glass Company, Dunkirk, Indiana, ca 1896; and Indiana Glass Company, Dunkirk, Indiana, ca 1904. This pattern has alternating panels with one stippled panel including two stars and moons; and the other panel is clear with a large teardrop. The bottom of the bowl is decorated only with teardrops.

Bowl

Item	Size	Crystal
Cake stand	8½"	$150.00
Bowl	8½"	40.00

SHUTTLE

OMN: Indiana Nr 29; AKA: Hearts of Loch Laven, Ribbed Asterisk and Concave.

Manufactured by: Indiana Tumbler and Goblet Factory, ca. 1896; and Indiana Glass, ca. 1898. The distinguishing pattern on this cake stand looks like a shuttle that was used (and is still used by some people) to make tatting lace for trimming on pillow cases, as well as other linens. Tatting is almost a lost art. The pattern is repeated on the base; there is a plain gallery.

Item	Crystal
Cake stand	$175.00

Pedestal

Top view of cake stand

SILVER QUEEN

AKA: Elmino

Manufactured by: Ripley and Company, Pittsburgh, Pennsylvania, ca. 1890. This is a very plain pattern with the exception of pleating around the edge of the bowl and just below the finial. This piece is enhanced by etching on the top.

Item	Size	Crystal	Crystal w/Etching
Cake stand		$95.00	$120.00
Butter dish	5¾" x 7¼"	40.00	65.00

Butter dish

SIX PANEL FINECUT

S

AKA: Daisy and Button Clear Stripes, Daisy with Amber Stripes.

Manufactured by: Dalzell, Leighton and Gilmore, 1888. This is a plain, but elegant pattern with the panels enhanced by amber stain. There is a plain gallery, and the pedestal is plain and very similar to those on plain salvers. See "Salvers, Plain" elsewhere in this book. The very attractive open compote has high and low scallops and the design is repeated on the base, which is so different from the cake stand. The covered compote is also enhanced with amber stain on both pieces, with the pattern repeated on the pedestal.

Item	Description	Size	Crystal	Amber Stain
Cake stand		7¼" x 7"	$100.00	$195.00
Compote		13" x 8¼"	70.00	100.00
	Covered	9" x 8¼"	125.00	225.00

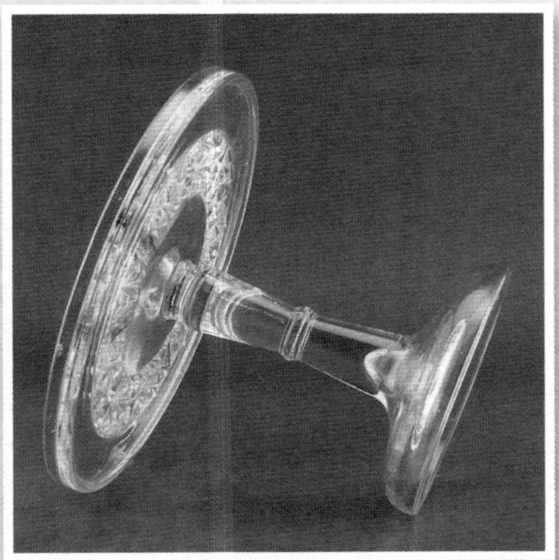

Pedestal

Top view of cake stand

Compote, covered

Compote, open

SKILTON

AKA: Early Oregon, Richards and Hartley's Oregon.

Manufactured by: Richards and Hartley Glass Company, Tarentum, Pennsylvania, ca. 1890. This bold pattern is greatly enhanced with ruby stain on the low standard compote.

Item	Description	Size	Crystal	Crystal w/Ruby
Cake stand			$175.00	$225.00
Compote	Open	7" x 4¾"	30.00	75.00

Compote

SLEWED HORSESHOE

OMN: United States Glass Nr 15111; AKA: Radiant Daisy, U. S. Peacock.

Manufactured by: United States Glass Company, Glassport, Pennsylvania, ca. 1908. This pattern looks like a horseshoe that is slightly askew, with what appears to be a shooting comet in the center of the horseshoe. Very elegant in gold trim.

Item	Description	Crystal	Crystal w/Gilding
Cake stand		$75.00	$85.00
Creamer	Berry	25.00	40.00
Sugar	Berry	25.00	45.00

Creamer and sugar

SNAIL

OMN: Duncan Nr 360 Ware; AKA: Compact, Double Snail, Idaho, Small Comet.

Manufactured by: George Duncan and Sons, Pittsburgh, Pennsylvania, ca. 1891. This pattern is aptly named with snails surrounding the bottom of the spooner.

Item	Size	Crystal	Crystal w/Ruby
Cake stand	9"	$150.00	
	10"	190.00	
Cake basket w/Pewter handle	9"	340.00	
	10"	360.00	
Spooner	3½" x 4¾"	55.00	$110.00

Spooner

SNOWFLAKE

OMN: Cambridge Nr 2635, Cambridge Snowflake, Snow-Flake, and Snowflake and Sunburst; AKA: Fernland – Toy Set.

Manufactured by: Cambridge Glass Company, ca 1906. The bowl is decorated in the center and in four panels around the bowl with snowflakes. The rim is scalloped.

Item	Size	Crystal
Cake stand	10" x 4¾"	$75.00
Child's creamer	3½" x 2¼"	35.00
Bowl		40.00

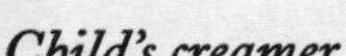

Child's creamer

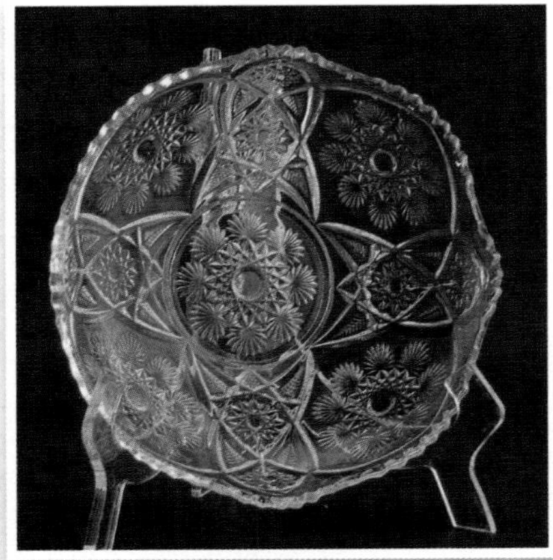

Bowl

SNOWFLOWER

OMN: United States Glass Nr 15135; AKA: Flower Fan.

Manufactured by: United States Glass Company, 1912. The clarity of this glass greatly enhances the Snowflower, which is comprised of six petals.

Butter dish

Item	Size	Crystal
Cake stand	9"	$65.00
	11"	85.00
Butter dish	8¼" x 5¾"	65.00

SPIRAL AND MALTESE CROSS

Manufactured by: Unknown, 1870s. Hard to distinguish in this pattern, but there is a Maltese Cross at the top of each panel. The spirals from the panels are repeated on the base.

Creamer

Item	Crystal	Amber
Cake stand	$60.00	$70.00
Creamer	35.00	40.00

SPIREA BAND

OMN: Earl; AKA: Nailhead Variant, Spirea, Square and Dot, Squared Dot.

Manufactured by: Bryce, Higbee and Company, Pittsburgh, Pennsylvania, ca. 1885. This pattern is very plain except for a band around the rim of the plate and surrounding the brandy well in the center. This pattern is very similar to Nr 6, one of the unidentified patterns. There is a plain gallery and pedestal.

Item	Size	Crystal	Amber	Blue	Vaseline
Cake stand	8"	$50.00	$60.00	$80.00	$100.00
	9"	60.00	70.00	95.00	115.00
	10"	70.00	80.00	110.00	125.00
	11"	90.00	95.00	140.00	150.00

Top view of cake stand

Pedestal

SPRIG

OMN: Bryce Royal; AKA: Indian Tree, Paneled Sprig.

Manufactured by: Bryce, Higbee and Company, Pittsburgh, Pennsylvania, ca. 1885. This cake stand has ten panels, with alternating panels containing a sprig of leaves and flowers. The pedestal is plain with descending rings down to the base.

Item	Size	Crystal
Cake stand	8"	$85.00
	9"	100.00
	10"	125.00
Compote (lid not shown)	7" x 6¾"	110.00

Top view of cake stand

Compote

S

SQUAT PINEAPPLE

AKA: Gem, Lone Star.

Manufactured by: McKee and Brothers, ca. 1898; National Glass, ca 1902; Federal Glass, ca 1914. One certainly could not derive the name from this pattern! This is a beautiful cake stand with deep, wide scallops.

Item	Size	Crystal	Green
Cake stand	8¾" x 4½"	$80.00	$95.00
Bowl	7½"	35.00	45.00

Stacked cake stands

Bowl

"S" RIB

Manufactured by: Dalzell, Gilmore and Leighton, 1889. The pedestal is comprised of several rings and the base has swirls that match the plate. There is a plain gallery with "ribs."

Item	Size	Crystal
Cake stand	9½" x 6½"	$80.00

Top view of cake stand

Pedestal

STARGLOW

OMN: United States Glass Nr 15120.

Manufactured by: United States Glass Company, Pittsburgh, Pennsylvania, ca. 1910. This is a very plain cake stand with six stars on the plate and a dainty scalloped gallery. The hollow pedestal has stars in alternating panels.

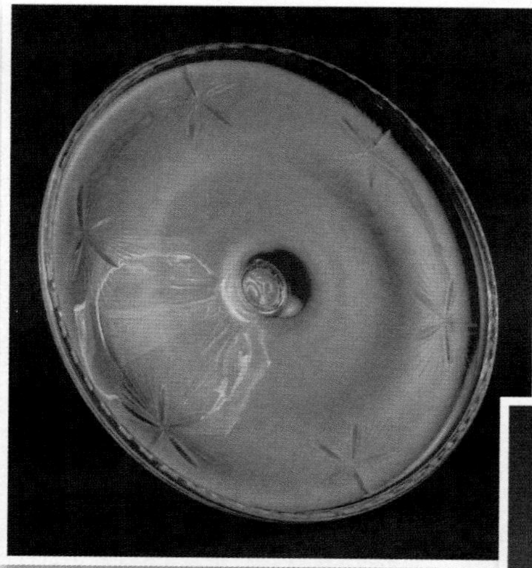

Top view of cake stand

Item	Size	Crystal
Cake stand	7"	$75.00
	8"	65.00
	9"	70.00
	10"	75.00
	11"	85.00
	12"	95.00

Pedestal

STAR IN A SQUARE

OMN: Duncan Nr 75; AKA: Star-in-Square.

Manufactured by: Duncan and Miller Company, ca. 1906. Aptly named, this is a truly elegant cake stand with a deep, scalloped skirt, which is gilded. The pattern is repeated on the pedestal.

Item	Size	Crystal	Crystal w/Gold
Cake stand	9½"	$110.00	$125.00

Pedestal

Top view of cake stand

STAR IN BULL'S EYE

OMN: United States Glass Nr 15092.

Manufactured by: United States Glass Company, Pittsburgh, Pennsylvania, ca 1905.

Item	Description	Size	Crystal
Cake stand			$90.00
Compote		6"	30.00
Pitcher	Water	½ gal.	65.00
Wine			25.00

Compote, interior

Wine

Pitcher

STAR IN DIAMOND

OMN: Gillander Nr 414; AKA: Barred Star, Spartan.

Manufactured by: Gillander and Sons, 1880s. The pattern is repeated on the pedestal and the base is paneled. There is a ¼" scalloped gallery.

Item	Size	Crystal
Cake stand	8¾" x 4¾"	$85.00

Top view of cake stand

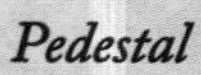

Pedestal

STAR OF DAVID

OMN: New Martinsville Nr 500, Wetzel.

Manufactured by: New Martinsville Glass Manufacturing Company, New Martinsville, West Virginia, 1905. The pattern derives its name from the star in the bottom of the bowl. Elegant pattern, especially trimmed in gold.

Item	Description	Size	Crystal	Crystal w/Gold
Cake stand			$150.00	
Bowl	Master berry	9¾" x 4½"	50.00	$65.00
	Berry		20.00	25.00

Bowls

STARRED BLOCK

AKA: Daisy and Button Petticoat, Daisy and Button with Petticoat Band, Daisy Band.

Manufactured by: Dalzell Brothers and Gilmore, ca 1885; Dalzell, Gilmore and Leighton, ca 1888. Found in Montgomery Ward catalog 1896. This stand can easily be confused with Pillow Encircled. On close examination, the gallery is plain, whereas the Pillow Encircled gallery has a design. The skirt flares out slightly beyond the gallery. Both cake stands have "arrows" radiating from the center of the plate; those on Starred Block are straight, while those on Pillow Encircled are curved. Both have deep brandy wells. Another pattern very similar to Starred Block is Daisy Band, featured in a wholesale house catalog dated 1886, with no manufacturer listed, and a cake plate was made with a wholesale price of fifty cents. Cake stand courtesy of John Nutter.

Item	Size	Crystal
Cake stand	10¼"	$225.00

Pedestal

Top view of cake stand

Top view Starred Block (left) and Pillow Encircled (right)

Side view Starred Block (left) and Pillow Encircled (right)

STARRED LOOP

OMN: Duncan Nr 45.

Manufactured by: George Duncan's Sons and Company, Washington, Pennsylvania, ca. 1895, and Duncan and Miller Glass Company, 1900. Wheat sheaves separate the four circles with stars encased. There is a scalloped skirt, and the pattern is repeated on the base.

Item	Size	Crystal
Cake stand	9¾"	$115.00

Top view of cake stand

Pedestal

STARS AND BARS

AKA: Daisy and Cube.

Manufactured by: Bellaire Goblet Company, 1890; and United States Glass Company, 1891. The cake stand is pictured in *Findlay Glass, The Glass Tableware Manufacturers, 1886 – 1902*, by James Measell and Don E. Smith.

Item	Description	Size	Crystal
Cake stand			$65.00
Compote	Covered	12" h x 7⅞"	65.00

Compote

STARS AND STRIPES

OMN: Kokomo Nr 209.

Manufactured by: Jenkins Glass Company, ca. 1899; Kokomo Glass Manufacturing Company, 1900; and Federal Glass Company, 1914. Pattern is alternating plain panels and panels with stars. Pattern is repeated on pedestal and base. There is a scalloped gallery.

Item	Size	Crystal
Cake stand	10"	$75.00

Pedestal

Top view of cake stand

THE STATES

OMN: United States Glass Nr 15093; AKA: Cane and Star Medallion.

Manufactured by: United States Glass Company, 1905. This pattern has alternating ovals with stars and cane. The butter dish is generously gilded.

Item	Size	Crystal	Crystal w/Gold
Cake stand		$75.00	$85.00
Bowl	4¼"	15.00	20.00
Butter dish	8¼" x 5"	95.00	110.00

Butter dish

Bowl

STERLING

AKA: Blazing Star, Pinwheels.

Manufactured by: Westmoreland Specialty Glass Company, 1896. This pattern is easily confused with Shoshone. In Shoshone the flowers are located at the point of the diamond; in Sterling, there are two flowers, top and bottom, between the diamonds. The pattern is repeated on the pedestal. The creamer and sugar originally had covers, which were interchangeable, and were made to contain their powdered (dry) mustard. There is a scalloped gallery and skirt.

Item	Size	Crystal
Cake stand	8¼" x 5¾"	$75.00
Creamer (no lid shown)	3¾" x 4¼"	65.00

Creamer

Top view of cake stand

Pedestal

STIPPLED BAR

OMN: United States Glass Nr 15044.

Manufactured by: United States Glass Company, 1895. This is an unusual cake stand with clear and stippled panels (bars). There are six clear bars radiating out from the center with serrated edges. The bars form a point on the underside of the plate, and extend about ½" beyond the edge of the plate. The round portion of the plate, with a gallery, is 8¾", and 9½" to the points of the bars. The stippled panels have ½" clear bars angled across. The stippled pattern is repeated on the base. The pedestal consists of six panels with serrated edges. The bottom edge of the plate, the extended edges, and the base are beaded. Very clear glass.

Item	Size	Crystal
Cake stand	9½" x 6¼"	$75.00
Fruit dish		20.00

Cake stand and fruit dish

Cake stand

STIPPLED FORGET-ME-NOT

AKA: Dot, Forget-Me-Not in Snow.

Manufactured by: Findlay Flint Glass Company, Findlay, Ohio, ca. 1890s. The surface of the plate is divided into four sections with sprays of forget-me-nots. Bars surround the rim of the plate, extending above and below the edge creating the gallery and skirt. The base also has bars.

Item	Size	Crystal
Cake stand	9"	$120.00
	10"	135.00
	12"	280.00

Top view of cake stand

Pedestal

SUNBEAM

Manufactured by: McKee and Brothers, 1898. This pattern is made in extended table service in crystal as well as emerald green. The vase and one plate are gilded. Note that the corners on the plate on the left have been turned in to make it appear round instead of square like the plate on the right.

Item	Size	Crystal
Cake stand	9¼"	$110.00
Plate	7"	35.00
Vase	6"	35.00

Vase and plates

SUNK DAISY

AKA: Daisy Coop, Kirkland, Sunken Daisy.

Manufactured by: Cooperative Flint Glass Company, 1896. This pattern comes in two variations; the first one shown is smaller with scalloped edges and the pattern is repeated on the pedestal and base. The second one has a slightly raised gallery and a scalloped skirt. A cake stand was for sale on an internet auction with red and blue dots that appeared to have been applied after market, as it was a very sloppy job of staining.

Item	Size	Crystal Gallery	Crystal Scalloped
Cake stand	8¾" x 3½"		$75.00
	9" x 6"	$95.00	
	10"	115.00	65.00
	11"		85.00

Stacked cake stands

Pedestal

Top view of cake stand

SUNK DIAMOND AND LATTICE

OMN: McKee Nr 900; AKA: National 900.

Manufactured by: McKee Glass Company, 1902.

Pitcher

Item	Crystal
Cake stand	$85.00
Pitcher	70.00

SURPRISE

Manufactured by: Bryce, Higbee Company, 1897. The only reference to this pattern is in *Bryce, Higbee and J. B. Higbee Glass* by Lola and Wayne Higby. They only have reference for three pieces, and indicate the pattern is rare. There is a slightly scalloped gallery. There is a pattern on the pedestal and base but it does not match the plate pattern.

Item	Size	Crystal
Cake stand	9½" x 5½"	$65.00

Top view of cake stand

Pedestal

SWAN

AKA: Plain Swan, Swan with Mesh.

Manufactured by: Canton Glass Company, 1882. A beautiful, long necked swan graces the center medallion on this two-handled spooner.

Item	Crystal
Cake stand	$275.00
Spooner	80.00

Spooner

SYLVAN

OMN: Fostoria 1119; AKA: English Hobnail Variant, Overall Diamond.

Manufactured by: Fostoria Glass Company, Moundsville, West Virginia, 1902. The picture tells it all — this is a gorgeous pattern generously gilded on the rim and finial.

Item	Description	Crystal
Cake stand		$75.00
Sugar	Covered, gold trim	65.00

Sugar

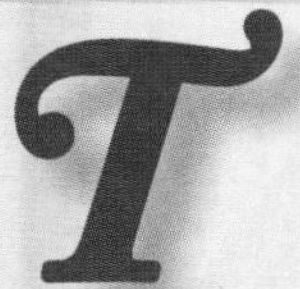

TARENTUM'S ATLANTA

AKA: Diamond and Teardrop, Royal Crystal, Shining Diamonds.

Manufactured by: Tarentum Glass Company, Tarentum, Pennsylvania, 1894. This is a very ornate cake stand. The pattern is repeated on the pedestal and base.

Item	Size	Crystal	Crystal w/Ruby
Cake stand	9"	$75.00	$165.00
	9¼"	85.00	190.00
	10"	110.00	250.00

Pedestal

Top view of cake stand

TARENTUM'S MANHATTAN

Manufactured by: Tarentum Glass Company, Tarentum, Pennsylvania, ca 1895. This is a very scarce pattern — the only cake stand in this pattern seen by the author. A truly magnificent size, it has a large scalloped gallery and a smaller scalloped skirt. The pattern, which resembles triangular saw blades, is repeated on the pedestal and base. There is a wide, deep brandy well. Thanks to Cindy Johnson for sharing this picture.

Item	Size	Crystal
Cake stand	10" x 6"	$175.00

Top view of cake stand

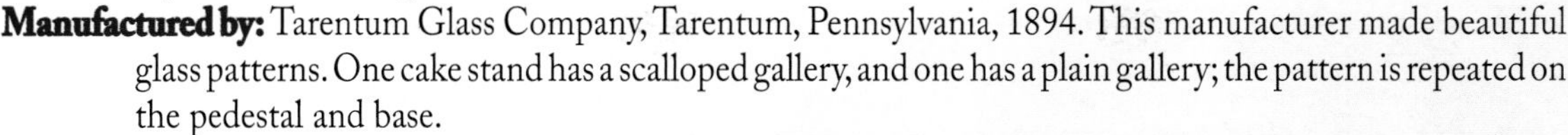

T

TARENTUM'S VIRGINIA

AKA: Many Diamonds, Virginia's Tarentum.

Manufactured by: Tarentum Glass Company, Tarentum, Pennsylvania, 1894. This manufacturer made beautiful glass patterns. One cake stand has a scalloped gallery, and one has a plain gallery; the pattern is repeated on the pedestal and base.

Item	Size	Crystal
Cake stand	10"	$80.00
Bowl	9½"	40.00

Top view of cake stand

Pedestal

Stacked cake stands

Cake stand and bowl

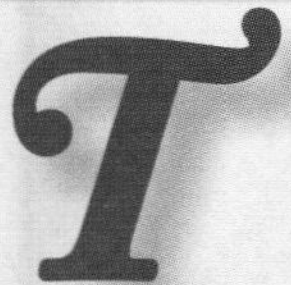

TAUNTON

AKA: Salient-Star, Scroll (O'Hara), Slashed Swirl Border.

Manufactured by: O'Hara Glass Company, Ltd, 1889. Beautiful clear glass, this pattern is a twisted rope around the rim and base of the bowl, as well as base of pedestal. The interior is similar to "S" Rib pattern.

Item	Size	Crystal
Cake stand		$90.00
Compote	11" x 7"	100.00

Compote

Compote, top removed

TEAR DROP AND TASSEL

AKA: Sampson.

Manufactured by: Indiana Tumbler and Goblet, 1900. An easy pattern to recognize as it is aptly named. Note the tiny beads on the rims.

Bowls

Item	Description	Size	Crystal
Cake stand			$175.00
Bowl	Sauce	4"	25.00

TEASEL

OMN: Bryce Nr 87; AKA: Short Teasel.

Manufactured by: Bryce Brothers Glass Company, ca. 1880s.

Item	Crystal
Cake stand	$55.00
Sugar (no lid shown)	40.00

Sugar

T

TEEPEE

OMN: Duncan Nr 128 – Arizona; AKA: Nemesis, Wigwam.

Manufactured by: George Duncan's Sons and Company, Washington, Pennsylvania, ca. 1896. It's easy to see how this pattern got its name, as six teepees are pictured on the top. This cake stand has a scalloped gallery.

Item	Description	Size	Crystal
Cake stand		9½" x 5"	$85.00
Nappy			30.00
	Handled		35.00
Biscuit/cracker		4¼" x 7½"	90.00

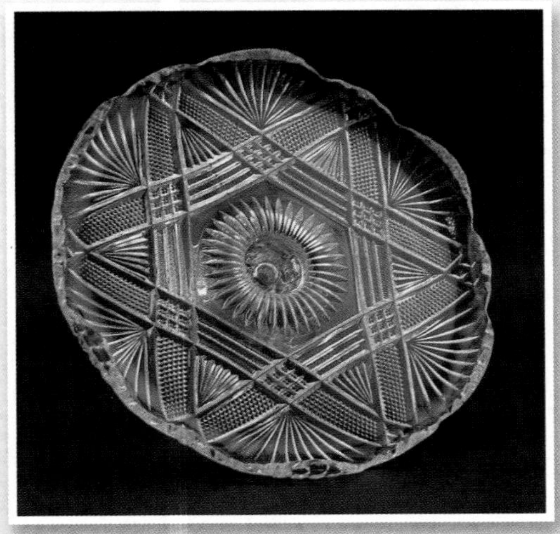

Top view of cake stand

Pedestal

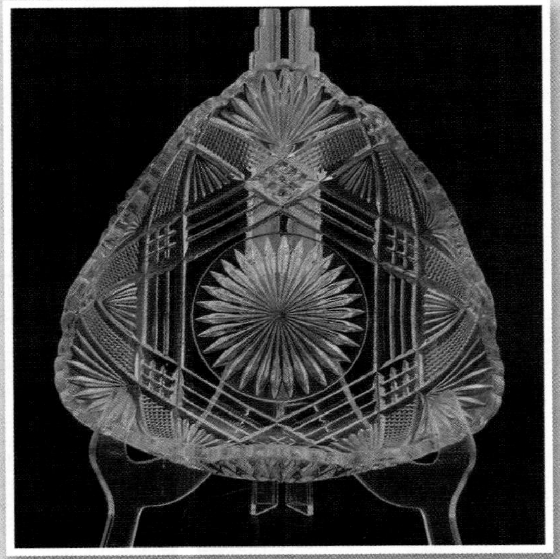

Nappy

Biscuit/cracker

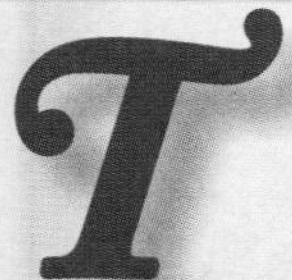

TENNESSEE

OMN: United States Glass Nr 15064 – Tennessee; AKA: Jewel and Crescent, Jeweled Rose(s), Scrolls with Bull's Eye.

Manufactured by: United States Glass Company, Pittsburgh, Pennsylvania, ca 1899. Very few pieces are seen in this pattern. This is the seventeenth in the "state series" patterns. This pattern has a scalloped gallery. The same scallops in the center of the plate are repeated on the pedestal.

Item	Size	Crystal
Cake stand	8½"	$75.00
	9½"	85.00
	10½"	125.00

Top view of cake stand

Pedestal

TEUTONIC

AKA: IHC, Long Star.

Manufactured by: McKee and Brothers Company, Jeannette, Pennsylvania, 1894. These four cake stands have similar patterns on the top, with different skirts, galleries, and pedestals. See the picture showing all four.

Top view of cake stand, plain rim

Item	Description	Size	Crystal
Cake stand	Scalloped rim	9"	$55.00
	Scalloped skirt	9¼"	70.00
	Plain rim	11"	65.00
	Serrated edge	11"	80.00
Celery tray	Scalloped edge	9½"	30.00

Top view of cake stand, serrated edge

Pedestal

Top view of cake stand, skirted, gallery

Top view of cake stand, serrated edge

Pedestal

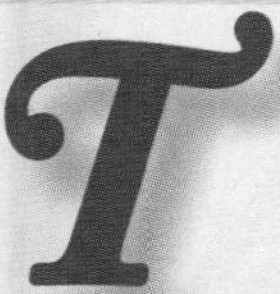

Cake stands, side by side

Three cake stands

Four cake stands

Celery tray

TEXAS

OMN: United States Glass Nr 15067 – Texas; AKA: Loop with Stippled Panels.
Manufactured by: United States Glass Company, ca. 1900. This is the twentieth in the "state series" patterns, and has been heavily reproduced.

Item	Description	Size	Crystal	Crystal w/Rose Blush
Cake stand	w/Galleried rim	9"	$160.00	$335.00
		9½"	175.00	350.00
		10"	215.00	375.00
		10½"	275.00	440.00
		11"	350.00	575.00
Sugar	Individual		40.00	75.00
	Table		160.00	295.00

Top view of cake stand

Pedestal

Sugar

TEXAS BULL'S-EYE

AKA: Bulls-Eye Variant, Filley, Notched Bull's Eye.
Manufactured by: Bryce Brothers, Pittsburgh, Pennsylvania, ca 1875 – 1880; A. J. Beatty and Sons, Steubenville, Ohio, ca 1888. The high standard cake stand is considered very rare. Celery courtesy of Carolyn Crozier.

Item	Size	Crystal
Cake stand		$185.00
Celery	4" x 8¾"	50.00

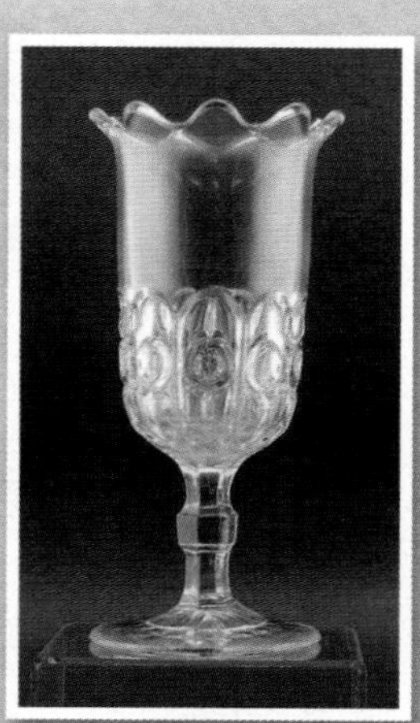

Celery

THREE FACE

OMN: Duncan Nr 400; AKA: The Sisters, Three Fates, Three Graces, Three Sisters.

Manufactured by: George Duncan and Sons, ca. 1878. This is a beautiful cake stand with a perfectly plain top with an extended scalloped skirt. The beauty is in the pedestal. The cake stand, compote, and many other pieces were reproduced. Some reproduced pieces are clearly marked with "MMA" – Metropolitan Museum of Art. The pattern is easily recognized with the faces midway down the pedestal. If found without frosted base, reduce the value by 25%. Note the detail in the hair in the close-up of the pedestal. The plain plate surface, skirt, and base are similar to Tree of Life with Hand, made by the same manufacturer.

Item	Description	Size	Crystal w/Frosting
Cake stand		8"	$550.00
		9"	375.00
		10¼"	425.00
		11"	555.00
Compote		6"	110.00
Creamer	w/Face	5½" x 6¾"	175.00
	w/o Face		275.00

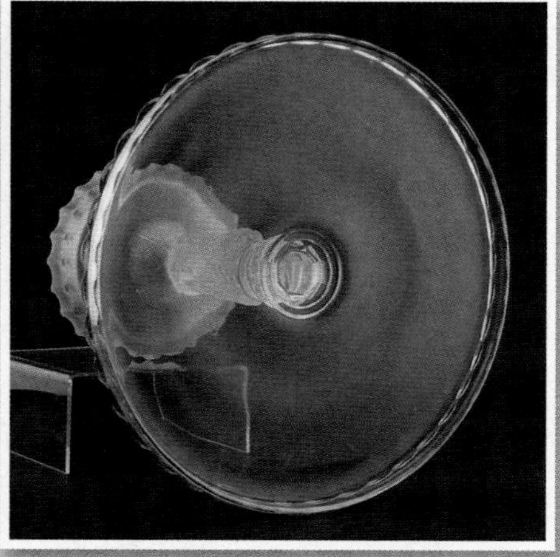

Top view of cake stand

Pedestal

Close-up of face on pedestal

Compote

Creamer

THREE-IN-ONE

OMN: Imperial Nr 1; AKA: Fancy Diamonds.

Manufactured by: Imperial Glass Company, Bellaire, Ohio, 1902. Usually you see how a pattern derived its name; not true, in this case. There is a scalloped skirt and plain gallery. A row of diamonds is on the outer rim of the plate, with a smaller row in the center surrounding the brandy well, with panels connecting the two rows. There is a band of diamonds at the top of the hollow pedestal and panels travel down the pedestal to a row of diamonds on the base.

Item	Size	Crystal
Cake stand	8"	$75.00
	9"	85.00
	10"	95.00
	13"	110.00
Butter dish (lid only)	6" x 5½"	80.00

Cake stand

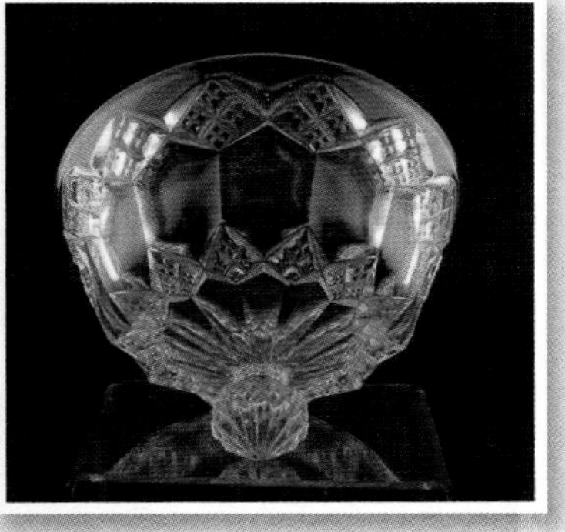

Butter dish

Pedestal

THUMBPRINT

Manufactured by: Unknown. The skirt on this cake stand has open scallops, which make it difficult to find it in perfect condition. No record of this pattern has been found, so the name may not be correct. This is an extremely heavy cake stand of thick glass with a massive pedestal with thumbprints on the pedestal and base.

Item	Crystal
Cake stand	$65.00

Pedestal

Cake stand

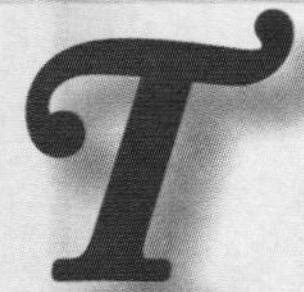

TORPEDO

OMN: Thompson Nr 17; AKA: Fisheye, Pigmy.

Manufactured by: Thompson Glass Company, ca. 1889 – 1893. This is an unusual pattern which is repeated on the hollow pedestal and base. There is a plain gallery. Pieces found in black amethyst or any other color would be considered rare.

Item	Description	Size	Crystal
Cake stand		9¼" x 6¼"	$180.00
		10"	210.00
Compote	Covered	7" x 13"	125.00

Compote

Top view of cake stand

Pedestal

TREE OF LIFE WITH HAND

Manufactured by: George A. Duncan and Sons, Pittsburgh, Pennsylvania, 1885. It has been difficult to determine the manufacturer. This is an outstanding cake stand that glows beautifully under a black light. The pedestal and base are clear, whereas all others seen have a frosted pedestal and base (as does the compote shown). The pedestal is stippled, with dainty double chains traveling up and down, and it is encircled with very feminine fingers. Where the pedestal joins the base, the same little double chains encircle the pedestal, separated by tiny grooves. The cake stand has a ½" gallery, which is plain, while the ½" skirt is scalloped. It is easy to see how the pattern got its name when you see the bowl of the open compote, which is in the Tree of Life pattern. The pedestal and base of the compote are frosted. Except for the pedestal, this is very similar to Three Face, made by the same manufacturer.

Item	Description	Size	Crystal	Crystal w/Frosting
Cake stand		10"	$300.00	$325.00
Compote	Open	10" x 10"	110.00	135.00

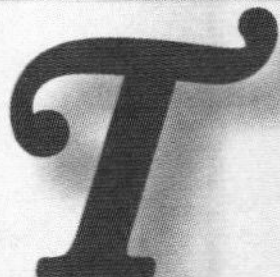

Pedestal

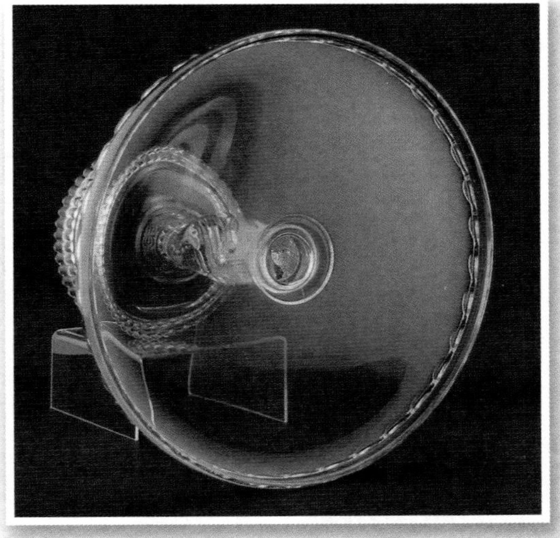
Top view of cake stand

Compote

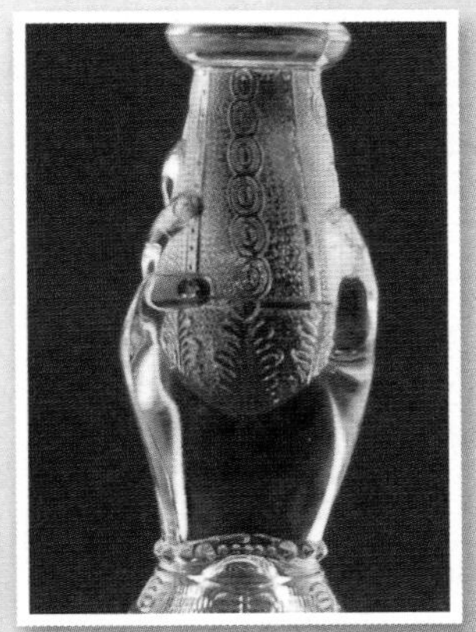
Close-up of pedestal

TRUMP

AKA: Mitered Prisms.
Manufactured by: Model Flint Glass Company, Findlay, Ohio, 1891.

Item	Size	Crystal
Cake stand	9"	$175.00
Spooner	6" x 4¼"	50.00

Spooner

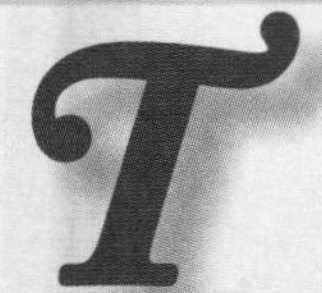

TRUNCATED CUBE

Manufactured by: Thompson Glass Nr 77, 1894. At first glance, this looks like Crystal Wedding. Courtesy of Ed and Sally Reid.

Item	Crystal
Cake stand	$195.00
Banana stand	175.00

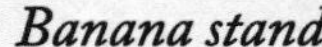

Banana stand

TWIN SNOWSHOES

OMN: United States Glass Nr 15139; AKA: Sunbeam.
Manufactured by: United States Glass Company, ca 1918. It is easy to see how this pattern got its name. Courtesy of Carolyn Crozier.

Item	Description	Size	Crystal
Cake stand			$65.00
Creamer	Individual	2½" x 3⅛"	35.00

Creamer

TWIN TEARDROPS

AKA: Anona.
Manufactured by: Bryce, Higbee and Company, ca 1905; J. B. Higbee Glass Company, ca 1907. There is a scalloped gallery. The pattern is repeated on the pedestal and base.

Item	Size	Crystal
Cake stand	9½"	$55.00
Cake plate	10½"	65.00
Celery vase	6"	55.00

Pedestal

Celery vase

Top view of cake stand

TWO PANEL

AKA: Daisy in Panel, Daisy in the Square.
Manufactured by: Richards and Hartley Glass Company, Tarentum, Pennsylvania, ca 1880s.

Item	Crystal
Cake stand	$125.00
Pitcher	70.00

Pitcher

TWO-PLY SWIRL

OMN: Duncan Nr 51.
Manufactured by: Duncan and Miller Glass Company, 1902. There is a plain gallery and scalloped skirt, and the pedestal is twisted.

Item	Size	Crystal
Cake stand	9½"	$70.00

Pedestal

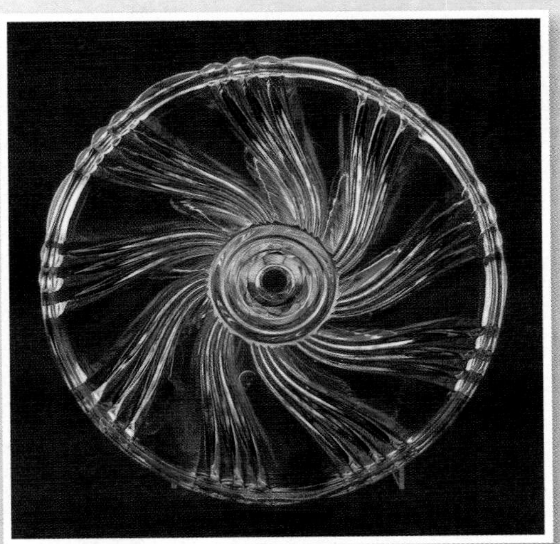

Top view of cake stand

UNIQUE

Manufactured by: Cooperative Flint Glass, 1898. This is a pretty cake stand with six large petals on the top of the plate, a scalloped skirt, and plain gallery. The pattern is repeated on the pedestal and base.

Item	Size	Crystal
Cake stand	10¼" x 5¾"	$175.00

Top view of cake stand

Pedestal

UNITED STATES COIN

OMN: United States Glass Nr 15005; AKA: American Coin, Coin (Dime), Coin (Half Dollar), Frosted Coin, Silver Age, The Silver Age.

Manufactured by: United States Glass Company, Pittsburgh, Pennsylvania, at Factory "H" and Factory "G," ca 1892. This pretty cake stand has a scalloped gallery with pictures of coins on the plate. Courtesy of Grace Guido.

Item	Size	Crystal	Crystal w/Frosting
Cake stand	10"	$425.00	$625.00

Top view of cake stand

UTAH

OMN: United States Glass 15080 – Utah; AKA: Frost(ed) Flower, Starlight, Twinkle Star.

Manufactured by: United States Glass Company, 1903. This is a very plain pattern with the dainty stars being the only decoration. This is the thirty-second in the "state series" of patterns. A rather plain pattern with dainty stars scattered over the surface of the plate.

Item	Size	Crystal High Standard	Crystal Low Standard
Cake stand	7"	$100.00	
	9"	125.00	$100.00
	10"	175.00	150.00
	11"		160.00

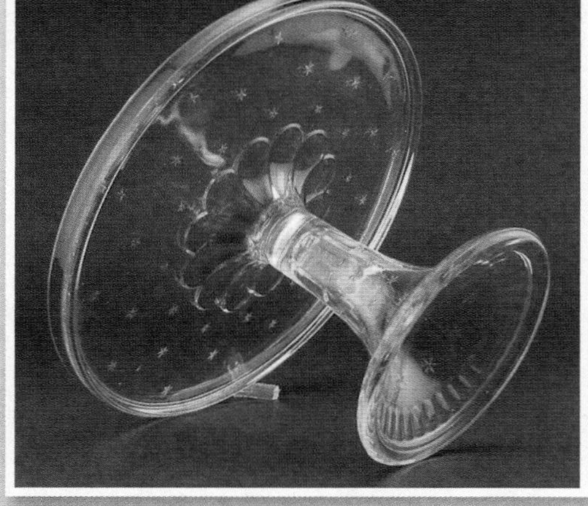

Cake stand

VALENCIA WAFFLE

OMN: Adams Nr 85; AKA: Block and Star, Hexagonal Block.

Manufactured by: Adams and Company, Pittsburgh, Pennsylvania, ca. 1885. This square pattern is decorated on the four corners of the hollow pedestal and square base.

Item	Description	Size	Crystal	Amber	Blue	Vaseline	Apple Green
Cake stand	Square	10"	$90.00	$120.00	$170.00	$200.00	$240.00
Compote	Covered (no lid shown)	8" x 8"	95.00	110.00	125.00	150.00	170.00

Pedestal

Compote, amber

VALENTINE

AKA: Northwood Nr 14.

Manufactured by: Northwood Glass Company, 1906. A beautiful scalloped bowl with valentines (hearts).

Item	Description	Size	Crystal
Cake plate		10"	$65.00
Bowl	Berry		40.00

Bowl

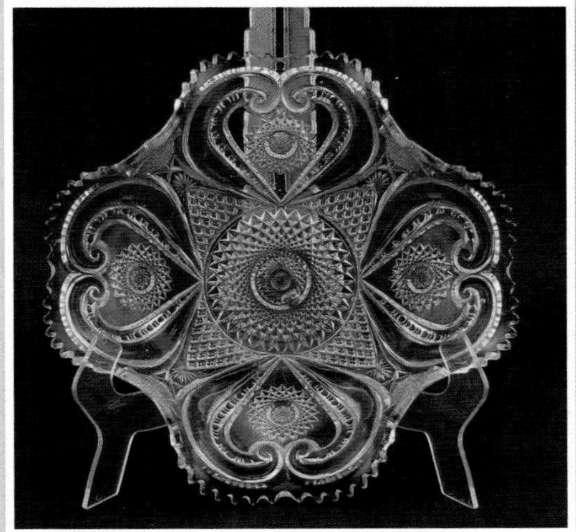

VALTEC

Manufactured by: McKee Glass Company, ca 1894. Like most cake stands, this has a scalloped gallery. The pedestal is plain with bars radiating out from the center of the base.

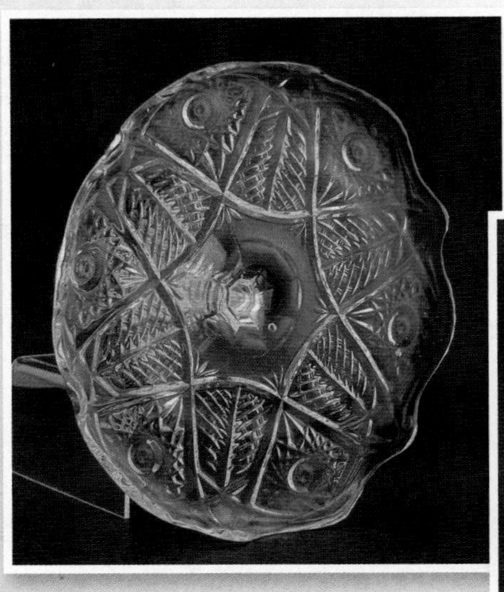

Top view of cake stand

Item	Size	Crystal
Cake stand	9"	$55.00
	10"	60.00

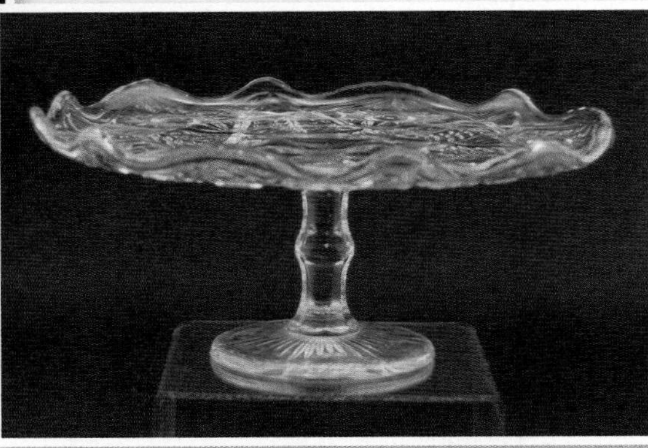

Pedestal

VIKING

OMN: Hobbs' Centennial; AKA: Bearded Head, Bearded Prophet, Old Man of the Mountain(s).

Manufactured by: Hobbs, Brockunier and Company, 1876. Easily identified by the bearded head on the pouring spout of the creamer. It rests on three feet.

Item	Crystal
Creamer	$110.00

Creamer

V-IN-HEART

Manufactured by: Bryce, Higbee and Company, ca. 1895.

Item	Size	Crystal
Cake stand	9½"	$60.00

Pedestal

Top view of cake stand

VIRGINIA

OMN: United States Glass Nr 15071 – Virginia; AKA: Banded Portland, Diamond Banded Portland, Maiden's Blush, Portland with Diamond Point Band.

Manufactured by: United States Glass Company, Pittsburgh, Pennsylvania, at Factories "G", "U," and "E," ca. 1901. This is the twenty-fourth in the "state series" patterns. Increase the value of pieces that are entirely flashed as is the toothpick pictured. Add 25% more for gilded items. Tankard courtesy of Patrick Ennis Marshall; toothpick courtesy of Sean Curtis Marshall; vase courtesy of Camille Virginia Marshall.

Item	Description	Size	Crystal	Crystal w/Rose Blush
Cake stand		10"	$110.00	$275.00
Creamer	Individual, oval		20.00	65.00
	Tankard		35.00	80.00
Olive dish			15.00	40.00
Syrup (lid not shown)			90.00	340.00
Toothpick			30.00	75.00
Vase	Short foot	6"	25.00	55.00

Syrup

Vase, creamer, and celery

Crystal with ruby flash tankard, toothpick, and vase

WASHINGTON (U.S. GLASS)

OMN: United States Glass Nr 15074; AKA: Beaded Base, Late Washington.

Manufactured by: United States Glass Company at Factory "F" and "K," Pittsburgh, Pennsylvania. This is the twenty-seventh in the "state series" patterns.

Item	Size	Crystal
Cake stand		$55.00
Sugar	4¼" x 7³⁄₁₆"	140.00

Sugar

WASHINGTON CENTENNIAL

AKA: Chain with Diamonds.
Manufactured by: Gillander and Sons, 1886.

Top view of cake stand

Item	Size	Crystal
Cake stand	8¼" x 5"	$160.00

Pedestal

WAVERLY

Manufactured by: Westmoreland Specialty Glass Company, Grapeville, Pennsylvania, 1896.

Item	Size	Crystal
Cake plate	9"	$35.00

Cake plate

WELLSBURG

OMN: Dalzell Nr 81; AKA: Daphne.
Manufactured by: Dalzell, Gilmore and Leighton, 1899; and National Glass Company, 1901. The pattern is alternating plain panels and panels with ovals, which are beaded on each side. The panel with ovals forms a scalloped gallery. The pattern on the plate is repeated down the hollow pedestal to the base. This pattern is similar to Broken Column and Nelly.

Item	Size	Crystal
Cake stand	11½" x 5½"	$85.00

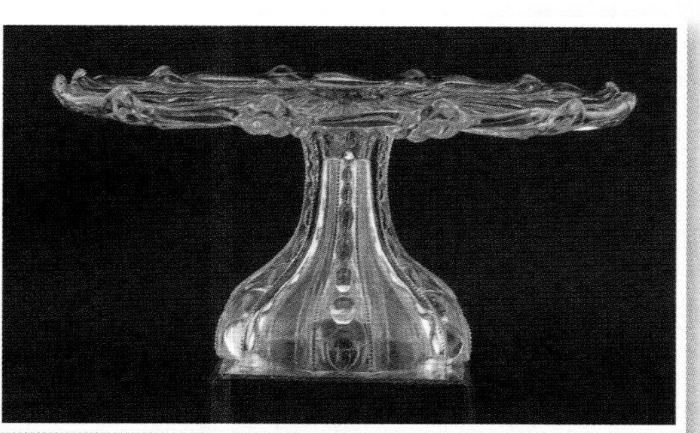

Pedestal

Top view of cake stand

WESTMORELAND NR 98

AKA: Late Westmoreland, New Westmoreland.

Manufactured by: Westmoreland Specialty Glass Company, ca 1898. This is a spectacular pattern; one of the most ornate patterns made. The pedestal and base are hollow. This pattern comes in two different styles: the one pictured which is scalloped, and one with a round edge, with a gallery.

Item	Size	Crystal
Cake stand	10½" x 5½"	$195.00
Banana stand	10" x 8¾"	180.00
Compote	9" x 8¾"	125.00

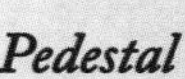

Pedestal

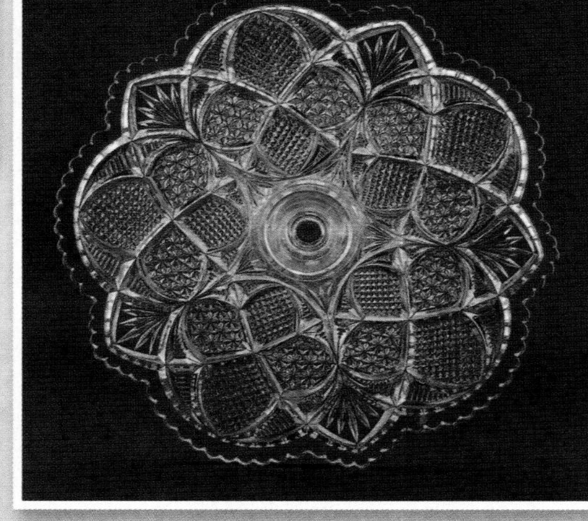

Top view of cake stand

Banana stand

Compote

WHEAT AND BARLEY

OMN: Duquesne; AKA: Hops and Barley, Oats and Barley.
Manufactured by: Bryce Brothers, Pittsburgh, Pennsylvania, ca. 1880s. Creamer courtesy of Carolyn Crozier.

Item	Size	Crystal	Amber	Blue	Canary
Cake stand	8"	$60.00	$70.00	$90.00	$100.00
	9"	67.00	80.00	110.00	130.00
	10"	95.00	120.00	150.00	160.00
Sugar (no lid shown)		80.00	90.00	110.00	125.00
Creamer	5" x 5"	65.00	65.00	85.00	95.00

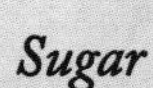

Sugar

Creamer

WHEAT SHEAF

Manufactured by: Unknown.

Item	Crystal
Bowl	$35.00

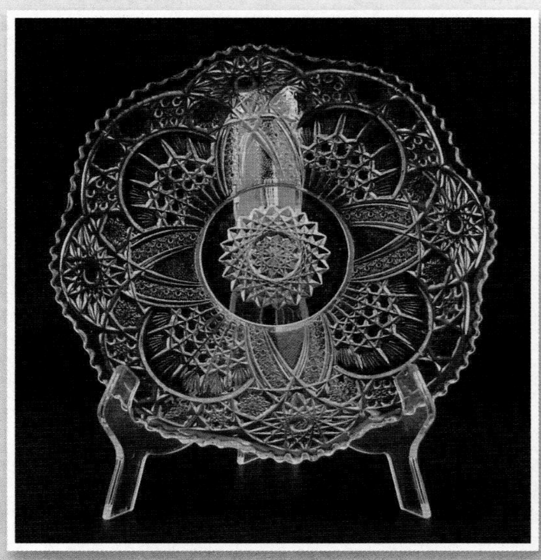

Bowl

WILDFLOWER

OMN: Adams Nr 140.
Manufactured by: Adams and Company, ca. 1874. This cake stand may have originally had a cover, as the scalloped edge extends beyond a small, plain gallery. A circle of wildflowers decorates the top of the plate and a circle of stars surrounds a portion of the pedestal. The base is panelled with scallops.

Item	Size	Crystal	Amber	Blue	Canary	Apple Green
Cake stand	10"	$145.00	$130.00	$195.00	$230.00	$230.00

Pedestal

Top view of cake stand

WILLOW OAK

OMN: Bryce Wreath; AKA: Acorn, Acorn and Oak Leaf, Oak Leaf, Stippled Daisy, Stippled Star, Thistle and Sunflower, Willow and Oak.

Manufactured by: Bryce Brothers, Pittsburgh, Pennsylvania, ca. late 1880s. The plate is divided into wide and narrow panels.

Item	Size	Crystal	Amber	Blue	Canary Yellow
Cake stand	8½"	$60.00	$80.00	$100.00	$115.00
	9"	70.00	100.00	125.00	150.00
	10"	75.00	110.00	140.00	175.00

Top view of cake stand

WILTEC

Manufactured by: McKee Glass Company, Jeannette, Pennsylvania, 1904.

Item	Crystal
Cake stand	$40.00
Sugar (no lid shown)	75.00

Sugar

WINGED SCROLL

OMN: Heisey Nr 1280.

Manufactured by: A. H. Heisey Glass Company, Newark, Ohio, ca 1899. This pattern is called Ivorina Verde when produced in custard glass.

Item	Size	Crystal	Green/Blue	Custard
Cake salver		$140.00	$275.00	$275.00
Cake basket		250.00	500.00	500.00
Butter dish	4¾" x 7½"	100.00	175.00	175.00

Butter dish

WISCONSIN

OMN: United States Glass Nr 15079 – Wisconsin; AKA: Beaded Dewdrop, Prism.

Manufactured by: United States Glass Company, ca. 1903. This is the thirty-first of the "state series" patterns. There is a beaded gallery. The pattern is comprised of beaded oval panels divided by teardrop designs. The pedestal is very unusual with beaded ovals; the pattern is repeated on the base.

Item	Size	Crystal
Cake stand	6½"	$75.00
	8½"	85.00
	9½"	100.00
	11½"	175.00

Pedestal

Top view of cake stand

WYOMING

OMN: United States Glass Nr 15081 – Wyoming; AKA: Bull's Eye, Enigma.

Manufactured by: United States Glass Company, Pittsburgh, Pennsylvania, at Factories "U" and "E," ca. 1903. This is the thirty-third pattern in the "state series." This pattern is easily identified by pictures of owls on the outer edge of the cake plate and pedestal. There is a scalloped gallery.

Item	Size	Crystal
Cake stand	9"	$95.00
	10"	110.00
	11"	140.00

Top view of cake stand

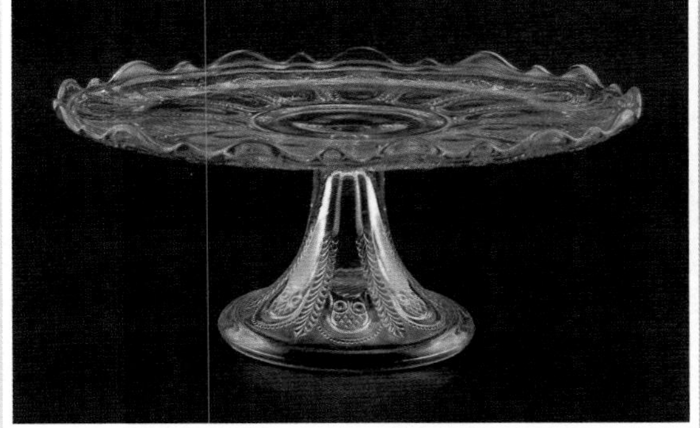

Pedestal

X-BULL'S EYE

AKA: Summit.

Manufactured by: Thompson Glass Company, Uniontown, Pennsylvania, 1889 – 1898. Alternating panels cover the top of the plate, narrow panels have four stars each; the other panels have stylistic arrows and bull's eyes. There is a scalloped gallery. The pattern is repeated on the base. Cake stand courtesy of Carolyn Crozier.

Item	Size	Crystal
Cake stand	10"	$55.00

Top view of cake stand

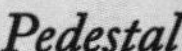

Pedestal

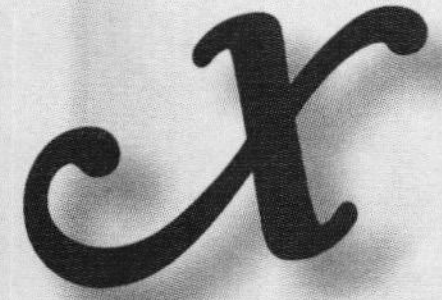

X-LOGS

AKA: Crossed Logs, Diamonds in Ovals, Prism Arc.
Manufactured by: Unknown, ca. 1880s.

Item	Description	Size	Crystal
Cake stand			$55.00
Bowl	Oval	8"	20.00
Relish		9"	15.00

Bowl and relish

X-RAY

Manufactured by: Riverside Glass Works, Wellsburg, West Virginia, ca. 1896. Although no information can be found on a cake salver, *Riverside Glass Works of Wellsburg, WV 1879 – 1907* by C. W. Gorham indicates that a cake salver was probably made.

Item	Size	Crystal	Amethyst	Emerald Green
Cake salver		$80.00	$225.00	$150.00
Butter dish	7¾" x 5¼"	70.00	185.00	130.00

Butter dish

Y

YALE

AKA: Crow Feet.

Manufactured by: McKee and Brothers, Pittsburgh, Pennsylvania, ca 1880s. Aptly named, this is also known as Crow Feet, which appear all over the plate. There is a plain gallery and extended scalloped edge, which may have originally accommodated a cover. The tall pedestal is plain, and the pattern is repeated on the base.

Item	Size	Crystal
Cake stand	10"	$65.00

Pedestal

Top view of cake stand

YUTEC

Manufactured by: McKee Brothers, ca 1909. This ornate cake stand has a scalloped gallery and a very wide hollow base.

Item	Size	Crystal
Cake stand	10¼" x 4½"	$65.00

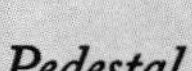

Pedestal

Top view of cake stand

ZIPPER CROSS

OMN: Paris; AKA: New Martinsville Nr 110, Roughneck.

Manufactured by: Bryce, Higbee and Company, 1899 – 1907; J. B. Higbee Glass Company, ca 1907; New Martinsville Glass Manufacturing Company, ca 1907. Pictured in Montgomery Ward catalog in 1900. This cake stand is scalloped with rows of "zippers" radiating from the center, with alternating plain panels. The pedestal and base have the same design as the top.

Item	Description	Size	Crystal
Cake stand		10"	$65.00
Banana stand	Child's	5¾" x 4½"	55.00
Celery vase			45.00

Child's banana stand

Pedestal

Banana stand and celery vase

Unidentified Patterns

We have been unable to identify these cake stands, but hope that you will be able to identify some or all of those listed. The value assigned is based on prices for comparable cake stands.

We may be contacted at:

Bettye James: bettye.james@verizon.net
Danny Cornelius: dndeapg@hughes.net

1 A cake stand from a three-part mold, the only design on this 9" cake stand is a "berry" type pattern consisting of seven berry seeds. This may be of English origin, as one was seen on the internet from England.

Item	Crystal
Cake stand	$35.00
Compote	25.00

Compote and pedestal

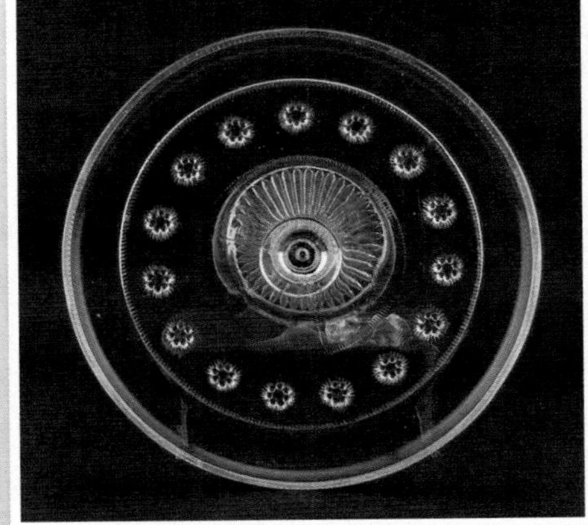

Cake stand

2 This dainty little cake stand is 8½" x 4" at the tallest scallop on the gallery. There are eight daisy and button panels divided by plain panels. The base of the pedestal is 4¼" and the pedestal has eight panels.

Item	Crystal
Cake stand	$45.00

Cake stand

Pedestal

3 The identity of this cake stand with buttons and petals is elusive. It stands 5" tall with a diameter of 11". The plate has a scalloped gallery, the pedestal is plain, and the 4¼" base has arrows (points) radiating from the center. It fluoresces under a black light.

Cake stand

ITEM	CRYSTAL
Cake stand	$65.00

Pedestal

4 This open compote with oval lens design should be identifiable; however, I have been unsuccessful. A cake stand in this pattern sold on a popular internet site in 2003, but was not identified. This pattern also comes with etching in the oval panels.

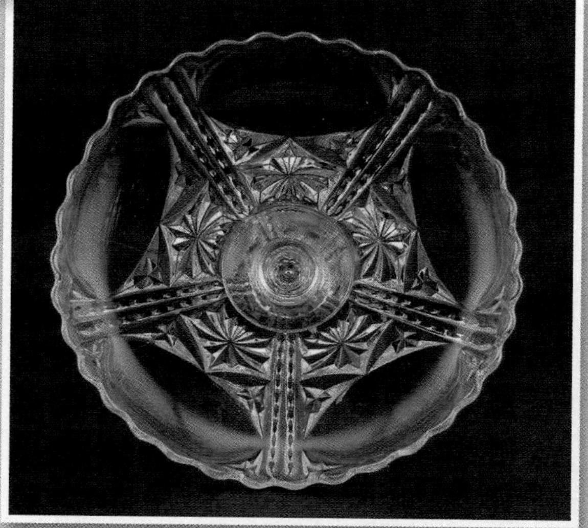

Compote interior

ITEM	CRYSTAL
Cake stand	$45.00
Compote	35.00

Pedestal

5

This dainty cake stand is 8" x 5". The approximate ½" gallery is pleated, while the base of the pedestal is scalloped. There are three long rays emanating from the center to the edge, with shorter rays in between that continue down into the pedestal about ¾" to a ring, with the remainder of the pedestal being plain until the scallops form. Each scallop has two rays.

Item	Crystal
Cake stand	$35.00

Pedestal

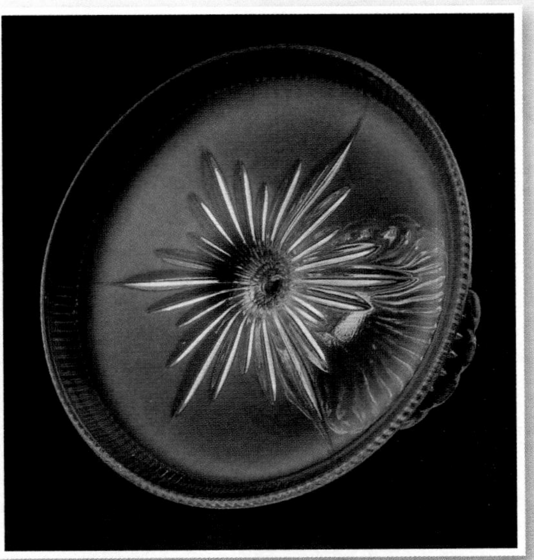

Cake stand

6

A most unusual cake stand — round with square blocks with stars and diamonds with crosses. There is a plain gallery. The pedestal base is rectangular.

Item	Size	Crystal
Cake stand	10¼" x 5¾"	$185.00
Celery		65.00

Celery

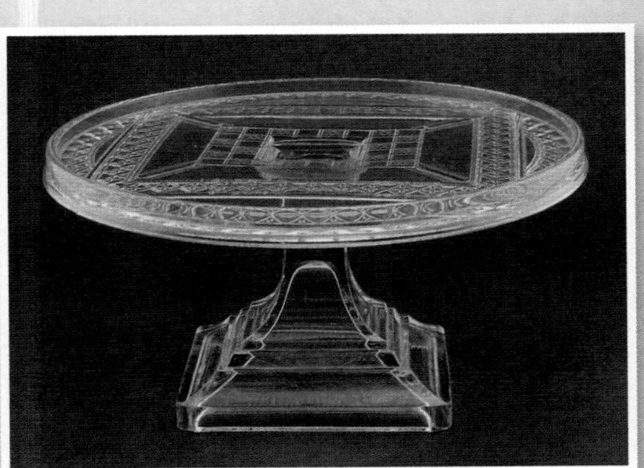

Pedestal

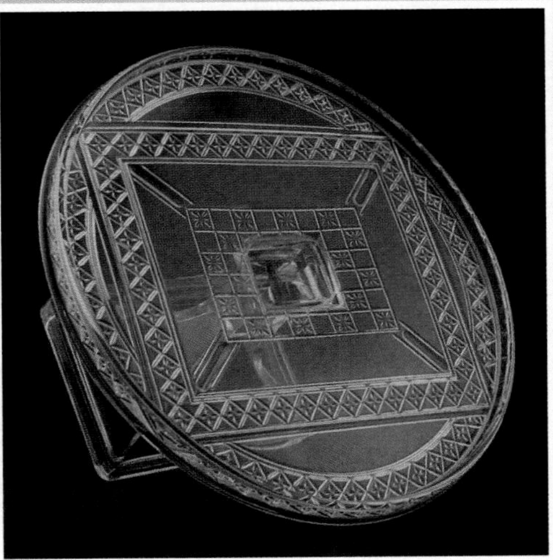

Cake stand

7

This cake stand has a raised, 12-scalloped gallery with six scallops in each scallop. It features squares (not diamonds) with 12 points radiating from the center. There are 12 points in the top, with fans in between each point. The pedestal is notched and the pattern is repeated on the base.

Item	Crystal
Cake stand	$145.00

Cake stand

Pedestal

8

This pattern is very lacy, similar to sheer Austrian window curtains. It has a raised, scalloped gallery. I cannot find the pattern in any of Kamm's books on pitchers.

Item	Size	Crystal
Cake stand	8¾"	$55.00
Pitcher		35.00

Cake stand

Cake stand and pitcher

9

This is a three-part mold with the design recessed in the center. There is a ½" scalloped gallery. The pedestal and base are comprised of panels. The design is similar to Cable made in the 1880s.

Item	Size	Crystal
Cake stand	9¾" x 4½"	$35.00

Pedestal

Cake stand

10

This cake stand has a scalloped gallery and panels with oval dots on the plate and pedestal base.

Item	Size	Crystal
Cake stand	9½" x 4½"	$65.00

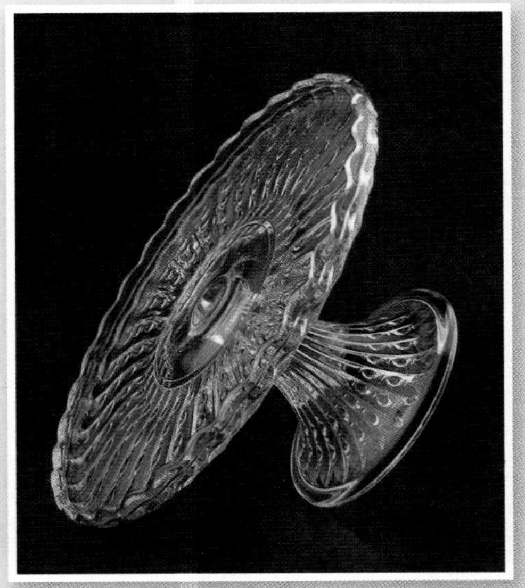

Pedestal

Cake stand

11

This is an elegant cake stand. There is a scalloped gallery. The design is repeated on the base. Courtesy of Carolyn Crozier.

Item	Size	Crystal
Cake stand	9½" x 5"	$55.00

Cake stand

Pedestal

12

This small cake stand is made from a three-part mold. The pattern is similar to Magna, but not as intricate. There is a small plain gallery.

Item	Crystal
Cake stand	$40.00

Cake stand

Pedestal

13

This is a plain salver, 10", with panels on the pedestal.

Item	Crystal
Cake stand	$115.00

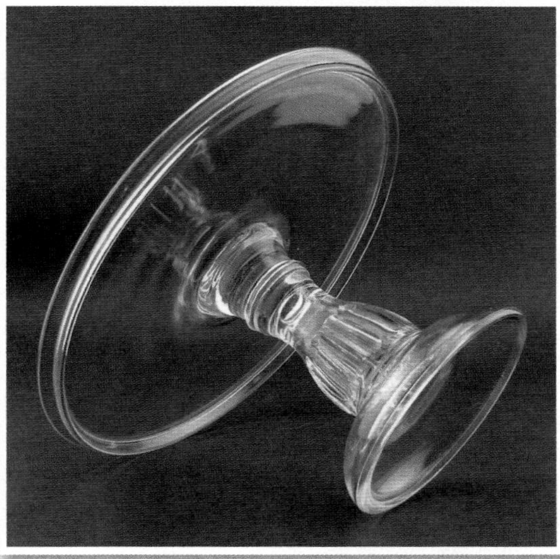

Cake stand

14

This cake stand is of beautiful, clear glass. It is made up of 12 plain panels and has a scalloped 1" skirt. There are scallops within the scallops, making a very plain, but beautiful, pattern. The pedestal is panelled.

Item	Size	Crystal
Cake stand	9½" x 5"	$75.00

Pedestal

Cake stand

15

This plain cake stand is quite impressive. It is made of very clear glass. There is a small decorative pattern in the very center of the plate top and around the base of the pedestal. There is a plain gallery.

Item	Size	Crystal
Cake stand	7⅝" x 9½"	$65.00

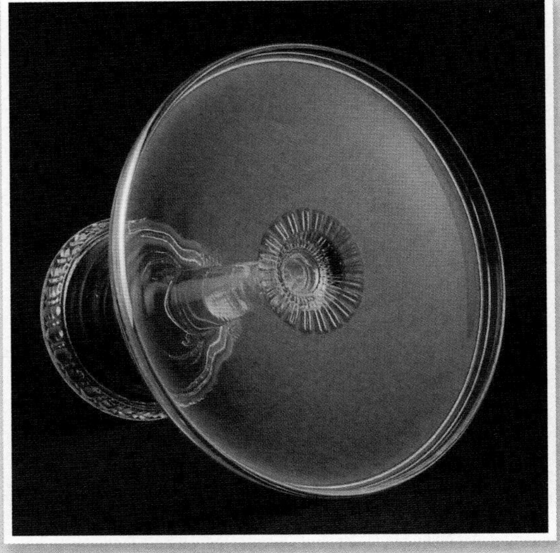

Cake stand

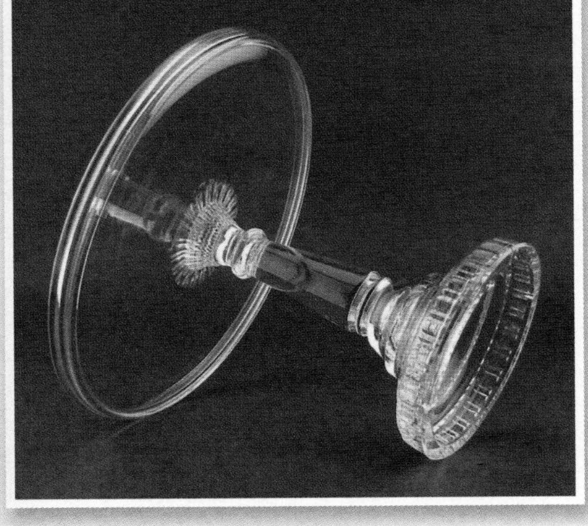

Pedestal

16

This pattern is similar to Brilliant as it has connecting ovals with a design in each. There is a scalloped gallery and a small brandy well.

Item	Size	Crystal
Cake stand	8" x 3¾"	$45.00

Cake stand

Pedestal

17 This beautiful cake stand is a very pretty green, with stippled background decorated with circles that, at first glance, appear to be roses. There are eight such circles around the perimeter and four smaller "roses" in triangles in the center. The pedestal base has alternating single rounded panels with two pointed panels.

Item	Size	Green
Cake stand	10"	$55.00

Pedestal

Cake stand

18 This is a beautiful design with an eight-sided star covering the top surface. The pattern is similar to Champion and Teepee. There is a scalloped gallery.

Item	Size	Crystal
Cake stand	8" x 3¼"	$35.00

Pedestal

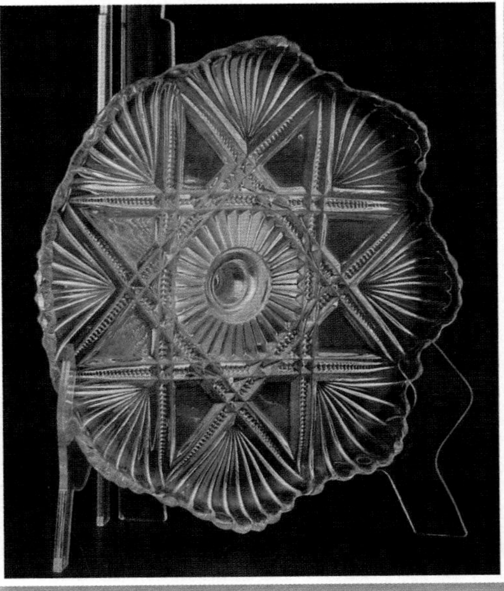
Cake stand

19 Although this cake stand contains flowers and sunbursts, it could not be identified. The flowers are surrounded by double parentheses in alternating scallops, while the remaining scallops contain a sunburst pattern. There is a scalloped gallery. The base of the pedestal has a sawtooth edge.

Item	Size	Crystal
Cake stand	10" x 5¼"	$55.00

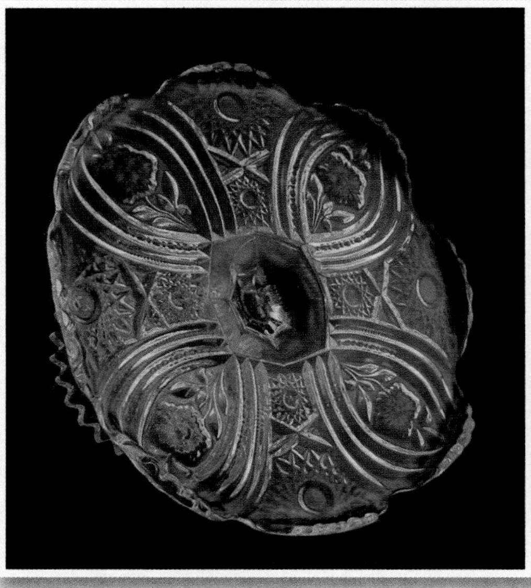
Cake stand

Pedestal

20 This detailed cake stand is divided into nine panels with a ten-pointed star in between each panel. There is a plain gallery.

Item	Size	Crystal
Cake stand	9" x 4½"	$35.00

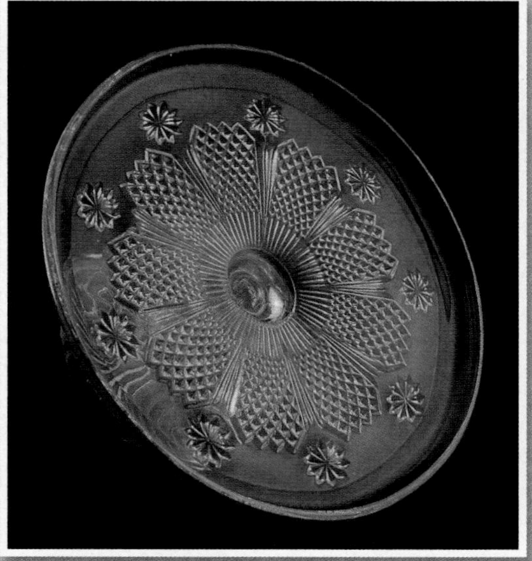
Cake stand

Pedestal

21 This petite cake stand has a scalloped gallery. It has alternating circles, plain, and diamonds.

Item	Size	Crystal
Cake stand	9" x 4½"	$55.00

Pedestal

Cake stand

22 This cake stand has a plain gallery and a scalloped skirt. Although the pattern is unknown, it is believed to be made by Hobbs, Brockunier and Company, 1880s, as the pedestal base is the same as Tree of Life with Hand made by Hobbs. It also has a similar scalloped skirt.

Item	Size	Crystal
Cake stand	8½" x 6½"	$55.00

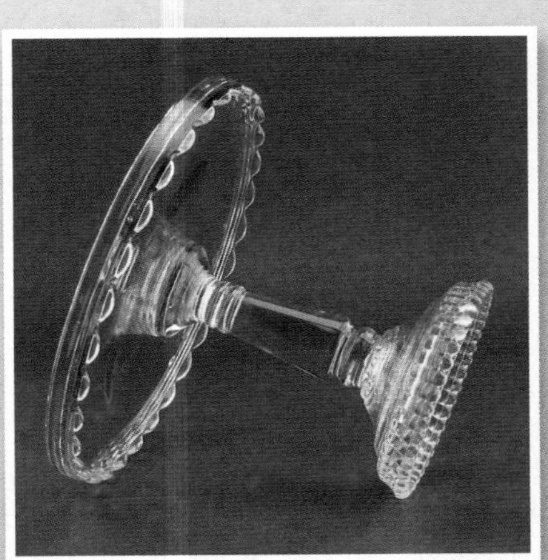

Pedestal

Cake stand

23

This cake stand has a panel across the surface with diamonds and fans.

Item	Size	Crystal
Cake stand	9½" x 4"	$55.00

Cake stand

24

This cake stand is 8½" x 2⅛" high with a scalloped edge. There are circles within circles.

Item	Crystal
Cake stand	$55.00

Cake stand

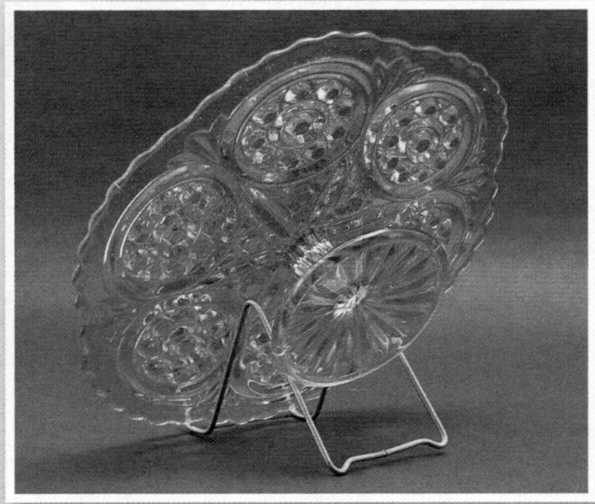

Pedestal

25

Formerly misidentified as Prism and Flute, this 9" cake stand is very plain except for the ridges on pedestal base and plate rim.

Item	Crystal
Cake stand	$50.00

Pedestal

Cake stand

Bibliography

American Historical Catalog Collection. *Pennsylvania Glassware 1870 – 1904*, 1972.
Barlow, Raymond and Joan E. Kaiser. *A Guide to Sandwich Glass, Pressed Tableware*, 1993.
Batty, Bob H. *A Complete Guide to Pressed Glass*, 1978.
Barnett, Jerry. *Paden City, The Color Company*, 1978.
Bond, Marcelle. *The Beauty of Albany Glass*, 1972.
Bones, Frances. *The Book of Duncan Glass*, 1973.
Bredehoft, Neila and Tom. *Glass Tumblers, 1860s to 1920s*, 2004.
———. *Tygart Valley Glass Company, EAPG from Grafton, WV, 1908 Catalog.*
Bredehoft, Neila. *The Collector's Encyclopedia of Heisey Glass, 1925 – 1938*, 1999.
Bredehoft, Neila and Tom, and Jo and Bob Sanford. *Glass Toothpick Holders, Identification and Values*, 1999.
Heisey Glass 1896 – 1957, Identification and Value Guide, 2001.
Bredehoft, Neila; Helen Jones and Dean Six. *L. G. Wright, The West Virginia Museum of American Glass, Limited, with Price Guide*, 2003.
Burkhomder, John R, and D, Thomas O'Connor. *Kemple Glass, 1945 – 1970*, 1997.
———. *Standard Encyclopedia of Pressed Glass 1860 – 1930*, 1999; 2nd Edition, 2000; and 3rd Edition 2003.
———. *Standard Encyclopedia of Millersburg Crystal, Identification and Values*, 2001.
Co-Operative Flint Glass Company Catalog, Beaver Falls, PA.
Dunbar, Shirley. *Heisey Glass, The Early Years: 1896 – 1924*, 2000.
Early American Pattern Glass Society News Journal, Volume 10, 2003.
Edwards, Bill and Mike Carwile. *Standard Encyclopedia of Pressed Glass 1860 – 1930*, 1999.
———. *Standard Encyclopedia of Pressed Glass, 1860 – 1930, Identification and Values*, 1999.
———. *Standard Encyclopedia of Pressed Glass, Second Edition, 1860 – 1930, Identification and Values*, 2000.
———. *Standard Encyclopedia of Pressed Glass, Third Edition, 1860 – 1930, Identification and Values*, 2003.
———. *Standard Encyclopedia of Pressed Glass, Fourth Edition, 1860 – 1930, Identification and Values*, 2005.
Gorham, C. W. *Riverside Glass Works of Wellsburg, WV 1879 – 1907*, 1995.
Hallock, Marilyn R. *Central Glass Company, The First 30 Years, 1863 – 1893*, 2002.
Hartley, Julia Magee and Mary Magee Cobb. *The States' Series Early American Pattern Glass*, 1976.
Heacock, William and Fred Bickenheuser. *Encyclopedia of Victorian Colored Pattern Glass, Book 5, US Glass from A – Z*, 1978.
Heacock, William, James Measell, Berry Wiggins. *Dugan/Diamond, The Story of Indiana, Pennsylvania Glass*, 1993.
———. *Encyclopedia of Victorian Colored Pattern Glass Book 6, Oil Cruets from A to Z*, 1981.
———. *Encyclopedia of Victorian Colored Pattern Glass Book 7, Ruby-Stained Glass from A to Z*, 1986.
———. *Fenton, the Second 25 Years*, 1980.
———.*Collecting Glass, Research, Reprints and Reviews, Volume 1, 1984 and 3*, 1986.
Hicks, Joyce A. *Just Jenkins*, 1988.
Higby, Lola and Wayne. *Bryce, Higbee and J. B. Higbee Glass*, 1998.
Hilton, Bing. *The Greentown Glass Company, History of the Indiana Tumbler and Goblet Company/Works*, 2002.
Hilton, Bing and Matthew Vieke. *The Greentown Glass Company, Price Adviser*, 2003.
Husfloen, Kyle. *Collector's Guide to American Pressed Glass, 1825 – 1915*, 1992.
Innes, Lowell. *Pittsburgh Glass, 1797 – 1891*, 1976.
Jenks, Bill and Jerry Luna. *Early American Pressed Glass 1850 – 1910*, 1990.
Kamm, Minnie Watson. *A Sixth Pattern Glass Book*, 1970.
Kamm-Wood. *Encyclopedia of Antique Pattern Glass, Volumes I and II*, 1961.
———. *The Years of Duncan, 1865 – 1955, Patterns Spanning the Ninety Years of Producing "The Loveliest Glassware in America."*
Krause, Gail. *Encyclopedia of Duncan Glass*, 1981.
———. *The Encyclopedia of Duncan Glass*, 1990.
Lee, Ruth Webb. *Victorian Glass*, 1946.
———. *Early American Pattern Glass, Enlarged and Revised*, 1958.
Lucas, Robert Irwin. *Tarentum Pattern Glass*, 1981.
McCain, Mollie Helen. *The Collector's Encyclopedia of Pattern Glass*, 1982.

———. *Field Guide to Pattern Glass*, 2000.
Measell, James and Don E. Smith. *Findlay Glass, The Glass Tableware Manufacturers, 1886 – 1902*, 1986.
———. *New Martinsville Glass, 1900 – 1944*, 1994.
Measell, James. *Greentown Glass, The Indiana Tumbler and Goblet Company*, 1979.
———. *Imperial Glass Encyclopedia, Volume 1, 1995; Volume II, 1997 and Volume III*, 1999.
Metz, Alice Hulett. *Early American Pattern Glass*, 2000.
———. *Much More Early American Pattern Glass, An Important American Heritage*, 2000.
Miller, Everett R. and Addie R. *The New Martinsville Glass Story, Book I*, 1972.
Miller, Robert W. *Wallace-Homestead Price Guide to Antiques and Pattern Glass, 4th Edition*, 1977.
———. *Wallace-Homestead Price Guide to Antiques, 1st Edition, 1971, and 6th Edition*, 1979.
Murphy, Catherine. *The Antique Traders Antiques and Collectibles Price Guide*, 1987.
News Journal EAPGS Vol 12, Nr 2, Summer 2005.
Pickvet, Mark. *Official Price Guide to Glassware, 3rd Edition*, 2000.
Pina, Leslie. *Fostoria Serving the American Table 1887 – 1986*, 1995.
Reilly, Darryl and Bill Jenks. *Early American Pattern Glass Collector's Identification and Price Guide, 2nd Edition*, 2002.
———. *U. S. Glass, The States Patterns, An Identification and Price Guide*, 1998.
Rinker, Harry L. *Warman's Antiques and Their Prices, 20th Edition*, 1986.
Revi, Albert Christian. *American Pressed Glass and Figure Bottles*, 1964.
Sanford, Jo and Bob. *The Canton Glass Company of Canton, Ohio, 1883 – 1890*, 1998.
Sanford, Jo and Bob and Barbara and Jim Payne. *The Artistic Glassware of Dalzell, Gilmore and Leighton*, 2006.
Schenning, Craig. *A Century of Indiana Glass*, 2005.
Schroy, Ellen Tischbein. *Warman's Pattern Glass*, 1993.
Spillman, Jane Shadel. *Adams and Company, A Closer Look,* in EAPG Newsletter, *The Glass Club Bulletin*, 1990 – 1991.
Stout, Sandra McPhee. *The Complete Book of McKee Glass*, 1972.
Sutton-Smith, Peter and Barbara. *Canadian Handbook of Pressed Tableware, Revised Edition*, ca 2000.
Teal, Ron Sr. *Albany Glass, Model Flint Glass Company of Albany, Indiana*, 1997.
The Cambridge Glass Company 1903 Catalog of Pressed and Blown Glassware, 1976.
The Glass Club Bulletin Nr 163, Winter/Fall 1990/1991, Computer Info Newsletter, reprint 2001.
The National Duncan Glass Journal Oct-Dec 2000.
United States Glass Company Catalogue Nr 135, Pressed and Blown Glassware, 1926.
Vogel, Clarence W. *Heisey's Early and Late Years 1896 – 1968.*
Weatherman, Hazel Marie. *Fostoria, First Fifty Years*, 1972.
Welker, John and Elizabeth. *Pressed Glass in America – Encyclopedia of the First Hundred Years: 1825 – 1925*, 1985.
Wilson, Chas West. *Westmoreland Glass, Identification and Value Guide*, 1996.

About the Authors

Bettye S. James resides in Lakeland, Florida, with her husband, Brad. They were charter members and former officers of the Depression ERA Collectibles Club, Manassas, Virginia. She is a former vice president and president of the Central Florida Glassaholics Club in Lakeland, and involved with the club's annual glass show. She initially collected glass of the Depression era. While progressing to other types of glass, her concentration focused on cake stands, primarily early American pattern glass.

She has amassed a collection of over 300 pedestal cake stands, the majority of which are in pattern glass, with the remainder in Depression, Elegant, and lead (crystal) glass. She has given programs on her cake stands to members of several local antique clubs in Lakeland. Add "dealer" to her resume of experience, as she has sold at flea markets in Florida, Pennsylvania, and Virginia. Unless otherwise attributed, all items are from the personal collections of Bettye S. James and Danny Cornelius.

Jane M. O'Brien and her husband, Tom, reside in Manassas, Virginia. She is a health educator by trade and co-owner of JK-Action, a provider of CPR and first aid training for local businesses. As a member of the faculty of the Training Center of the American Heart Association, she is involved in training and updating instructors and promoting CPR with the fire and rescue departments, a local hospital, and within the community. For 25 years, she taught group fitness classes.

She has collected glass and antiques for several years. In the beginning, her glass collection consisted of bowls, platters, and other serving pieces in various patterns. Eventually, as most collectors do, she focused on a select few patterns of Depression glass. Although her passion is Depression glass, she loves the uniqueness and elegance of early American pattern glass, especially the pieces handed down from her grandmother. She and Tom have spent many long weekends searching for special treasures in Adamstown, Pennsylvania, at antique stores and flea markets.

Index

Popular names are in bold.
Additional known names (**popular name**).